D1461156

NEW
MATHS
IN ACTION

S1³

Members of the
Mathematics in Action Group
associated with this book:

D. Brown
R.D. Howat
G. Marra
E.C.K. Mullan
R. Murray
K. Nisbet
D. Thomas
J. Thomson

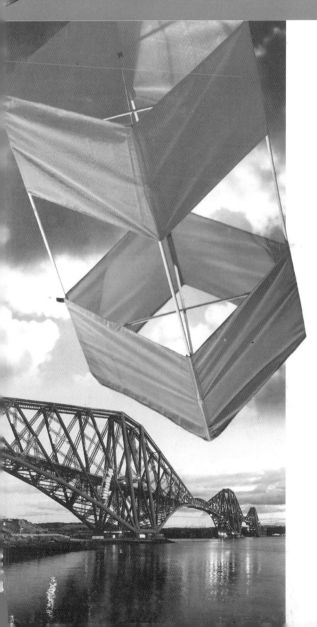

Published in 2002 by:
Nelson Thornes Ltd
Delta Place
27 Bath Road
CHELTENHAM
GL53 7TH
United Kingdom

13 / 10 9 8 7 6

A catalogue record of this book is available from the British Library

ISBN 978 0 7487 6517 1

Illustrations by Ian Foulis, Oxford Designers and Illustrators, Peters and Zabransky
Page make-up by Tech-Set Ltd

Printed in China

Acknowledgements

The publishers thank the following for permission to reproduce copyright material.
Corel (NT): 204, 232; Digital Vision (NT): 108; Hulton Getty: 20, 73 (top left); Magic Eye Inc.: 266; Mary Evans Picture Library: 148, 188; Serge Mehl: 59; www.florence-nightingale.co.uk: 73 (bottom right).

The publishers have made every effort to contact copyright holders but apologise if any have been overlooked.

Contents

Introduction

The principal aim of this resource is to provide a comprehensive coverage of Level E attainment targets as defined in the 5-14 National Guidelines. This includes materials not mentioned explicitly in section 2 of these Guidelines, but which the authors feel are essential, indispensable aspects for the proper development and understanding of mathematics. As suggested by the Guidelines, natural opportunities are taken to introduce new content and depth. Common vocabulary associated with each topic is emphasised and tools to assist in communication, e.g. notation and conventions, are promoted. Opportunities to exercise mental agility and non-calculator skills are provided, especially in chapters developing the attainment outcome Number, Money, Measurement. Problem solving and Enquiry is catered for throughout the resource through *Challenges*, *Brainstormers* and *Investigations*.

An opportunity to develop the mathematics to level F is provided in each chapter. Here, unless it is essential, technical vocabulary is not included. Problem solving, investigation and abstraction are also kept to a minimum. All targets are visited to the standard required by the National assessments.

Each chapter follows the same structure.
> *Looking Back* – establishes the knowledge and skills required to proceed with the topic. Questions in this section may examine a lower level or an essential topic at the same level.
> *Level E Exercises* – comprehensive and graded.
> *Level F Exercises* – establish the basic mathematical skills required at this level.
> *Check-Up* – provides a diagnostic test ensuring that all attainment targets are known before progression to the next topic. Level F questions are indicated by green question numbers.

Contexts have been chosen to show students the variety of places where maths may be applied. *Brainstormers*, *Challenges*, *Puzzles* and *Investigations* appear throughout the text, providing stimulating and motivating opportunities to enrich mathematical experience.

A Teacher Resource Pack providing material for homework, extension and preparation for assessment is available. The pack also contains a section that examines problems exemplifying the strategies listed on page 13 of the National Guidelines.

1 Whole numbers

Through the ages, people have kept a record of things using numbers. The numbers we use today are thought to have been invented in India by the Hindus and brought to Europe in the eighth century by Arab traders and travellers.

1 Looking back ◀◀

Exercise 1.1

No working allowed until question **6**.

1 Write down the answer to:
   a $26 + 38$ **b** $73 - 37$ **c** $78 + 95$ **d** $650 - 280$

2 Calculate:
   a 390×10 **b** 497×100 **c** 240×1000
   d $8600 \div 10$ **e** $96\,400 \div 100$ **f** $105\,000 \div 1000$

3 Write down the answer to:
   a 365×20 **b** 38×400 **c** $7500 \div 50$ **d** $74\,100 \div 300$

4 Greg made two phone calls. One lasted 57 minutes and the other lasted 65 minutes.
   What was the total length of the two calls in minutes?

5 Chris weighs 62 kg. His sister Laura weighs 47 kg.
   What is the difference in their weights?

6 Calculate:
   a $4326 + 3085$ **b** $8163 - 2571$ **c** 3465×8 **d** $4302 \div 9$

7 Katie made 1967 minutes of calls on her mobile phone.
   She is charged 7 pence per minute.
   How much did she have to pay for her calls?

8 There are 7000 leaflets and 8 volunteers to deliver them.
   How many leaflets should each volunteer be given if they all
   have to deliver the same number?

9 In the year 2000 the estimated population of Scotland's four largest cities was:
   Edinburgh 445 400,   Glasgow 678 700,
   Aberdeen 223 200,   Dundee 170 700.
   a What was the total population of the four cities?
   b The population of Scotland in 2000 was estimated at 5 728 000.
      How many of the population did not live in one of these four cities?

10 A garage bought 55 000 litres of petrol at 87 pence a litre and sold it at 96
    pence a litre. Calculate:
    a the amount paid by the garage for the petrol
    b the amount collected by the garage on selling the petrol
    c the profit made by the garage.
    Give your answers in pounds (£).

11 The population of the USA in the year 2000 was estimated at two hundred
    and seventy-four million and thirty thousand.
    The population of the UK was estimated at fifty-eight million, nine hundred
    and forty thousand.
    a How many more people lived in the USA than in the UK in the year 2000?
    b How many short of sixty million was the UK population?

12 Last year Ann earned £23 244. How much did she earn in
    a a month   b a week?

13 This year Ann will earn £24 057. How much will she earn in
    a a month   b a week?
    Round both answers to the nearest pound (£).

2 Mental calculations

Remember to look for shortcuts.

> Examples $32 \times 80 = 32 \times 8 \times 10 = 256 \times 10 = 2560$
> $480 \div 80 = 480 \div 10 \div 8 = 48 \div 8 = 6$
> $96 + 35 = 90 + 30 + 6 + 5 = 120 + 11 = 131$
> $72 - 45 = 72 - 40 - 2 - 3 = 30 - 3 = 27$

No calculators are allowed when doing mental
calculations, and you cannot write down any working.

Exercise 2.1

1 Add 87 and 94.

2 From 92 subtract 37.

3 Find the sum of 66 and 77.

4 What is the difference between 71 and 27?

5 Multiply 85 by 30.

6 What is the product of 176 and 600?

7 Divide 1040 by 80.

8 Divide 36 000 by 100.

9 Multiply 550 by 1000.

10 What is the product of 280 and 90?

11 Divide 93 200 by 400.

12 Divide a quarter of a million by 10.

Exercise 2.2

1 Last week 78 mm of rain fell and 84 mm fell this week. How much rain fell altogether?

2 There were 28 hours of sunshine last week and 81 hours of sunshine this week. What's the difference?

3 Sara drove 96 km to her gran's house and then 67 km to her friend's. How many kilometres did Sara drive altogether?

4 A baker baked 85 pies and sold 58 of them. How many pies did he have left?

5 If 47 people each paid £40 for a train journey, how much was paid altogether?

6 A store bought 600 computer games for £49 each. How much was paid in total for the games?

7 £6153 is shared among 70 people. How much does each person receive?

8 A school paid £1870 for 50 tables. How much did one table cost?

9 One torch battery cost 85 pence. How much will ten cost?

10 A metal washer weighs 108 grams. How much do 100 of the washers weigh?

11 One sheet of card costs 11 pence. How much will 1000 of the sheets of card cost?

12 One hundred calculators cost £485. What should be the cost of one calculator?

3 Whole number calculations

Lay all working out clearly.

| Examples | | | | |

$$7472$$
$$+ 6{,}5{,}6{,}9$$
$$\overline{14041}$$

$$\overset{6}{7}{}^{1}4\overset{6}{7}{}^{1}2$$
$$- 6569$$
$$\overline{903}$$

$$8572$$
$$\times \;_{3}\;_{4}\;_{1}6$$
$$\overline{51432}$$

$$\begin{array}{r} 256 \\ 8\overline{)2\,0^{4}4^{4}8} \end{array}$$

Exercise 3.1

1 Calculate:

  a $8738 + 9685$ **b** $7051 - 3184$ **c** 9806×7 **d** $4284 \div 9$

2 Re-write the following, replacing the dots with the correct numbers:

  a $316\bullet$ **b** $251\bullet$ **c** $\bullet\bullet4\bullet$ **d** $7\bullet56 \div 8 = 95\bullet$

     $+\bullet9\bullet3$ $-\;\bullet86$ $\times 7$

     $\overline{6\bullet11}$ $\overline{\bullet8\bullet8}$ $\overline{\bullet6922}$

3 Ann and Babs fly out from London, Ann to Chicago and Babs to Perth in Australia. They then meet up in Johannesburg.

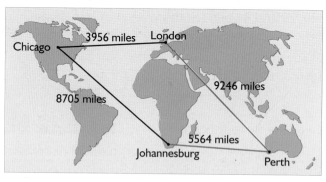

How many more miles does Babs fly than Ann?

4 A car was bought for £12 050 and sold for £9975.
Calculate the loss made on the deal.

5 The populations of the countries forming the UK were estimated in the year 2000 as:

    England   49 392 000   Northern Ireland 1 664 000
    Scotland   5 728 000   Wales   2 946 000

  a Write the populations of England and Scotland in words.

  b If the population of Wales had been 10 000 less, what would it have been?

  c What was the total population of the four countries in the year 2000?

Exercise 3.2

1 The attendances at five Scottish Cup matches played one Saturday were:

7095, 14 689, 57 283, 8065 and 6728.

   a How many watched the five games?

   b Divide the total above by 5 to find the average attendance.

   c How many of the attendances were above the average?

   d What was the difference between the largest and the smallest crowd?

   e The price of a ticket was £15 for an adult and £8 for a senior citizen
or a child.
Half the people watching were adults and the rest senior citizens
or children.
How much was collected altogether in ticket money?

2 A lorry can carry no more than 16 tonnes of stone chips. How many lorry
journeys are needed to transport all 875 tonnes of chips from a quarry to a
road development?

3 The dimensions, to the nearest metre, of some of the famous football pitches
in Scotland are:

Hampden Park	105 m by 69 m	Love St	110 m by 68 m
Fir Park	101 m by 69 m	Rugby Park	108 m by 68 m
Dens Park	103 m by 68 m	Tannadice Park	101 m by 66 m

Which of these pitches has the greatest area and which has the smallest area?
Assume all pitches are rectangular.

4 A rectangular field has dimensions 450 metres by 325 metres.
Calculate the area of the field and give your answer in hectares.
(1 hectare = 10 000 square metres)

5 A Hollywood movie made £350 million at the box office in ticket sales.
It cost £185 250 000 to make.
Calculate the profit made on the movie.

6 Chloe has an annual salary of £19 684.
How much does she earn in a month, to the nearest pound (£)?

7 A manufacturer makes 3 875 000 washers.
They are put into packets of 25.

   a How many packets will there be?

   b Each packet is sold for £2.
How much money is made from the washers?

8 **a** 65 830 curtain hooks are put into packs of 24.
How many packs are obtained?

   b A railway carriage can seat 78 passengers.
How many carriages are needed on a train to seat 500 passengers?

4 Squares, cubes and square roots

> When we multiply a number by itself, we are said to **square** the number.

Examples   Square 3 and we get $3 \times 3 = 9$.
Square 5 and we get $5 \times 5 = 25$.

We write $3^2 = 3 \times 3 = 9$ and we say '3 **squared** equals 9',
$5^2 = 5 \times 5 = 25$ and we say '5 **squared** equals 25'.

The small number is often referred to as a **power** or **index**.

We can say 3^2 is '3 to the power 2',
5^2 is '5 to the power 2'.

For any number a, $a^2 = a \times a$ (a^2 is the second power of a)
Similarly $a^3 = a \times a \times a$ (a^3 is the third power of a)
a^3 is read as 'a cubed' or 'a to the power 3'.

Examples $2^3 = 2 \times 2 \times 2 = 8$ $5^3 = 5 \times 5 \times 5 = 125$

Exercise 4.1

No calculators unless the question asks you to use one!

1   Calculate:

   a 4^2 **b** 3^3 **c** 6^2 **d** 7^3 **e** 8^2
   f 10^3 **g** 100^2 **h** $(5 - 3)^3$ **i** $9^2 - 7^2$ **j** $(1^3 + 3^2)^3$

2   Find the value of each expression when $a = 2$ and $b = 4$.

   a $a^2 + b^2$ **b** $b^3 - b^2$ **c** $(ab)^2$ **d** a^2b^2 **e** $2b^3$
   f $(a + b)^2$ **g** $5a^3b^2$ **h** $3a^3b$ **i** $(a + b)^3$ **j** $a^3 + b^3$

3   **a** For a square of side L cm, what does
      L^2 cm^2 represent?

   b For a cube of side L cm, what does
      L^3 cm^3 represent?

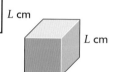

L cm

L cm

If we use a calculator, the button $\boxed{x^2}$ will give us the square number.
$\boxed{5}\,\boxed{x^2}$ will give the value 25.

Alternatively, $\boxed{x^y}$ will give us squares and cubes of numbers.

Examples $\boxed{6}\,\boxed{x^y}\,\boxed{2}\,\boxed{=}$ $6^2 = 36$
$\boxed{6}\,\boxed{x^y}\,\boxed{3}\,\boxed{=}$ $6^3 = 216$

4 A square play area of side 18 metres is to be laid with square rubber tiles of side 1 metre. How many tiles are needed?

   a Use the x^2 key on your calculator to evaluate 18^2.

   b Another square play area is laid with tiles.
It is 23 metres long.
Use your calculator to calculate how many tiles are needed for this play area.

   c Use your calculator to find the value of each of the following:
    i 100^2 **ii** 1000^2 **iii** 1934^2

5 Use the x^y key on your calculator to evaluate:

   a 5^3 **b** 10^3 **c** 9^3 **d** 15^3 **e** 25^2

   f 12^3 **g** $(5 + 3)^3$ **h** $5^3 + 3^3$ **i** $7^3 - 6^3$ **j** $2 \times 4^3 - 4 \times 3^2$

6 A number, when squared, has the value 289 ($x^2 = 289$).
What is the number?

> The button $\boxed{\sqrt{}}$ on the calculator will give us the answer.
>
>
>
> $\boxed{\sqrt{}}\,\boxed{289}$ will give the value 17.
>
> So $17^2 = 289$
>
> We say the **square root** of 289 is 17, because $17^2 = 289$.

Without using a calculator, write down the values of:

   a $\sqrt{1}$ **b** $\sqrt{4}$ **c** $\sqrt{16}$

   d $\sqrt{49}$ **e** $\sqrt{64}$ **f** $\sqrt{100}$

7 Use the $\sqrt{}$ key on your calculator to find:

   a $\sqrt{625}$ **b** $\sqrt{961}$ **c** $\sqrt{2025}$ **d** $\sqrt{4096}$

   e $\sqrt{400}$ **f** $\sqrt{2500}$ **g** $\sqrt{(3^2 + 4^2)}$ **h** $\sqrt{(3^2 + 3^3)}$

8 $\sqrt{10}$ lies between 3 and 4 because $\sqrt{10}$ lies between $\sqrt{9}$ and $\sqrt{16}$.
Between which pair of whole numbers does each of these square roots lie?

   a $\sqrt{6}$ **b** $\sqrt{20}$ **c** $\sqrt{30}$

   d $\sqrt{70}$ **e** $\sqrt{90}$ **f** $\sqrt{102}$

9 Copy and complete each table:

   a

x	121		729		676
$\sqrt{x}$		16		21	

   b

x^2		144		2304
x	17		23	

10 a A square has an area of 361 cm². Find the length of its side.
 b Find the side of the square with area:
   i 1764 cm² **ii** 961 m²   **iii** 4356 cm²

11 A garden is square with an area of 1089 m².
 A central square with an area of 729 m²
 is dug out.
 The border is uniform, which means it is
 the same width all round.
 What is the width of the border?

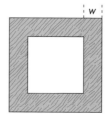

12 A box in the shape of a cube is made from
 square plastic sheets of area 3600 cm².
 Calculate:

 a the length of a side of the square
 b the volume of the box.

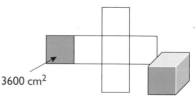

3600 cm²

Challenge

Andrew's dad wanted help to lay 25 concrete slabs in his garden.
Andrew offered to help if he was paid 1p for the first slab, 2p for the second,
4p for the third, 8p for the fourth, and so on.
Should Andrew's dad agree to this method of payment?
How much will it cost him if Andrew helps lay all 25 slabs?

A calculator crossword
Copy the grid onto squared paper.
Use your calculator for the calculations, and after each one turn it upside
down and read the word needed to fit into the grid.

Clues across	Clues down
1 42 876 ÷ 12	2 7035 ÷ 21
4 14 906 ÷ 29	3 37 205 617 + 40 140 046
5 184 977 ÷ 279	6 9247 − 5871
7 615 293 × 9	8 8063 ÷ 11
11 7092 − 6757	9 10 609 × 5
13 12 167 − 8407	10 102 341 − 47 265
14 32 719 + 20 788	
15 1015 × 7	

(Grid: numbered cells 1, 2, 3, 4, 5, 6, 7, 8, 9, 10, 11, 12, 13, 14, 15; cell 12 across filled with **H E L L O**)

Can you invent a clue for 12 across?
(Hint: it is not a whole number!)

F

5 Factors and prime factors

1, 2, 3 and 6 are the whole numbers that divide 6 evenly, i.e. they divide 6 without a remainder.

$6 \div 1 = 6$ $6 \div 2 = 3$ $6 \div 3 = 2$ $6 \div 6 = 1$

1, 2, 3 and 6 are called the **factors** of 6.

Example 1   List the factors of 8.   **Example 2** List the factors of 20.

Answer: 1, 2, 4, 8   *Answer:* 1, 2, 4, 5, 10, 20

Exercise 5.1

1   List all the factors of:

a 10	**b** 13	**c** 16	**d** 18
e 24	**f** 30	**g** 31	**h** 64
i 100	**j** 400	**k** 360	

2   What whole number less than 100 has most factors?

3   Make a list of the first ten whole numbers that have an odd number of factors. What is special about these numbers?

4   Which number has only one factor?

5   **a**   List all the numbers less than 20 that have only two factors. You should have found eight of them.

> These numbers are examples of **prime numbers**.
> A prime number is a whole number divisible only by itself and 1.

   b   What is the only even number that is a prime number?

6   Follow these instructions to write down the prime numbers less than 100.
   a   Write down the number 2.
   b   Write down all the odd numbers from 3 to 99.
   c   Circle the number 2, the lowest prime number.
   d   Circle the number 3, the lowest unmarked number on the list, and score out its multiples from the list.
   e   Circle the number 5, the lowest unmarked number on the list, and score out its multiples.
   f   Circle the number 7, the lowest unmarked number on the list, and score out its multiples.
   g   11 is now the lowest unmarked number. All its multiples are scored out already, or bigger than 100. Circle 11 and all the other unmarked numbers.

F

7

> To test if a number, n, is prime, we need only try to divide it by all the prime numbers less than or equal to $\sqrt{n}$.
>
> If none of these divides n evenly, then n itself is prime.

Example

To see if 211 is prime we need only try 2, 3, 5, 7, 11, 13. ($\sqrt{211} = 14.5$ to 1 d.p.)

Which of the following are prime numbers?

a 109   **b** 167   **c** 227   **d** 299   **e** 311

8 A **prime factor** is a factor which is a prime number.
2 and 3 are prime factors of 12.
Write down the prime factors of:

a 6   **b** 8   **c** 20   **d** 36   **e** 70   **f** 90.

9 We can write any whole number as a **product** of prime factors, i.e. as prime factors multiplied together.

Examples   Consider 84.

$84 = 2 \times 42$

$= 2 \times 2 \times 21$

$= 2 \times 2 \times 3 \times 7$

$= 2^2 \times 3 \times 7$

2	84
2	42
3	21
7	7
	1

Consider 90.

$90 = 2 \times 45$

$= 2 \times 5 \times 9$

$= 2 \times 5 \times 3 \times 3$

$= 2 \times 3^2 \times 5$

2	90
5	45
3	9
3	3
	1

Write each of these numbers as a product of prime factors. Give your answer in index form where appropriate.

a 12   **b** 18   **c** 30   **d** 16   **e** 50   **f** 72   **g** 84   **h** 184

Challenges

1 Find the smallest whole number that has all of 1, 2, 3, 4, 5, 6, 7, 8 and 9 as factors.

2 What is the lowest number that has a remainder of 1 when it is divided by 2, *and* a remainder of 2 when divided by 3, *and* a remainder of 3 when divided by 4, *and* a remainder of 4 when divided by 5?

3 Find four 4-digit numbers that have only prime factors.

4 Search the web to find out what you can about the Great Internet Mersenne Prime Search (GIMPS). You may like to join the search. In 2001 a student in Canada found the largest known prime to date.
Key words: "Largest known primes".

$$2^{13466917} - 1$$

$\longleftarrow$ 13466917 terms $\longrightarrow$

This is $2 \times 2 \times 2 \times \dots \dots 2 \times 2 - 1$

It has 4 053 946 digits ... and it would fill a paperback to write down.

6 Working with integers: below zero

Reminders

Example 1

Water freezes to ice at zero degrees Celsius (0 °C).
On a really cold day the temperature can drop below zero.
Three degrees below zero is written as −3 °C.
We read −3 °C as *'negative 3 °C'* or '3 degrees *below zero'*.

Example 2

The depth to which a submarine dives is given as its depth below sea level.
A submarine 500 metres below sea level is at −500 metres.

Example 3

A company can make a profit or a loss.
A loss of £1000 is often denoted as a profit of −£1000.

The examples above show us where negative numbers can be used.
Positive and negative whole numbers are called **integers**.
These can be represented on a number line.

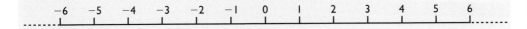

F

Adding integers with a number line

Start at the first number and do as the second number tells you (where 2 means
go 2 to the right, −2 means go 2 to the left).

Example 1

−3 + 2 means −3 add 2
Start at −3 and go 2 to the right.
−3 + 2 = −1

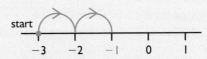

Example 2

4 + (−6) means 4 add (−6)
Start at 4 and go 6 to the left.
4 + (−6) = −2

Example 3

−1 + (−3) means (−1) add (−3)
Start at −1 and go 3 to the left.
−1 + (−3) = −4

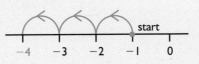

Exercise 6.1

Use a number line to help you do these calculations.

1 $2 + (-2)$ **2** $5 + (-1)$ **3** $4 + (-3)$ **4** $6 + (-1)$

5 $1 + (-4)$ **6** $3 + (-4)$ **7** $3 + (-1)$ **8** $2 + (-5)$

9 $6 + (-8)$ **10** $-1 + 5$ **11** $-3 + 4$ **12** $-6 + 3$

13 $-7 + 2$ **14** $-3 + (-2)$ **15** $-5 + (-1)$ **16** $-4 + (-4)$

17 $-2 + (-7)$ **18** $0 + (-9)$

19 Perform each pair of calculations. You may use a number line to help you.

    a **i** $5 + (-3)$ **ii** $5 - 3$ **b** **i** $7 + (-2)$ **ii** $7 - 2$

    c **i** $6 + (-1)$ **ii** $6 - 1$ **d** **i** $3 + (-3)$ **ii** $3 - 3$

    e **i** $4 + (-2)$ **ii** $4 - 2$ **f** **i** $0 + (-4)$ **ii** $0 - 4$

Exercise 6.2

1 Copy and continue the following sequences for three more terms.

    a $5, 4, 3, 2, 1, 0, \_, \_, \_$ **b** $10, 8, 6, 4, 2, 0, \_, \_, \_$

    c $15, 12, 9, 6, 3, 0, \_, \_, \_$ **d** $9, 5, 1, -3, \_, \_, \_$

2 Copy and complete each list of subtractions by looking for the pattern:

    a $3 - 1 = , 2 - 1 = , 1 - 1 = , 0 - 1 = , -1 - 1 = , -2 - 1 = , -3 - 1 = ,$
       $-4 - 1 =$

    b $4 - 2 = , 3 - 2 = , 2 - 2 = , 1 - 2 = , 0 - 2 = , -1 - 2 = , -2 - 2 = ,$
       $-3 - 2 =$

    c $4 - 3 = , 3 - 3 = , 2 - 3 = , 1 - 3 = , 0 - 3 = , -1 - 3 = , -2 - 3 = ,$
       $-3 - 3 =$

    d $4 - 4 = , 3 - 4 = , 2 - 4 = , 1 - 4 = , 0 - 4 = , -1 - 4 = , -2 - 4 = ,$
       $-3 - 4 =$

3 Perform each pair of calculations. You may find results found in question **2** helpful with parts **ii**.

    a **i** $-4 + (-1)$ **ii** $-4 - 1$ **b** **i** $-3 + (-2)$ **ii** $-3 - 2$

    c **i** $-3 + (-3)$ **ii** $-3 - 3$ **d** **i** $-3 + (-4)$ **ii** $-3 - 4$

4 Copy and complete each list of subtractions by looking for the pattern:

    a $6 - 4 = , 6 - 3 = , 6 - 2 = , 6 - 1 = , 6 - 0 = , 6 - (-1) = , 6 - (-2) = ,$
       $6 - (-3) =$

    b $8 - 4 = , 8 - 3 = , 8 - 2 = , 8 - 1 = , 8 - 0 = , 8 - (-1) = , 8 - (-2) = ,$
       $8 - (-3) =$

    c $5 - 4 = , 5 - 3 = , 5 - 2 = , 5 - 1 = , 5 - 0 = , 5 - (-1) = , 5 - (-2) = ,$
       $5 - (-3) =$

    d $-4 - 4 = , -4 - 3 = , -4 - 2 = , -4 - 1 = , -4 - 0 = , -4 - (-1) = ,$
       $-4 - (-2) =$

F

5 Perform each pair of calculations. You may find results found in question **4** helpful with parts **ii**.

  a **i** $6 + 3$ **ii** $6 - (-3)$ **b** **i** $8 + 3$ **ii** $8 - (-3)$

  c **i** $5 + 3$ **ii** $5 - (-3)$ **d** **i** $-4 + 2$ **ii** $-4 - (-2)$

7 Subtracting integers

From the above we see that for each subtraction we can always find an addition which gives the same answer.

Instead of subtracting a number, we can **add its negative**.

$$a - b = a + (-b)$$
$$\text{and} \quad a - (-b) = a + b$$

Once the subtraction has been exchanged for an addition, we can use the number line as before.

Exercise 7.1

1 Use a number line to help you do these calculations.

  a $2 - 5$ **b** $1 - 3$ **c** $-2 - 1$ **d** $-3 - 3$

  e $-4 - 5$ **f** $-1 - 7$ **g** $2 - (-1)$ **h** $3 - (-4)$

  i $5 - (-5)$ **j** $-1 - (-4)$ **k** $-8 - (-3)$ **l** $-2 - (-2)$

2 Write down the answer to each of the following:

  a $3 - 4$ **b** $4 - 8$ **c** $1 - 7$ **d** $2 - 5$

  e $-3 + 4$ **f** $-2 + 7$ **g** $-1 + 9$ **h** $-6 + 7$

  i $0 - 5$ **j** $-3 - 4$ **k** $-4 - 3$ **l** $-6 - 1$

3 Evaluate:

  a $7 + (-4)$ **b** $6 + (-1)$ **c** $3 - (-1)$ **d** $1 - (-3)$

  e $5 + (-5)$ **f** $5 + (-7)$ **g** $2 + (-8)$ **h** $3 + (-9)$

  i $0 - (-4)$ **j** $-1 - (-5)$ **k** $-3 - (-4)$ **l** $-2 - (-6)$

  m $-2 + (-3)$ **n** $-5 + (-2)$ **o** $-4 + (-1)$ **p** $-2 + (-7)$

4 Find the value of:

  a $-14 + 19$ **b** $-27 + 12$ **c** $-43 + 29$ **d** $17 - 31$

  e $19 - 41$ **f** $11 - 30$ **g** $-16 - 17$ **h** $-23 - 18$

5 Simplify:

  a $18 + (-17)$ **b** $23 - (-15)$ **c** $-46 + (-25)$

  d $-17 - (-23)$ **e** $-36 + (-27)$ **f** $-37 - (-15)$

6 Find the answer to $3 - (-5) + (-1) - (-6) - 8 + (-3) - (-2) - 4$.

7 Brutus was born in 32 BC and died in AD 39.
What age was Brutus when he died?

8 Cleo was born in 93 BC and died when she was 68 years old.
In what year did Cleo die?

9 Helen died in AD 23 aged 65 years. When was she born?

10 A submarine is at −350 m.
A helicopter directly above the submarine is at a height of 250 m.
What is their distance apart?

8 Multiplying integers

When we study this pattern:

$5 \times 5 = 25$
$5 \times 4 = 20$
$5 \times 3 = 15$
$5 \times 2 = 10$
$5 \times 1 = 5$
$5 \times 0 = 0$

we can see a pattern that continues like this:

$5 \times 0 = 0$
$5 \times -1 = -5$
$5 \times -2 = -10$
$5 \times -3 = -15$
$5 \times -4 = -20$
$5 \times -5 = -25$

Exercise 8.1

F

1 a By looking for patterns in the rows, copy and complete the table down to the green line.

b By looking for patterns in the columns, complete the table below the green line.

c Use your table to state the value of
   i -5×3
   ii $4 \times (-2)$
   iii $-4 \times (-3)$
   iv $-3 \times (-4)$

d What can be said about all the answers in the
   i pale green areas
   ii dark green areas?

e What can be said about the pair
   i 5×3 and $-5 \times (-3)$
   ii -5×3 and $5 \times (-5)$?

f We know that $5 \times 3 = 3 \times 5$.
Is this true for -5×3 and $3 \times (-5)$?

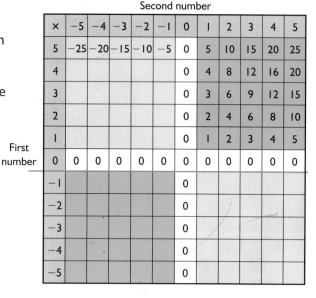

Second number

×	−5	−4	−3	−2	−1	0	1	2	3	4	5
5	−25	−20	−15	−10	−5	0	5	10	15	20	25
4						0	4	8	12	16	20
3						0	3	6	9	12	15
2						0	2	4	6	8	10
1						0	1	2	3	4	5
0	0	0	0	0	0	0	0	0	0	0	0
−1						0					
−2						0					
−3						0					
−4						0					
−5						0					

First number

2

> From the table we see that when we multiply two numbers:
> - with the *same* sign, the result is *positive*,
>   e.g. $3 \times 4 = 12$ and $-2 \times (-5) = 10$
> - with *opposite* signs, the result is *negative*,
>   e.g. $-3 \times 4 = -12$ and $2 \times (-5) = -10$

Use this rule to calculate these.

a -3×2	**b** 2×6	**c** $-4 \times (-5)$	**d** $4 \times (-6)$
e -6×8	**f** 7×9	**g** $-5 \times (-9)$	**h** $8 \times (-7)$
i -10×21	**j** 16×12	**k** $-14 \times (-8)$	**l** $17 \times (-5)$

9 Dividing integers

We know that ...   if $8 \times 4 = 32$ then $32 \div 4 = 8$

Similarly
- If $8 \times (-4) = -32$ then $-32 \div (-4) = 8$
- If $-8 \times 4 = -32$ then $-32 \div 4 = -8$
- If $-8 \times (-4) = 32$ then $32 \div (-4) = -8$

> When we divide two numbers:
> - with the *same* sign, the result is *positive*, e.g. $12 \div 4 = 3$ and $-15 \div (-3) = 5$
> - with *opposite* signs, the result is *negative*, e.g. $-12 \div 4 = -3$ and $15 \div (-3) = -5$

F

Exercise 9.1

1 Write down the answers to the following:

a $24 \div 6$	**b** $-24 \div 8$	**c** $-24 \div (-2)$	**d** $24 \div (-1)$
e $-30 \div (-6)$	**f** $-14 \div 7$	**g** $42 \div (-3)$	**h** $-50 \div (-5)$
i $72 \div 12$	**j** $17 \div (-1)$	**k** $56 \div (-8)$	**l** $-48 \div 8$

2 Calculate each pair of expressions.

a i $(24 \div 4) \div 2$ **ii** $24 \div (4 \div 2)$

b i $(100 \div (-50)) \div 2$ **ii** $100 \div (-50 \div 2)$

c i $(-60 \div (-6)) \div (-2)$ **ii** $-60 \div (-6 \div (-2))$

3 a In general, is $(a \div b) \div c = a \div (b \div c)$?

b How would you interpret $24 \div 4 \div 2$?

> To avoid ambiguity use brackets.

4 Evaluate:

a $7 \times (-2)$	**b** $(-3) \times 6$	**c** $(-2) \times (-8)$	**d** $(-12) \div 6$
e $20 \div (-10)$	**f** $(-18) \div (-9)$	**g** $(-4) \times 8$	**h** $(-7) \times (-7)$
i $28 \div (-4)$	**j** $(-36) \div 9$	**k** $12 \times (-1)$	**l** $0 \times (-3)$

m $2 \times (-3) \times 4$ **n** $(-1) \times (-1) \times (-1)$ **o** $4 \times (-6) \times (-3)$

p $(-5) \times 2 \times (-6)$ **q** $(12 \div (-3)) \div (-2)$ **r** $((-36) \div (-1)) \div (-9)$

s $((-24) \div 8) \div (-3)$ **t** $(18 \div (-2)) \div 3$

u $(-2)^3$ **v** $(-3)^2$

10 Sum, difference, product and quotient

The **sum** is what you get when you **add** numbers together.

> **Example 1**   The *sum* of 3, 8 and 7 is 18.

The **difference** is the result of **subtracting** one number from another.

> **Example 2**   The *difference* between 8 and 13 (when 8 is subtracted from 13) is 5.

The **product** is the result of **multiplying** numbers together.

> **Example 3**   The *product* of 2, 4 and 10 is 80.

The **quotient** is the result of **dividing** one number by another.

> **Example 4**   When 30 is divided by 3, the *quotient* is 10.

Exercise 10.1

1 Find the sum of:

    a 9 and 12   **b** -3 and 7   **c** 11 and -8

    d -14 and -7 **e** -1, 3 and 7   **f** -6, -2 and 3

2 Find the difference when:

    a 8 is subtracted from 15   **b** -7 is subtracted from 10

    c 6 is taken away from -2 **d** -4 is subtracted from -1

3 Find the product of:

    a 7 and -2 **b** -3 and 8   **c** -6 and -9

    d -5, 3 and -4 **e** -9, -4 and -3 **f** 12, -4 and 5

4 Find the quotient:

    a $35 \div 5$ **b** $-40 \div 8$ **c** $36 \div (-4)$ **d** $-81 \div (-3)$

F

Challenges

1 Find two numbers whose difference is 6 and whose sum is 14.
2 Find two numbers whose difference is −6 and whose sum is 2.
3 Find two numbers whose product is 12 and whose quotient is 3.
4 Find two numbers whose product is 24 and whose sum is 11.
5 In each of these magic integer squares, each row and column and main diagonal add to give the same magic total.
Copy and complete each square.

a

0		
	−1	
−4		−2

b

−6	4	2
−2		

c

		19
14		−6
		−1

11 More mental calculations

In the following exercises write down your answer to each question without the help of a calculator or any written working.

Exercise 11.1

1 What is the cost of 9 tapes at £9.99 each?

2 What is 8000 minus 150?

3 What is the value of 10^3?

4 Write down the value of $\sqrt{2500}$.

5 What factor, other than 1, is common to both 98 and 105?

6 What is $25 - 84$?

7 Calculate $(-27) + 45$.

8 Take 37 away from (-26).

9 Two different numbers when squared give the answer 1. What are they?

10 Decrease (-5) by 7.

11 What is $(-198) \div 6$?

12 Find the product of 8 and $((-6) + (-6))$.

Exercise 11.2

1 One pen costs 99p. What is the cost of 40 pens?

2 What is 10 000 minus 320?

3 What is the value of 40^2?

4 Calculate $8^2 - 4^3$.

5 Write down the prime factors of 84.

6 What is $(-100) + 36$?

7 Find the value of $73 - (-48)$.

8 Evaluate $(-54) - 67$.

9 Increase (-9) by 15.

10 Calculate $(-2) \times (-7) \times (-6)$.

11 Divide the product of 7 and (-8) by 4.

12 Calculate the value of $1^3 + 2^3 + 3^3$.

F
E

CHECK-UP

1 Write down the answer to:

    a $78 + 36$ **b** $93 - 47$ **c** 306×10

    d $28\,000 \div 100$ **e** $750 \div 30$ **f** $36\,000 \div 400$

    g 230×1000 **h** 38×200 **i** $1800 \div 60$

    j $700\,000 \div 10$

2 Write down the answer to six million divided by 1000.

3 Calculate:

    a $7846 + 8098$ **b** $7023 - 5876$

    c 6978×8 **d** $3752 \div 7$

4 Emir's salary last year was £9803. His salary has been increased by £1278. What is Emir's new salary?

5 The distance by air from London to Tokyo is 6218 miles. From London to Montreal it is 3252 miles. Calculate the difference in these two distances.

6 The distance from Vienna to Lisbon by road is 2935 km. Heinrich made seven return journeys between the two cities last year. How far did he travel altogether?

7 A road relay race covers a distance of 15 000 metres.
There are eight runners in each team.
How far does each runner cover if they all run the same distance?

8 In the year 2000, the population of Denmark was 5 378 000 and
the population of the Netherlands was 15 875 000.

  a What was the total population of the two countries in 2000?
  b How many more people lived in the Netherlands?

9 Barpey Homes built and sold 189 similar houses last year.
Each cost £59 750 to build and each was sold for £68 900.

  a How much did it cost to build all the houses?
  b How much did Barpey get for selling all the houses?
  c What was the profit?

10 Write down the value of:

a 3^2	**b** 4^3	**c** $2^3 - 1^3$
d $(3^2 - 2^3)^3$	**e** $\sqrt{81}$	**f** $\sqrt{900}$
g $\sqrt{1\,000\,000}$	**h** $\sqrt{(5^2 - 3^2)}$	

11 List all the factors of:

  a 12   **b** 80   **c** 90

12 Write down the prime factors of:

  a 24   **b** 42   **c** 96

13 Write as a product of prime factors in index form:

  a 20   **b** 48   **c** 60

14 Write down the sum or difference:

a $7 + (-3)$	**b** $2 + (-8)$	**c** $(-1) + (-3)$	**d** $-4 + 9$
e $-3 - 8$	**f** $-6 + 1$	**g** $7 - 8$	**h** $2 - (-1)$
i $(-4) - (-7)$	**j** $(-6) - (-1)$		

15 Write down the product or quotient:

a $3 \times (-4)$	**b** -2×6	**c** $-7 \times (-5)$	**d** $12 \div (-6)$
e $-14 \div 7$	**f** $-24 \div (-3)$	**g** $0 \div (-2)$	**h** $5 \times (-4) \times 6$
i $-7 \times 2 \times (-3)$	**j** $(-4)^3$		

16 Marcus celebrated his 36th birthday in 24 BC.
When did he celebrate his 70th birthday?

17 A submarine is 385 metres below sea level.
A plane is 4985 metres above sea level and directly above the submarine.
How far apart are the plane and the submarine?

E
F

(2) Decimals

Decimal fractions first appeared around AD 1400. Arabic mathematicians left a space between the whole number and the decimal part:

3 1415

Around 1530 a vertical bar was used:

3│1415

It was only in 1616, when John Napier of Edinburgh produced his tables, that the decimal point appeared in print for the first time.

3·1415

John Napier

---

1 Looking back ◄◄

Exercise 1.1

1 To which number does each arrow point?

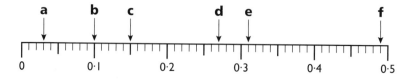

2 In the number 2·34 the 2 stands for units.
What is the value of **a** the 3 **b** the 4?

3 These are the 100 m times for four sprinters:
   a List the runners in order, winner first.
   b Who won and by how many seconds?

John	10·12 s
Earl	9·88 s
Asif	10·05 s
Mike	9·90 s

4 Louise weighs 57·8 kg. Her rucksack weighs 18·5 kg.
Calculate the total weight.

5 Jack's training shoes cost £36·25. Jill's cost £28·99.
  a How much more expensive are Jack's trainers?
  b Calculate the total cost.

6 Each can of fruit juice holds 0·25 litre.
Calculate the total volume of   **a** 10 **b** 100 **c** 1000 cans.

7 Audio cassettes are on special offer. You can buy 10 for £12.90 or 100 for £99.
  a How much is one cassette on the   **i** 10 **ii** 100 offer?
  b How much is saved on each cassette if 100 are bought rather than 10?
  c Calculate the cost of 1000 cassettes using each offer.

8 One lap of a motorbike track is 3·68 km long.
Calculate the distance travelled when a bike completes
  a 5 **b** 8 laps.

9 Keith calculates that on his cycling holiday he will travel 479·5 km.
He wants to cycle the same distance each day for 7 days.
How far should he cycle per day?

10 Robert's truck weighs 3·62 tonnes.
It is carrying a load of 2·7 tonnes.
By how much is the total weight under the limit?

11 Phil works out that buying and developing a film with 24 photos costs £6·48 compared with the cost of £9 for a film with 36 photos.
Calculate the cost of a single photo for a film with
  a 24 **b** 36 photos.

Weak Bridge
Limit 8 tonnes

2 Adding and subtracting without a calculator

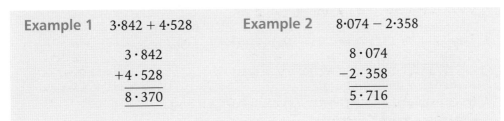

tenths   hundredths

So far we've used *tenths* and *hundredths*. 63·29

thousandths

Now we are going to use *thousandths*. 63·295

Example 1 3·842 + 4·528

   3·842
+4·528
────
8·370

Example 2 8·074 − 2·358

  8·074
−2·358
────
5·716

(2)

Exercise 2.1

1 Calculate

   a 2·415 + 3·216   **b** 3·063 + 4·341

   c 5·735 + 2·425   **d** 1·967 + 6·748

2 Calculate

   a 6·578 − 2·474   **b** 8·357 − 3·319

   c 9·408 − 7·684   **d** 7·002 − 6·869

3 At midnight the temperature is 9·7 °C. By 11 a.m. it has risen to 17·2 °C.

   a Calculate the rise in temperature.

   b By late afternoon it has risen by a further 11·9 °C.
Calculate the new temperature.

4 Diane lists what she spent on clothes last month.

       Shoes   £25·99
       Skirt   £16·75
       Top   £9·99

   Calculate   **a** the total amount spent   **b** how much is left from £60.

5 Calculate

   a the total volume

   b the difference in volume of the two milk cartons.

6 A garage door is 2·2 metres wide.
A truck is 1·896 metres wide.
Calculate the gap when the truck enters the garage.
(Hint: use 2·200.)

7 A gold prospector discovers three nuggets weighing 9·389 g, 7·569 g and 8·732 g.
Calculate the total weight.

8 The cost of telephone calls is given to a tenth of a penny.
Calculate the cost of these calls.

   a £2·448 + £0·750   **b** £1·029 + £0·438 + £0·660

   c £1·655 + £2·540 + £0·839   **d** £0·870 + £2·703 + £3·520 + £1·965

9 These populations are in millions.

   Edinburgh   0·420 m   Glasgow   0·765 m
   London   6·771 m   Manchester   2·581 m

   Calculate the difference between

   a Glasgow and Edinburgh

   b Glasgow and Manchester

   c London and Manchester.

E

10 The table gives the charges for one unit of gas.

	Monthly	Quarterly
Excluding tax	1·730p	1·750p
Including tax	1·817p	1·838p

   a Calculate the tax per unit on
   i quarterly
   ii monthly payments.

   b How much per unit is saved by paying monthly rather than quarterly
   i excluding
   ii including tax?

Example 3   2·73 + 5·708

$$2\cdot730$$
$$+5\cdot708$$
$$\overline{8\cdot438}$$

Example 4   7·04 − 4·524

Add trailing zeros.

$$7\cdot040$$
$$-4\cdot524$$
$$\overline{2\cdot516}$$

Exercise 2.2

1 **a** 3·75 + 4·827
  b 6·434 + 5·7
  c 4·3 + 0·528 + 2·78
  d 6 + 1·43 + 0·859

2 **a** 6·25 − 4·716
  b 8·153 − 6·64
  c 9·1 − 7·536
  d 8 − 5·555

3 1 ounce = 0·028 kg   1 pound = 0·454 kg   1 stone = 6·35 kg
   How many kilograms make 1 stone + 1 pound + 1 ounce?

4 Two radio masts A and B are 9 km apart.
   Point P is 3·725 km from A.
   Point Q is 4·135 km from B.
   A, B, P and Q lie in a straight line.

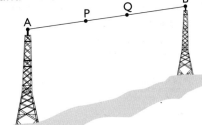

   Calculate the distance between P and Q.

5 Find the next two numbers.
   a 0·125   0·375   0·625   0·875   1·125   ...   ...
   b 0·864   1·344   1·824   2·304   ...   ...

Brainstormers

Find the digit to replace each *.
  a   2·6*0 + 1·*19 = *·46*
  b   4·2*6 + *·34* = 7·*41
  c   *·8*3 + 4·*4* = 7·140
  d   *·5** + 2·*68 = 8·142
  e   *·84* − 2·*54 = 4·4*3
  f   7·*2* − *·136 = 5·5*1
  g   *·0*2 − 3·*2* = 4·114
  h   9·*0* − *·9*6 = 0·388

E

3 Adding and subtracting on the calculator

Exercise 3.1

1 Copy and complete these magic squares.

a

	0·9	
	0·5	
	0·1	0·8

b

		2·4
	1·5	
0·6		1·8

2 Find the next three terms in these sequences.

a 1·5   2·25   3   3·75 ... ...

b 0·125   0·25   0·375   0·5 ... ...

3 **a** A mountain bike costs £245·99 plus £43·05 tax. Calculate the total cost.

    b Another bike costs £324·83 including £48·38 tax. Calculate the price before tax.

4

COMPUTER SYSTEM

Normal Price £1849·99

SALE

COMPUTER SYSTEM

including computer	£985.00
printer	£125.75
scanner	£74.99
digital camera	£238.65

PRICE £

Rachel can't read the sale price.

    a Calculate the total sale price of the system.

    b How much would Rachel save if she buys it?

5 Between which two suitcases is the difference in weight the least?

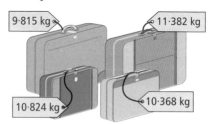

9·815 kg   11·382 kg   10·824 kg   10·368 kg

6 Calculate the perimeters of these shapes.

a

6·375 m   7·225 m   6·875 m

b

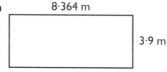

8·364 m   3·9 m

Exercise 3.2

1 The Dow Jones Index shows how the USA stock market is doing.
At the start of trading the Index stands at 10 742·38.

    a During the day it rises by 95·76. Calculate the new Index.

    b The highest value for the year is 11 310·64. The lowest value is 9796·83.
       Calculate the difference between these two values.

2 **a**

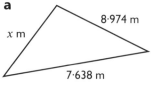

    Perimeter is 20 m.
    Find x.

    b

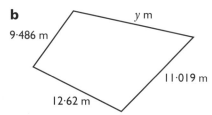

    Perimeter is 40 m.
    Find y.

3 These are the times of a team of 400 m runners: 48·76 s, 50·12 s, 51·27 s
and 49·63 s.

    a Calculate the total time for the 4 × 400 m event.

    b The team wanted to beat 200 s.
       By how much were they above or below 200 s?

4 These are the weights, in kilograms, of two tug-o-war teams.
Great Grippers   104·7, 112·25, 96·8 and 94·75
The Heavies   102·4, 99·52, 98·75 and 103·45.

    Which is the heavier team and by how much?

5 The map shows five villages and the distances between them.

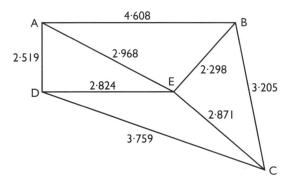

All distances are in kilometres.

Starting at A and finishing anywhere, find the shortest route which visits
B, C, D and E.
What is the total distance of this route?

E

4 Rounding to 1 decimal place

> Examine the digit in the second decimal place.
> ● If it is 4 or less then round down.
> ● If it is more than 4 then round up.

Example

Round each number to 1 decimal place.
   a 7·28   **b** 0·7498   **c** 0·850 64

a   The second decimal place is 8 ... (more than 4, so round up)
     7·28 = 7·3 (to 1 d.p.)
b   The second decimal place is 4 ... (not more than 4, so round down)
     0·7498 = 0·7 (to 1 d.p.)
c   The second decimal place is 5 ... (more than 4, so round up)
     0·850 64 = 0·9 (to 1 d.p.)

Exercise 4.1

1   Round each of these numbers to 1 decimal place.
    a 5·27   **b** 8·94   **c** 6·15   **d** 0·638
    e 0·9701   **f** 60·051   **g** 372·999

2   The table shows how to convert from *imperial* lengths to *metric* lengths.

inches → cm	× 2·54
feet → m	× 0·3048
yards → m	× 0·9144
miles → km	× 1·6093

    Round each of these multipliers to 1 decimal place.

3   These are the times of four runners in a 100 m
    sprint.

Wayne	9·98 s
Rick	10·06 s
Karl	9·95 s
Jim	9·94 s

    a Round each time to 1 decimal place.
    b Do the rounded times show how close the
       race was?

4   Carry out each calculation and then round your answer to
    1 decimal place.
    a 2·84 + 1·37   **b** 8·02 + 0·27   **c** 9·83 − 5·29   **d** 23·65 − 9·09
    e 7·36 × 8   **f** 63·09 × 26   **g** 26 ÷ 7   **h** 50·3 ÷ 9

5 **a** Round the weights of the suitcases to 1 decimal place.

b Use your answers to **a** to estimate the total weight of the two cases.

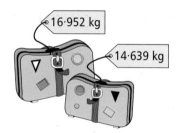

16·952 kg

14·639 kg

6 Jamie measures his distances for each part of the triple jump.

   Hop   3·18 m   Step   2·82 m   Jump   3·95 m

a Round each part to 1 decimal place.

b Estimate the total length of the jump.

7 In a science experiment Cara has 1·362 litres of a chemical solution in a beaker.

She removes 0·875 litre.

a Round the volumes to 1 decimal place.

b Estimate the volume left.

5 Multiplying and dividing by 10, 100 and 1000

Reminder   3·14 × 10 = 31·4   3·14 × 100 = 314·0
                    2·54 ÷ 10 = 0·254   2·54 ÷ 100 = 0·0254

> For ×1000 move the decimal point 3 places to the right.
> For ÷1000 move the decimal point 3 places to the left.

Example 1   3·14 × 1000 = 3140·0 or 3140

Example 2   2·54 ÷ 1000 = 0·002 54

Exercise 5.1

Do these without writing down any working.

1 1 km = 0·62 mile

Copy and complete:

a 10 km = ... miles   **b** 100 km = ... miles
c 1000 km = ... miles   **d** 1 m = ... mile (1000 m = 1 km)

2 1 litre = 1·7598 pints

Copy and complete:

a 10 litres = ... pints   **b** 100 litres = ... pints
c 1000 litres = ... pints   **d** 1 ml = ... pint (1000 ml = 1 litre)

E

3 1 cm = 0·3937 inch.   1 cm = 10 mm.   1 m = 100 cm.   1 km = 1000 m.

Copy and complete:

a 1 mm = ... inch   **b** 1 m = ... inches   **c** 1 km = ... inches

4 1 g = 0·0322 ounce.   1000 mg = 1 g.   1000 g = 1 kg.   1000 kg = 1 tonne.

Copy and complete:

a 1 mg = ... ounce   **b** 1 kg = ... ounces   **c** 1 tonne = ... ounces

5 A 1000 ml bottle of perfume costs £75. Calculate the cost of 1 ml in pence.

6 Dylan checks the currency exchange rates.
$1 buys 116·98 yen. $1 buys 1·085 euros.
How many   **a** yen   **b** euros will he get for $1000?

7 Mr Jackson is paid a car allowance of 37·8p per mile.
How much does he receive in a month when he drives 1000 miles?
(Give your answer in £.)

Exercise 5.2

1 Copy and complete:

a 7·5 × 100 ÷ 10 = ...   **b** (0·63 ÷ 1000) × 10 = ...

c 450 ÷ 1000 × 100 = ...   **d** (0·099 ÷ 100) × 1000 = ...

e (73 ÷ 10) ÷ 100 = ...   **f** ((8·72 ÷ 1000) ÷ 10) × 100 = ...

2 In cycling, the men's record for the 1000 m flying start is 58·269 s.
The women's record is 70·463 s.
Write down   **a** the men's
                    b the women's time for   **i** 1 m   **ii** 100 m.

3 Erica buys a 1000 ml can of paint for £12·65.

a How much does 1 ml cost?
   Write your answer in pence, rounded to 1 decimal place.

b What is the cost of   **i** 10 ml   **ii** 100 ml of paint?

6 Multiplying and dividing a decimal by a whole number

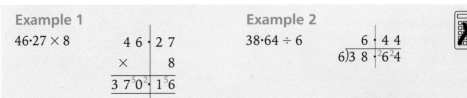

Example 1

46·27 × 8

```
    4 6 · 2 7
  ×       8
  ─────────────
  3 7⁵0²· 1⁵6
```

Example 2

38·64 ÷ 6

```
      6 · 4 4
  6)3 8 ·²6²4
```

When multiplying or dividing by a whole number, keep the decimal points in line.

Exercise 6.1

1 a $2 \cdot 17 \times 4$ **b** $60 \cdot 52 \times 3$ **c** $42 \cdot 37 \times 6$
   d $17 \cdot 38 \times 5$ **e** $13 \cdot 89 \times 7$ **f** $47 \cdot 68 \times 9$

2 a $42 \cdot 18 \div 2$ **b** $45 \cdot 42 \div 3$ **c** $70 \cdot 25 \div 5$
   d $50 \cdot 28 \div 6$ **e** $38 \cdot 01 \div 7$ **f** $91 \cdot 84 \div 8$

3 Hayley buys two new cycle tyres for £12·75 each.
Calculate the total cost.

4 Ian hires a boat for 3 hours. It costs him £14·25.
How much is that for each hour?

5 1 litre = 2·272 pints.
Meg buys 9 litres of milk.
How much is this in pints?

6 Calculate the cost for
   a 4 adults
   b 6 children.

Theatre Tickets

| Adults | £12·65 |
| Children | £7·85 |

7 Samantha pays £44·10 for 6 months of Internet use.
What is the cost for each month?

8 How much is saved by hiring skis at
the weekly price rather than paying
for seven separate days?

Ski Hire

£6.95 per day

£29.95 for 1 week

9 Usman drives an Escort with a 4 cylinder, 1·4 litre engine.
We can work out the capacity of each cylinder by dividing the engine size by
the number of cylinders.
   a Copy and complete: Each cylinder has a capacity of $1 \cdot 4 \div 4 = \dots$ litres.
   b Find the capacity of each cylinder for a Jaguar with a 6 cylinder,
3·3 litre engine.
   c Repeat for a 4 cylinder Astra with a 1·7 litre engine.
   d Repeat for an 8 litre Chevrolet with a 5·4 litre engine.

E

10 Janice wants to hire a bike.

    a Which is the cheaper offer per day?   **b** By how much?

11

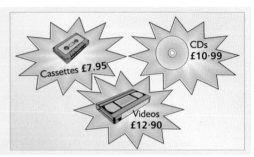

> **Example**
>
> Estimate the cost of 6 CDs,
> then calculate the actual cost.
> Estimation: £10·99 → £11.
> £11 × 6 = £66
> Actual cost:
> (£11 × 6) − (1p × 6) = £65·94

Estimate and then calculate the cost of   **a** 9 cassettes   **b** 8 videos.

12 Estimate and then calculate the areas of these rectangles.
Lengths are in centimetres. (Area = length × breadth)

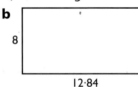

a
4
8·35

b
8
12·84

c
6
28·78

13 Leanne runs 5 laps of the school running track.
Her times are: 30·5 s, 32·8 s, 29·7 s, 33·4 s and 34·4 s.
Calculate her average lap time.

14 Erica changes £8 for $11·04.
    a How much is £1 worth in dollars?
    b How many dollars would she get for £5?

Brainstormers

Find the value of each *.

1   **a**   *3·*   **b**   1·**   **c**   *6·*   **d**   1·4*
        × 2   × 3   × 5   × 6
        ‾‾‾‾   ‾‾‾‾   ‾‾‾‾   ‾‾‾‾
        87·4   5·91   82·5   *·94

2 **a**   31·*   **b**   *0·8   **c**   1·5*   **d**   1·7*
     2)*3·6   5)5*·0   4)*·12   3)*·25

7 Multiplying and dividing on the calculator

Exercise 7.1

1. The Jacksons take out an interest free loan of £1980 to buy a computer.
   Calculate how much they would have to repay per month if they make
   a 36 **b** 24 **c** 12 monthly payments.

2. A can of orange contains 0·33 of a litre.
   Calculate the total volume in a pack of
   a 16 **b** 200 **c** 140 cans.

3. The maximum length of Scotland is 274 miles.
   The maximum width is 154 miles.
   1 mile = 1·6 km.
   Calculate the maximum
   a length
   b width in kilometres.

4. The £97·50 cost of hiring a minibus for the 15 players of a rugby team is
   shared between the players.
   How much does each of them pay?

5. Four teachers and 36 students of the Valley High School go to watch a play at
   a theatre.
   Tickets are £14·50 for each adult and £8·75 for each student.
   Calculate the total cost.

6. The Scottish Southern Upland Way is 323 km long.
   A walker plans to do it in 14 days.
   Calculate the average distance to be walked each day, correct to 1 decimal place.

7. Hannah wants to buy a mountain bike on easy terms.
   The store has two plans:

   52 weeks at £5·75 per week
   or 12 months at £24·50 per month

   a Calculate the total cost of each plan.

   b Which is the better offer and by how much?

8. One lap of a running track is 400 m.
   A runner completes 25 laps at an average time of 72·45 s per lap.
   Calculate:
   a how far he has run
   b the total time taken in **i** seconds **ii** minutes and seconds.

Exercise 7.2

1 The speed of jet aircraft is often measured in Mach numbers where
Mach 1 = 1193·3 km/h.
Change these Mach numbers to km/h, rounded to the nearest whole number.
  a Mach 2 (1193·3 × 2)   **b** Mach 3
  c Mach 1·5   **d** Mach 1·85

2 A 150 g jar of coffee costs £2·82.
Calculate the cost, in pence, per gram.

3 An 8 minute phone call costs 55·2p.
Calculate the cost per   **a** minute   **b** second.

4 A unit of electricity costs 6·175p.
  a Calculate the cost of
    i 65   **ii** 250   **iii** 600 units.
  b Write each answer in pounds (£), rounded to the nearest penny.

5 **a** Hank changes $250 into Japanese currency and receives 28 833·25 yen.
How much is $1 worth in yen?
  b Hillary changes $320 into euro and is given 503·68.
How much is $1 worth in euro?

6 The distance round the trunk of a tree is measured to be 3·36 m.
  a If the tree is 80 years old, what is its average growth, in centimetres,
per year?
  b A neighbouring 120-year-old tree is calculated to have grown at 3·9 cm
per year.
Calculate the distance, in metres, round this tree.

7 Ged fills the fuel tank of his car. It takes 68·19 litres.
He calculates that this is equal to 15 gallons.
  a How many litres are equal to 1 gallon?
  b Change 8·5 gallons to litres.

8 Mr Pearson pays £36 for his 250 km rail journey.
Mrs Morrison travels 280 km and her ticket
costs £38·08.

  a Calculate the cost per kilometre for each of them.
  b Who gets the better deal and by how much per kilometre?

9 Copy and complete this gas bill.
90 days at 7·46p per day = £...
3815 units at 1·08p per unit = £...
Total = £... (to the nearest penny)

Challenges

1 a Chris weighs 6 stone and 13 pounds. There are 14 pounds in a stone.
      His weight in pounds = 6 × 14 + 13 = 97 pounds.
      1 pound = 0·455 kg.
      Calculate his weight in kilograms.
   b Repeat the above steps for Alice who weighs 5 stone 10 pounds.
   c Can you write down the steps to change from kilograms to stones and
      pounds?
   d Weigh yourself in kilograms and convert it to stones and pounds.

2 1 inch = 2·54 cm. 1 foot = 12 inches.
   a Marie is 1·58 m tall. Convert her height into
      i inches (to the nearest inch)   ii feet and inches.
   b Khan is 5 feet 9 inches tall. Convert his height to metres. Give your
      answer to 2 d.p.
   c Measure your own height in metres and convert it to feet and inches.
   d Measure the height of a friend in feet and inches and convert it to metres.

8 Adding and subtracting: being more precise

E
F

Example   2·4 + 0·75 + 0·968

```
2 · 400     Make sure the points are in line.
0 · 750     Add trailing zeros.
0 · 968
4 · 118
```

Exercise 8.1

1 Calculate:
   a 6·3 + 7·38 + 0·864   b 0·079 + 5·86 + 0·9   c 73 + 5·08 + 0·46

2 Calculate:
   a 8·5 + 7·42 − 6·482   b 8·006 − 7·05 + 0·638   c 86 − 9·58 − 47·4

3 The total weight of the three bags is 8·1 kg.
   Calculate the weight of the third bag.

1·74 kg

3·065 kg

4 The length of a piston rod should be 1·5 m.
It must not be 0·085 m greater or less than this.
Calculate **a** the maximum **b** the minimum length of the rod.

5 Find the missing numbers in these sequences.
    a 0·009, 0·012, ..., 0·018, ...   **b** ..., 0·05, 0·075, 0·1, ...
    c ..., ..., 0·075, 0·09, 0·105   **d** ..., 0·22, ..., 0·39, 0·475

6 a The temperature in Inverness one day is −2·5 °C.
    In Fort William it is 1·5 °C.
    What is the difference in temperature?
    b The temperature in Oban on the same day is 2 °C.
    In Perth it is 2·5 °C colder.
    What is the temperature in Perth?

7 Mal keeps a record of his bank account.
    a In column 1, '+' indicates money put in
and '−' indicates money taken out.
What do these signs mean in column 2?
    b Copy and complete the table.

Debit/Credit	Balance
	+10·00
+5·50	
−12·00	
+4·00	
−10·00	

8 The table shows the temperature at midnight in three cities.
    a Calculate the difference in temperature
between
    i Glasgow and Moscow
    ii Glasgow and Chicago
    iii Moscow and Chicago.
    b Calculate the temperature in each city if
the temperature rises by 6·5 °C.

City	Temperature (°C)
Glasgow	2·6
Moscow	−13·8
Chicago	−4·5

9 To convert from degrees Celsius to degrees Kelvin, add 273·15.
    a Convert these temperatures to °K:
    i 30 °C   **ii** 19·5 °C   **iii** −50 °C   **iv** −125·5 °C
    b Convert these temperatures to °C:
    i 300 °K   **ii** 26·15 °K   **iii** 100 °K   **iv** 26·9 °K

10 The table shows how the value of a company changes over five weeks.

Week	1	2	3	4	5
Gain/loss	+£1·754m	−£0·485m	−£0·823m	+£2·873m	−£1·980m

The amounts are in million pounds and '−' means a decrease in value.
Calculate the overall gain or loss.

F

9 Rounding to more than 1 decimal place

Example

Round 6·2539 to   **a** 2   **b** 3 decimal places.

To round to 2 decimal places, look at the third digit after the point. Here it is not more than 4 so round down.

$$6·2539 = 6·25 \text{ (to 2 d.p.)}$$

To round to 3 decimal places, look at the fourth digit after point. Here it is greater than 4 so round up.

$$6·2539 = 6·254 \text{ (to 3 d.p.)}$$

Exercise 9.1

1 Round these numbers to 2 decimal places.

   a 6·136   **b** 0·421   **c** 9·348

   d 12·675   **e** 64·8082   **f** 70·9849

2 Round these numbers to 3 decimal places.

   a 4·8326   **b** 31·6372   **c** 80·2615

   d 0·077 28   **e** 42·999 99   **f** 0·527 541

3 Round these to the number of decimal places given in the brackets.

   a 57·054 (2)   **b** 3·0909 (3)   **c** 0·006 37 (4)

   d 4·108 25 (4)   **e** 409·399 99 (4)

4

Exchange rates	
pound/dollar	1·4689
pound/euro	1·5709
euro/dollar	0·9351

Round these rates to
a 2
b 3 decimal places.

5 These are the numbers to multiply by to convert from metric to imperial weights.

grams	→	ounces	0·0322
kilograms	→	pounds	2·2046
tonnes	→	tons	0·9842

Round these numbers to   **a** 2   **b** 3 decimal places

6 Here are two mathematical numbers you may meet. They are written to 9 decimal places.

$$\pi = 3·141\ 592\ 654 \quad e = 2·718\ 281\ 828$$

Round each of them to   **a** 1   **b** 2   **c** 3   **d** 4 decimal places.

F

10 Further multiplication and division

> **Example 1** $4 \cdot 2 \times 30 = 4 \cdot 2 \times 10 \times 3 = 42 \times 3 = 126$
>
> **Example 2** $0 \cdot 03 \times 0 \cdot 004 \rightarrow 3 \times 4 = 12$
> There are five digits after a decimal point in the question so there
> should be five digits after the decimal point in the answer $\rightarrow 0 \cdot 000\ 12$
>
> **Example 3** $28 \div 0 \cdot 7 = 280 \div 7$ ($\times$ both numbers by 10) $= 40$
>
> **Example 4** $0 \cdot 006 \div 0 \cdot 02 = 0 \cdot 6 \div 2$ ($\times$ both numbers by 100) $= 0 \cdot 3$

Exercise 10.1

1   Calculate:

a $0 \cdot 4 \times 20$	**b** $0 \cdot 4 \times 200$	**c** $0 \cdot 4 \times 2000$	**d** $1 \cdot 2 \times 40$
e $1 \cdot 2 \times 400$	**f** $1 \cdot 2 \times 4000$	**g** $4 \cdot 3 \times 50$	**h** $8 \cdot 1 \times 300$
i $0 \cdot 2 \times 0 \cdot 3$	**j** $0 \cdot 2 \times 0 \cdot 03$	**k** $0 \cdot 8 \times 0 \cdot 6$	**l** $0 \cdot 08 \times 0 \cdot 06$
m $600 \times 0 \cdot 04$			

2   Calculate:

a $8 \div 0 \cdot 2$	**b** $8 \div 0 \cdot 02$	**c** $8 \div 0 \cdot 002$	**d** $2 \cdot 4 \div 0 \cdot 3$
e $2 \cdot 4 \div 0 \cdot 03$	**f** $2 \cdot 4 \div 0 \cdot 003$	**g** $6 \cdot 4 \div 0 \cdot 4$	**h** $7 \cdot 5 \div 0 \cdot 05$
i $0 \cdot 6 \div 0 \cdot 2$	**j** $0 \cdot 6 \div 0 \cdot 02$	**k** $0 \cdot 06 \div 0 \cdot 2$	**l** $2 \cdot 4 \div 0 \cdot 4$
m $0 \cdot 48 \div 0 \cdot 008$			

3   The volume of a bottle of perfume is $0 \cdot 02$ litre.
   What is the volume of
   a 4   **b** 40   **c** 400 bottles?

4   A packet of salt weighs $0 \cdot 4$ kg.
   How many packets can be filled from a container holding
   a 8 kg   **b** 80 kg   **c** 800 kg?

5   Calculate the area of each of these rectangles (area = length $\times$ breadth).

   a 0·9 m, 0·4 m
   b 1·6 m, 0·3 m
   c 1·5 m, 0·8 m

6   **a**   800 paper clips weigh 40 g. Calculate the weight of one paper clip.
   b   5000 staples weigh 150 g. Calculate the weight of one staple.

7 Calculate:

a the total of the 36 monthly payments

b the total including the final payment

c how much more than the cash price is repaid and comment on this advert.

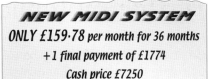

NEW MIDI SYSTEM
ONLY £159·78 per month for 36 months
+1 final payment of £1774
Cash price £7250

8 To calculate the Value Added Tax (VAT) on goods and services, multiply by 0·175. Calculate the tax, to the nearest penny, on:

a a mobile phone at £46·76

b a pager at £25·99

c a CD copier at £89·87.

Exercise 10.2

1 Calculate:

a $6 \cdot 3 \times 500$	**b** $0 \cdot 04 \times 6000$	**c** $74 \cdot 2 \times 60$
d $0 \cdot 16 \times 0 \cdot 008$	**e** $700 \times 0 \cdot 35$	**f** $6 \cdot 5 \times 90\,000$
g $0 \cdot 012 \times 0 \cdot 04$	**h** $0 \cdot 2 \times 0 \cdot 4 \times 0 \cdot 6$	**i** $400 \times 0 \cdot 05 \times 0 \cdot 006$

2 Calculate:

a $200 \div 0 \cdot 4$	**b** $24 \cdot 2 \div 0 \cdot 002$	**c** $0 \cdot 045 \div 0 \cdot 9$
d $5640 \div 0 \cdot 05$	**e** $0 \cdot 852 \div 0 \cdot 003$	**f** $8400 \div 0 \cdot 7$
g $0 \cdot 0528 \div 80$	**h** $5 \cdot 34 \div 600$	

3 Copy and complete:

a $2 \cdot 3 \div$ ___ $= 0 \cdot 023$	**b** $2 \cdot 3 \times$ ___ $= 23$
c $7 \cdot 1 \div$ ___ $= 0 \cdot 0071$	**d** $7 \cdot 1 \times$ ___ $= 7100$
e ___ $\times 10 = 8 \cdot 6$	**f** ___ $\div 10 = 5 \cdot 6$
g ___ $\times 100 = 54$	**h** ___ $\div 100 = 0 \cdot 93$
i ___ $\times 1000 = 9$	**j** ___ $\div 1000 = 0 \cdot 07$

4 A stalagmite has grown 15 cm in 3000 years.
Calculate its average growth per year.

5 The area of a rectangle = length × breadth.
Calculate these areas:

a

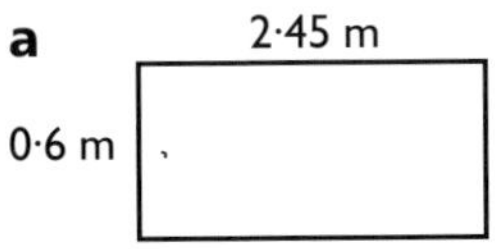

b

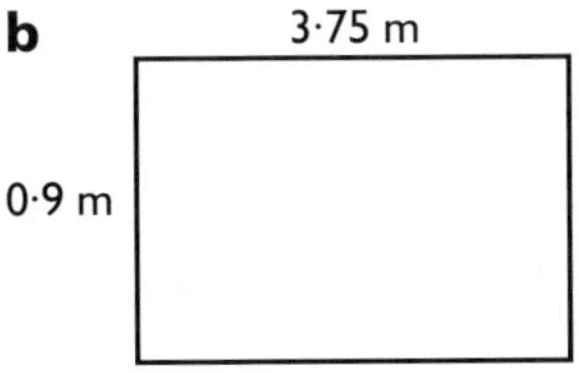

c

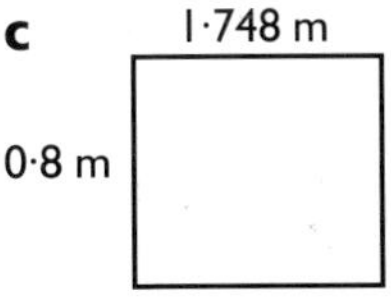

6 a One night in winter, Lin calculated the change in temperature in the 8 hours from nightfall to midnight to be $-1.5\,°C$ per hour. Calculate the total change in temperature.

b On another night the total change was $-20\,°C$ over 8 hours. Calculate the average change per hour.

7 On the foreign exchange, £1 buys: 67·74 rupees; 2·32 Swiss francs; 165·25 yen.

a Which country uses **i** rupees **ii** yen?

b On holiday, Yvonne changes £200 into Swiss francs.
i How many francs does she receive?
She spends 420 francs and then changes the remainder into pounds at the same rate.
ii How much has she got in pounds and pence?

c Going abroad, Robert changes £500 into rupees.
i How many rupees does he get?
When he gets home he changes the money he has left back into pounds and receives £12.
ii How many rupees has he spent?

d How many pounds do you need to change to become a yen millionaire?

Investigation

Increase or decrease?

When 6·4 is multiplied by 1, the result is 6·4.
When 6·4 is multiplied by 1·1, the result is 7·04 ... bigger than 6·4.
When 6·4 is multiplied by 0·9, the result is 5·76 ... less than 6·4.

1 Is the result bigger or smaller than 6·4 when 6·4 is multiplied by:
  a 3·9   **b** 0·99   **c** 5·6   **d** 0·1
  e 12·0   **f** 0·999   **g** 0·0   **h** 1·0?

2 Is the result bigger or smaller than 0·4 when 0·4 is multiplied by:
  a 4·9   **b** 0·99   **c** 3·2   **d** 0·01
  e 12·0   **f** 0·999   **g** 0·0   **h** 1·0?

3 Assuming that we are only working with positive numbers and zero, copy and complete the following sentences.
  a Multiplying one number by another which is greater than   has an increasing effect on that number.
  b Multiplying one number by another which is   than   has a decreasing effect on that number.

4 Work out similar rules when negative numbers are included. (Remember that, for example, -5 is less than -4.)

5 Investigate the effect of division on a number in a similar fashion.

11 Significant figures

Any number is made up of digits or figures.
We say a digit, or figure, is **significant** if it gives an idea of   i   quantity or
                                                                       ii   accuracy.

When zeros are used only to position the decimal point they are not regarded as
significant.

Example 1

702 cm has 3 significant figures.
70·2 cm has 3 significant figures.
7·02 cm has 3 significant figures.
0·702 cm has 3 significant figures ... the leading zero positions the decimal point.
702·0 cm has 4 significant figures ... the trailing zero tells you the measurement
                                        is more accurate than 702 cm.

When working with whole numbers you need more information before you can
tell if trailing zeros are significant.

Example 2

1600 cm measured to the nearest 100 cm has
2 significant figures (think of 16 hundred).
1600 cm measured to the nearest 10 cm has
3 significant figures (think of 160 tens).
The figures on a 50p coin are both significant ... there is exactly 50p.
'360° make one revolution' ... there are 3 significant figures in the '360'.
'52 × 7 is roughly 360' ... there are 2 significant figures in the '360'.

Example 3

7285 people attend a sports event.
To the nearest thousand: 7285 = 7000 to 1 significant figure (1 s.f.)
To the nearest hundred: 7285 = 7300 to 2 s.f.
To the nearest ten: 7285 = 7290 to 3 s.f.
The thickness of a piece of paper was measured as 0·001 026 cm.

0·001 026 = 0·001 to 1 significant figure (1 s.f.)
0·001 026 = 0·0010 to 2 s.f.
0·001 026 = 0·001 03 to 3 s.f.

Exercise 11.1

1   Round each number to 1 significant figure:

    a 728   **b** 39   **c** 8072   **d** 57 020   **e** 619 801

    f 5·67   **g** 0·084   **h** 23·4   **i** 40·08   **j** 0·005 005

2   Round to 2 significant figures:

    a 317   **b** 4608   **c** 14 099   **d** 999   **e** 305 590

    f 3·84   **g** 0·0602   **h** 37·41   **i** 3·084   **j** 0·005 96

F

3   Round to 3 significant figures:
   a 7029   **b** 14 929   **c** 289 500   **d** 999 999 **e** 3 671 683
   f 0·040 14 **g** 0·4597   **h** 2·0414   **i** 0·002 406 6

4   **a** Round to 1 s.f.   **i** 285   **ii** 23
   b Use your answers to part **a** to help you estimate the value of £285 × 23.
   c Compare your estimate with the actual answer.

5   Estimate the area of a rectangle 6·8 cm by 3·1 cm.

6   The Science Department buys 28 books costing £7·90 each.
   a Write   **i** 28   **ii** 7·90 to 1 significant figure.
   b Estimate the total cost.

7   The Maths Department orders 53 new graphic calculators each costing £88·15.
   a Write   **i** 53   **ii** 88·15 to 1 significant figure.
   b Estimate the total cost of the calculators.

12 Scientific notation

Scientists often have to work with very large and very small numbers.

Example 1

'The sun is 93 000 000 miles away.'
An astronomer may write 'The sun is $9·3 \times 10^7$ miles away.'
We would move the point 7 places to the
right to get the *normal* way of writing it. **9 3 0 0 0 0 0 0·**

Example 2

'A millilitre of helium weighs 0·000 18 g.'
A chemist may write 'A millilitre of helium
weighs $1·8 \times 10^{-4}$ g.'
We would move the point 4 places to the left to **0·0 0 0 1 8**
get the *normal* way of writing it.

Note that to write a number in **scientific notation**
- we write down the significant figures
- we put the point after the first figure
- we write '×10'
- we give the 10 an index which tells you how to move the point to get the *normal* form of the number.

Example 3

Express the following in scientific notation:
a 34 000   **b** 0·000 000 456

Answer: **a** $3·4 \times 10^4$ **b** $4·56 \times 10^{-7}$

Exercise 12.1

1 Express each of these numbers in the normal way of writing numbers.

    a $2 \cdot 3 \times 10^5$ **b** $1 \cdot 7 \times 10^8$ **c** $5 \cdot 31 \times 10^6$ **d** $1 \cdot 14 \times 10^7$

    e $8 \cdot 01 \times 10^{-3}$ **f** $3 \cdot 0 \times 10^{-6}$ **g** $9 \cdot 43 \times 10^{-4}$ **h** $1 \cdot 08 \times 10^{-1}$

    i $4 \cdot 97 \times 10^{-8}$ **j** $6 \cdot 5 \times 10^7$ **k** $7 \cdot 09 \times 10^{-5}$ **l** $5 \cdot 0 \times 10^1$

    m $6 \cdot 45 \times 10^{-2}$ **n** $1 \cdot 69 \times 10^5$ **o** $8 \cdot 41 \times 10^{-1}$ **p** $9 \cdot 99 \times 10^8$

2 Express each of these numbers in scientific notation.

    a 34 900   **b** 97 000 000   **c** 610 000   **d** 514

    e 0·876   **f** 0·041   **g** 0·000 32   **h** 0·000 561

    i 0·004 56   **j** 789·00   **k** 0·000 006   **l** 3·78

    m 0·005 67   **n** 0·876   **o** 56·7   **p** 512 300 000

3 Round each number to 3 significant figures and express it in scientific notation.

    a 356 129   **b** 85 992 364   **c** 912 271   **d** 9348

    e 0·745 67   **f** 0·079 112   **g** 0·000 079 54   **h** 0·006 912

    i 0·009 999 9   **j** 794·76   **k** 9354·75   **l** 0·891 28

    m 1·4597   **n** 0·118 722   **o** 37·67   **p** 91 928 384

4 Write out the following sentences, expressing the numbers in the normal way.

    a An oxygen molecule has a diameter of $3 \cdot 0 \times 10^{-10}$ m.

    b Saturn is $8 \cdot 86 \times 10^8$ miles from the sun.

F

CHECK-UP

1 Calculate:

    a 3·859 + 2·926   **b** 6·52 − 4·617   **c** 0·263 × 10

    d 52 ÷ 1000   **e** 8·2 × 100   **f** 13·62 × 7

    g 93·52 ÷ 8.

2 Calculate:

    a the sum

    b the difference of the weights of the suitcases.

7·628 kg   9·125 kg

3 £1 buys 2·4785 Swiss francs.
How many francs you would get for

    a £10 **b** £100 **c** £1000?

4 Anna's car travels 1000 miles and uses 128·5 litres of petrol.
Calculate the amount of petrol needed for

    a 100 miles   **b** 10 miles   **c** 1 mile.

5 A tank holds 94·5 litres of oil. It fills 6 cans of equal size.
Calculate the volume of each of the cans.

6 Calculate the total cost of buying the bike.

Mountain Bike
9 monthly payments of
£28·95

7 In the triple jump Raj records these lengths:
Hop 3·362 m; Step 4·819 m; Jump 5·054 m.

    a Write each of these lengths to 1 decimal place.

    b Use your answers to **a** to estimate the total length jumped.

8 Mr Stone owns two lorries. One weighs 38·75 tonnes.
The other weighs 42·125 tonnes. Calculate:

    a the total weight **b** the difference in weight of the lorries.

9 How many bottles, each of volume 0·75 litre, can be filled from a tank holding

    a 22·5 litres   **b** 42·75 litres   **c** 72·6 litres?

10 Copy and complete this electricity bill.

    91 days at 9·125p per day £...
    78 units at 6·175p per unit £...
              Total £... (to the nearest penny)

11 On Monday, £1 buys $1·381. On Tuesday, £1 buys $1·379.

    a Calculate the amount the pound (£) has changed.

    b On Wednesday, the pound (£) rises by $0·058.
Calculate its new value.

12 A medicine spoon holds 0·005 litre. How many spoonfuls are there in a bottle which holds:

   a   0·3 litre   b   0·25 litre   c   0·375 litre?

13 Gill's car averages 9·6 km per litre.

   a   How far will it go on

       i   40 litres   ii   600 litres   iii   2000 litres?

   b   A litre costs £0·85. Calculate the cost of

       i   40 litres   ii   600 litres   iii   2000 litres.

14 A plumber charges £83·50 for 5 hours of work.

   a   What is the hourly rate?

   b   How much would the charge be for 8 hours at the same rate?

15 A marathon is 26 miles 385 yards long.
1 mile = 1·6093 km. 1 yard = 0·0009 km.
How long is a marathon in kilometres?

16 Round each of the following to

     i   1 significant figure   ii   2 significant figures.

   a   341   b   3·07   c   0·006 15   d   0·0704   e   93 420 000

17 Express these numbers in scientific notation:

   a   34 500 000   b   0·003 91

18 Express these numbers in normal form:

   a $7·61 \times 10^{5}$ b $4·97 \times 10^{-3}$

F

③ Angles

The people of Babylon in 600 BC were great students of astronomy. They taught the Greeks that the night sky could be divided into the 12 signs of the zodiac, and that each part could be subdivided into 30 smaller parts called degrees.

12 × 30° = 360°

---

1 Looking back ◀◀

Some definitions

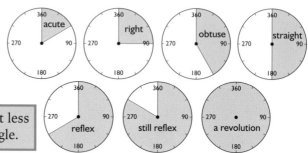

> An angle greater than 180° but less than 360° is called a **reflex** angle.

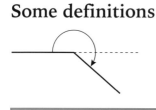

35° is the complement of 55° and 55° is the complement of 35°.

$(90 - x)°$ is the complement of $x°$ and $x°$ is the complement of $(90 - x)°$ where x is less than or equal to 90.

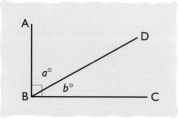

> When two angles add to make 90° they are called **complementary**.

∠ABD + ∠DBC = 90°
∠ABD is the **complement** of ∠DBC.

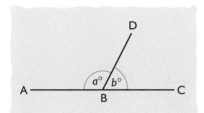

$(180 - x)°$ is the supplement of $x°$
and $x°$ is the supplement of $(180 - x)°$
where x is less than or equal to 180.

$\angle ABD + \angle DBC = 180°$
$\angle ABD$ is the **supplement** of $\angle DBC$.

When two angles add to make 180°
they are called **supplementary**.

AC crosses DE at B.
$\angle ABD$ is the supplement of $\angle DBC$.
$\angle ABD$ is the supplement of $\angle ABE$.

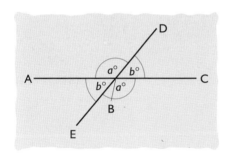

The amount one side of the see-saw goes up
is matched by the amount the other side
goes down.

So $\angle DBC = \angle ABE$.
B is the vertex of both $\angle DBC$ and $\angle ABE$.
$\angle DBC$ and $\angle ABE$ are **vertically opposite** angles.

Vertically opposite angles are equal.

E

Exercise 1.1

1   State the type of each angle below.

a   **b**   **c**   **d**   **e**

          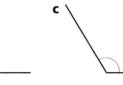   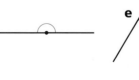

f 72°   **g** 172°   **h** 272°   **i** 91°   **j** 181°

2 Calculate the size of each labelled angle.

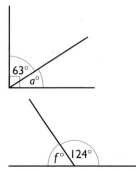

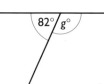
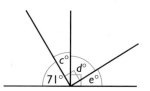
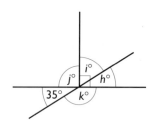

3 State the complement of

   a 74°
         b 40°
         c $x°$

   d $(90 - y)°$
     e $(20 - x)°$
    f $(x + 40)°$.

4 State the supplement of

   a 55°
         b 175°
       c $x°$

   d $(180 - y)°$
    e $(90 - x)°$
    f $(x + 90)°$.

5 a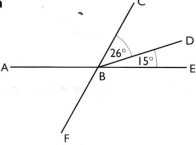

ABE and CBF are straight lines.
Calculate the size of

  i the acute angle ABF

 ii the reflex angle ABC.

b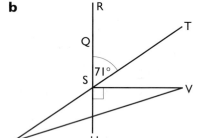

PST and RSU are straight lines.
Calculate the size of

  i the acute angle PSU

 ii the reflex angle TSU.

6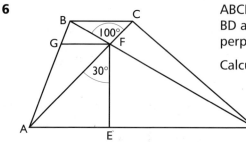

ABCD is a four-sided figure with diagonals
BD and AC crossing at F. The line GF is
perpendicular to the line EF.

Calculate the size of **a** the acute angle CFD

                           b the obtuse angle BFE.

7 Calculate the value of x in each case.

a

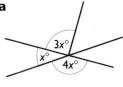

b

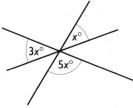

c

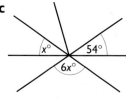

8 Calculate the value of x, y and z in each case.

a

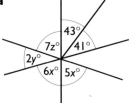

b

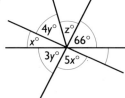

c

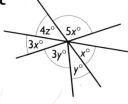

Challenge

A pair of scissors is an example of vertically opposite angles in action. (Think about the cutting edges.)

Can you name at least five other cases of vertically opposite angles in the real world?

E

2 Angles associated with parallel lines

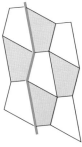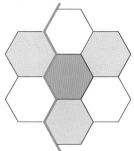

A shape is said to tile when congruent (identical) examples fit together to fill space without overlapping or leaving spaces.
The boundary between tiles may wobble and weave as highlighted above.

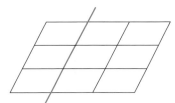

When parallelograms tile, the boundaries form straight lines.
These form a very useful pattern of angles.

Since each tile is identical, the pattern of angles round each vertex must be identical.

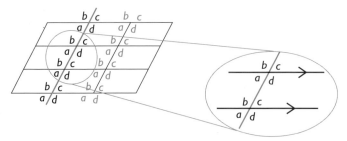

When a line cuts across two parallel lines, identical patterns of angles are formed at the intersections.
The cutting line is often called a **transversal**.

E

Example

Given that the lines AC and DF are parallel, and that $\angle ABG = 70°$, find all the marked angles in the diagram.

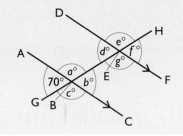

Answer

$a° = 180 - 70 = 110°$ (supplementary)
$b° = 70°$ (vertically opposite)
$c° = a° = 110°$ (vertically opposite)

Since AC and DF are parallel, the pattern of angles round B is the same as the pattern of angles round E, so

$d° = 70°$
$e° = a° = 110°$
$f° = b° = 70°$
$g° = c° = 110°$

Exercise 2.1

1 Calculate the size of each lettered angle in the diagrams below.

a

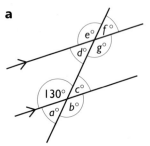

b

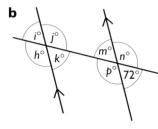

c

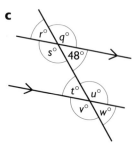

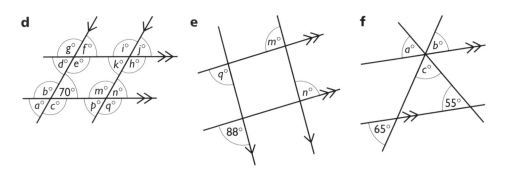

d   **e**   **f**

2   Calculate the size of each lettered angle.

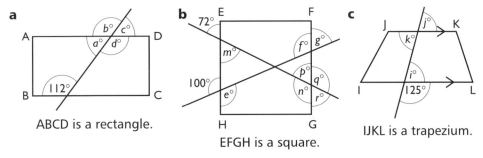

a

ABCD is a rectangle.

b

EFGH is a square.

c

IJKL is a trapezium.

3   The clothes-horse can take various positions. Lines that look parallel are parallel.

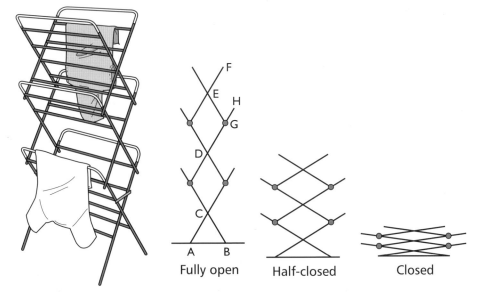

Fully open   Half-closed   Closed

a   Fully open, ∠ ACB = 28°.
   i   What is the size of ∠FEG?   **ii**   What is the size of ∠EGH?

b   Half-closed, ∠ACB = 143°. What now is the size of
   i   ∠FEG   **ii**   ∠EGH?

c   When closed, ∠FEG = 3°. Calculate the sizes of ∠ACB and ∠EGH.

Sometimes adding your own lines will help solve a problem.

Example

AB is parallel to CD.
∠APQ = 140°. ∠DRQ = 30°.
Calculate the size of ∠PQR.

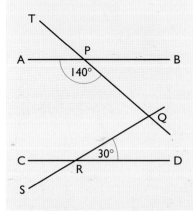

Answer

Add a line EF, parallel to AB, passing through Q. Complete the pattern of angles round P and round R.

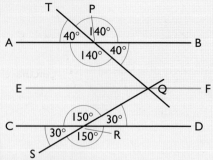

∠PQE = ∠TPA = 40°
(The pattern round Q is the same as the pattern round P, ignoring line QR.)
∠RQE = ∠SRC = 30°
(The pattern round Q is the same as the pattern round R, ignoring line QP.)
∠PQR = ∠PQE + ∠RQE = 40° + 30° = 70°

Exercise 2.2

1

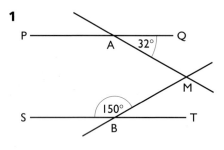

PQ is parallel to ST. ∠SBM = 150°. ∠QAM = 32°. Calculate the sizes of all the angles round M.

2

Calculate the sizes of all the angles round A.

3

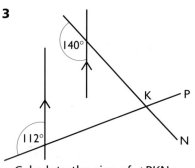

Calculate the size of ∠PKN.

4

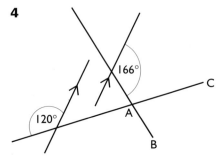

Calculate the sizes of all the angles round A.

50

3 Corresponding angles

Consider this diagram:

By extending each line we see that $a = b$.

Each corresponds to the top left-hand angle in a congruent tiling.

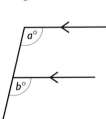
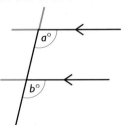
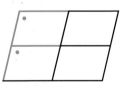

When parallel lines are crossed by a transversal, **corresponding** angles are equal.

Examples of corresponding angles

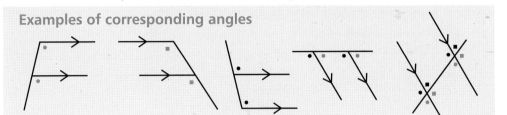

Exercise 3.1

1 Name pairs of corresponding angles in these diagrams.

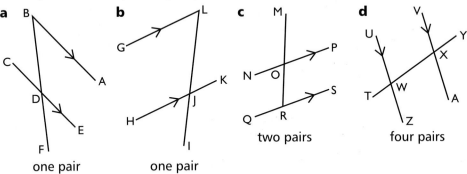

a one pair **b** one pair **c** two pairs **d** four pairs

2 Calculate the size of each of the lettered angles by considering corresponding angles.

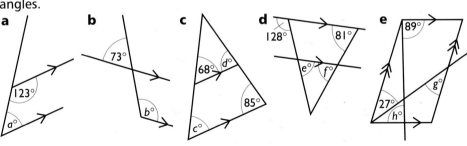

3 On the gable-end of a factory you can see that the south-facing part of the roof has a shallower slope than the north-facing part. The struts AB and CD are parallel. CF is parallel to EB.

Calculate the size of:

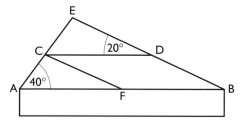

a ∠ECD

b ∠EBA

c ∠CFA

4 The figure PQRS is a parallelogram – its opposite sides are parallel.

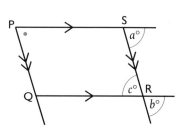

a If ∠QPS = 50° calculate the size of
   i   *a*   **ii** *b*   **iii** *c*
   giving a reason for each answer.

b If, instead, ∠QPS = 60° calculate the size of
   i   *a*   **ii** *b*   **iii** *c*

c If ∠QPS = *x*° calculate the size of
   i   *a*   **ii** *b*   **iii** *c*

d What can be said about angles which are diagonally opposite in a parallelogram?

4 Alternate angles

Consider this diagram:

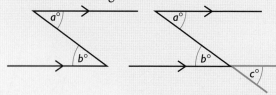

Extend two lines to make the angle marked *c*°.

$a° = c°$ (corresponding angles)
$b° = c°$ (vertically opposite angles)
and so $a° = b°$
Such pairs of angles are called **alternate** angles.

When parallel lines are crossed by a transversal, **alternate** angles are equal.

Examples of alternate angles

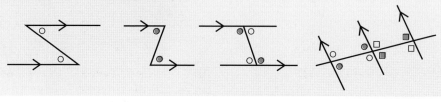

Exercise 4.1

1 Identify the alternate angles in each diagram.

a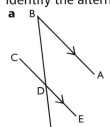

one pair

b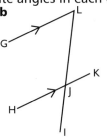

one pair

c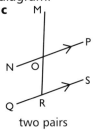

two pairs

d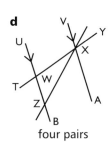

four pairs

2 Calculate the size of each labelled angle with the help of alternate angles.

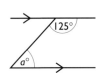 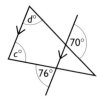 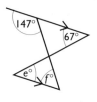

3 **a** By extending the line PQ, calculate the size of $\angle$SRQ.
   b By a suitable extension, calculate $p°$ and $q°$.

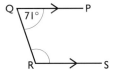 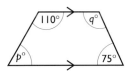

4 Take any triangle ABC with angles $a°$, $b°$ and $c°$.
   Draw the line DE through A parallel to BC.

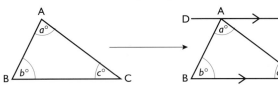

Use alternate angles to prove that the sum of the angles of any triangle is 180°.

5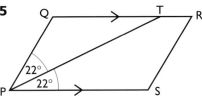

What kind of triangle is PQT?

6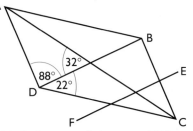

ABCD is a parallelogram. FE is parallel to DB. Calculate the sizes of as many angles in the diagram as you can.

E

5 Mixed examples

In each of the questions below, give reasons for your answers, for example: alternate angles, corresponding angles, vertically opposite angles, complementary angles, supplementary angles, third angle in a triangle.
It can often help to draw extra lines in a diagram.
Describe any such additions you make.

Exercise 5.1

1 Calculate the sizes of all the angles round

   a T   **b** V.

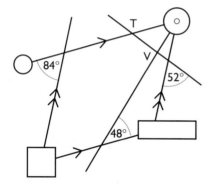

2 DE is parallel to CB.
ACF and ABG are straight lines.

  a Calculate the size of

    i a **ii** g **iii** b
    iv f **v** c
    giving a reason for each answer.

  b Calculate $a + b + c$.

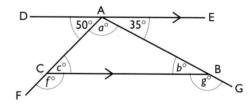

Brainstormer

Repeat question **2** with $\angle DAF = x°$ and $\angle EAG = y°$.

---

3 What is the value of $x°$?

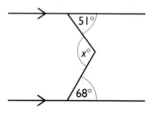

Hint: make additions to the diagram as shown here and calculate $p°$ and $q°$ first.

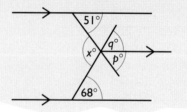

4 Calculate the value of x in each case by first making suitable additions to the diagram.

  a

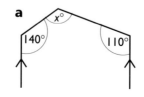

  b

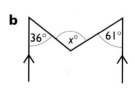

5 How does a camera work?

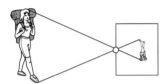

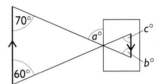

Light comes from an object, passes through the lens of a camera and makes an image on the film.

Using this simplified diagram, find the size of each lettered angle.

6 A pantograph is a copying instrument. The instrument is fixed to the table at C. A pen at B traces a picture and another pen at A will draw an enlargement of the same picture.

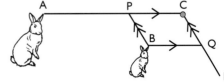

  a When ∠APB = 112° calculate   **i** ∠PBQ   **ii** ∠BQC.
  b When ∠PCQ = 24° calculate   **i** ∠APB   **ii** ∠BQR.
  c Name four pairs of angles which will remain equal to each other no matter how much B is moved.

7 A snooker ball bounces off the cushion as shown.
Calculate the value of x.

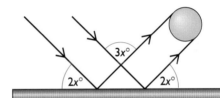

8 A star is made from two congruent rhombuses as shown.
The angle at A is 40°.
The star has quarter-turn symmetry.

Calculate the size of all the angles round B.

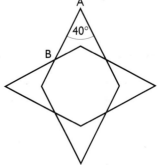

9 ABCD is a parallelogram.
PQRS is a V-kite.
AB is parallel to PS.
∠BAN = 80°. ∠ANQ = 95°.
Calculate the size of every other angle in the diagram.

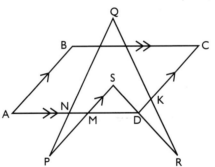

F

6 The sum of the angles of a polygon

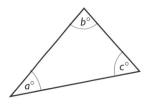 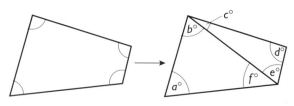

A quadrilateral can be split into two triangles.

> The sum of the angles of a triangle is 180°.

> So the sum of the angles of a quadrilateral is $2 \times 180° = 360°$.

If the quadrilateral is **regular** (all sides equal and all angles equal) then each angle is $360° \div 4 = 90°$.

F

A pentagon splits into 3 triangles, so $3 \times 180° = 540°$.

Each angle in a regular pentagon is $540° \div 5 = 108°$.

The angles inside a shape are known as **interior** angles.

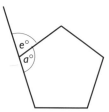

exterior angle = $e°$
interior angle = $a°$

When one side of a polygon is extended, the angle formed between the extension and the next side is called an **exterior** angle.

Investigation

1 What can be said about the interior angle and exterior angle in a regular pentagon?
2 Is this true about all regular polygons?
3 Copy and complete this table.

Regular polygon Number of sides	N	3	4	5	6	7	8	9	10
interior angle	$a°$	60°	90°	108°					
exterior angle	$e°$	120°	90°	72°					

4 For a *regular polygon*, what is the connection between
   a the number of sides, N, and the size of the interior angle, $a°$?
   b the number of sides, N, and the size of the exterior angle, $e°$?

5 The pre-decimal threepenny piece was a regular 12-sided polygon.
   Calculate the size of one of its
   a interior   b exterior angles.

CHECK-UP

1 State the relationship between the following angle pairs, e.g. $a°$ and $b°$ are supplementary.

a   b   c   d   e

2 Calculate the size of each lettered angle.

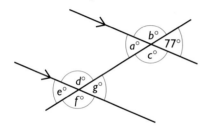

3 Name a pair of
   a corresponding angles
   b alternate angles.

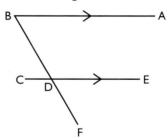

4 Calculate the value of x.

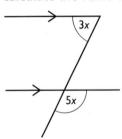

5 Calculate the size of

a ∠QTS

b ∠TPR

c ∠PRQ

d ∠TSQ

e ∠TSR.

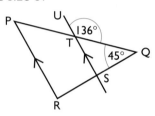

6 By adding suitable lines, calculate the reflex angle XYZ.

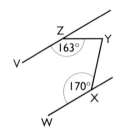

7 Calculate the size of as many angles as possible.

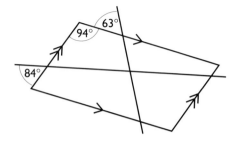

8 The 50p coin is based on a regular heptagon (7-sided polygon).
Calculate, to 1 decimal place, the size of one of its

a interior angles

b exterior angles.

(4) Letters and numbers

Around AD 800, the mathematician Abu Ja'far Muhammad ibn Musa al-Khwarizmi wrote a book called *Hisab al'jabr w'al-muqabala* from which we get our word 'algebra'. It is considered the first book to be written on algebra.

From his name, al-Khwarizmi, we get the word algorism.

Al-Khwarizmi

1 Looking back ◀◀

Exercise 1.1

1 What number is represented by each letter?

a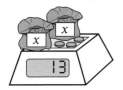

b 25, 21, t, 13, 9, ...

c
	$- 4$	
x	12	8
21	17	y

$+ 5$

d Ian is 2 m tall.
The tree in his garden is x m tall and is three times as tall as the fence. Ian's height is 1 m less than the height of the fence.

2 Find the missing expressions:

a IN x ─ subtract 5 ─ OUT

b IN ─ subtract 6 ─ OUT y

c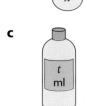

t ml

20 ml has been used. How much is left?

d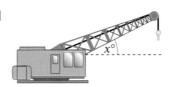

$x°$

The crane jib was heightened by 12°. What is the new angle?

e IN k ─ $\times 8$ ─ OUT

f

140 cm

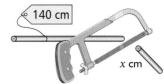

x cm

What length is left?

3 Find the value of:

   a $10 - y$ when $y = 4$ **b** $4a + 2$ when $a = 3$

   c $\frac{1}{2}x - 3$ when $x = 10$ **d** $8k - 7$ when $k = 3$

2 A variety of expressions

> **Example**
>
> Evaluate (find the value of) $30 - 2a + 3b$ when $a = 4$ and $b = 5$.
>
> **Answer:** $30 - 2a + 3b$
> $= 30 - 2 \times 4 + 3 \times 5$
> $= 30 - 8 + 15$
> $= 37$

Exercise 2.1

1 Evaluate:

   a $12 - 3a$ when $a = 3$

   b $4x - 2y$ when $x = 5$ and $y = 3$

   c $8 + 3m - 2n$ when $m = 4$ and $n = 6$

2 $a = 1$, $b = 3$, $c = 5$, $d = 8$ and $e = 7$
Evaluate these expressions:

a $5b + 2$	**b** $d + 3b$	**c** $12 - 2c$
d $3b + 2e$	**e** $5d - 3b$	**f** $5b + 2c - 3d$
g $100 - 8d - 3b$	**h** $4a - b + 3c + 12$	**i** $32 - 4d + 7e - 3b$
j $10a - 2 + 4b - d$	**k** $4b + c - 2d$	**l** $5e - 30 + 5c$
m $12c - 20b$	**n** $100 - 10c - 7e$	

Challenge

Copy and complete

a

$10 - x$			9	4
x	3	8		
y	5	2	4	
$2x + 3y$				24

b

$21 - 4a$	a	b	$3a - b$
	4	5	
	1	2	
1		9	
9			2

3 Like terms

This quadrilateral is made with four straws.
Its perimeter is therefore $(2x + 3y + 4x + 2y)$ cm.
This can be simplified to give $(6x + 5y)$ cm in total.

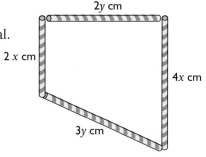

2y cm

2 x cm

4x cm

3y cm

Notice:
- $2x$ and $4x$ are **like** terms and can be combined to give $6x$
- $2y$ and $3y$ are **like** terms and can be combined to give $5y$
- $6x$ and $5y$ are **unlike** terms and cannot be combined.

Example 1 Simplify $7x - 3x$
Answer: $4x$

Example 2 Simplify $7x - 3x + 2y$
Answer: $4x + 2y$

Example 3 Simplify $8y + 7x - 3x$
Answer: $8y + 4x$

Example 4 Simplify $8y + 7x - 3x - 3y$
Answer: $5y + 4x$

Exercise 3.1

E

1 Simplify each of the following:
a $2x + 5x$	**b** $3p + 7p$	**c** $6y - 3y$
d $8x - 2x$	**e** $6x + 2x + x$	**f** $5x + 2x - x$
g $5a - 2a + a$	**h** $3x - 2x + x$	**i** $3b + 6b - 2b$
j $k + 4k - 3k$	**k** $b + 7b - 3b$	**l** $3z - 5z + 4z$

2 Match the expressions on the left with the simplified expressions on the right:

a
  i $2x + y - x + 3y$ **A** $2x + 3y$
  ii $5y + x - 2y + x$ **B** $3x + 2y$
  iii $x + y + 3x + y - x$ **C** $x + 4y$
  iv $7y + x + 4x - 3y - 2x$ **D** $3x + 4y$

b
  i $4m + n - 3m + n$ **A** $m + 2n$
  ii $3n + 2m - m - 2n$ **B** $2m + n$
  iii $5m - 2n - 3m + 3n$ **C** $m + n$
  iv $12n - 3m - 9n + 4m$ **D** $m + 3n$

3 Simplify these expressions:
a $4a - 2 + a$ ($4a$ and 2 are unlike terms)	**b** $3b + 2a - b + a$
c $12 - a + 3 + 4a$	**d** $2x - 3y + x$
e $m - 2n + m + 3$	**f** $5k + 7 - k + 2m + 3$
g $4p + 3q - 2p + 3 - q$	**h** $5y + 8x - 2y - 8x$
i $7 + 2y + 3a - 2y + 1$	**j** $8w + 3z - 8w + 3z + w + 5z$
k $10 - 3x + 8x - 2$	**l** $2n - r + 7n + 2r - 9n - r$

4 Write expressions for the balance in the bank accounts each day from Monday to Friday:

Account 1			Account 2		
Day	**Action**	**Amount (£)**	**Day**	**Action**	**Amount (£)**
Monday	puts in £x	x	Monday	puts in £$(x + 2y)$	x
Tuesday	takes out £8		Tuesday	takes out £y	
Wednesday	puts in £$3x$		Wednesday	puts in £$(x + 4)$	
Thursday	puts in £10		Thursday	takes out £$2x$	
Friday	takes out £2		Friday	puts in £$(3y - 4)$	

Challenge

Example

Do you see how this diagram is built up?

Now complete these arrow puzzles:

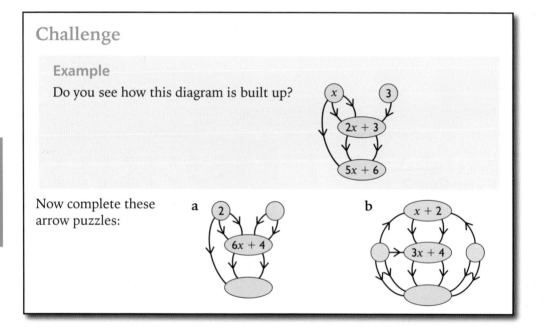

4 Ordering the operations

In a string of calculations with various steps, an order has been agreed.

Does your calculator know this order?

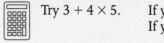 Try $3 + 4 \times 5$. If your calculator says 23, then it knows the rules.
If your calculator says 35, then it doesn't.

E

Example 1	$8 + 5 \times 2$	Example 2	$(8 + 5) \times 2$
	$= 8 + 10$		$= 13 \times 2$
	$= 18$		$= 26$

Example 3 $(8 + 5) \times (6 - 3) + 1$

$= 13 \times 3 + 1$

$= 39 + 1$

$= 40$

Example 4 $\dfrac{5 + 4}{3} = \dfrac{(5 + 4)}{3}$

$= \dfrac{9}{3}$

$= 9 \div 3$

$= 3$

Example 5 $\dfrac{4 + 8}{4 - 1} = \dfrac{(4 + 8)}{(4 - 1)}$

$= \dfrac{12}{3}$

$= 12 \div 3$

$= 4$

Example 6 $8(5 - 2)$

$= 8 \times (5 - 2)$

$= 8 \div 3$

$= 24$

Exercise 4.1

1 Calculate:

   a $10 - 4 \times 2$ **b** $10 - \dfrac{4}{2}$ **c** $\dfrac{10 - 4}{2}$

   d $(10 - 4) \times 2$ **e** $10 \times (4 - 2)$ **f** $10 - 4 + 2$

   g $10 + 4 - 2$ **h** $10 \times 4 - 2$ **i** $10 - 4 - 2$

   j $10 - (4 - 2)$ **k** $\dfrac{10}{4 - 2}$ **l** $\dfrac{4}{10 - 2}$

2 If $m = 5$ and $n = 3$ calculate:

Reminder:
mn means $m \times n$

   a $5(m + 2)$ **b** $15 - mn$ **c** $(5 - m) \times n$

   d $\dfrac{m + n}{2}$ **e** $\dfrac{6}{m - n}$ **f** $m - (n + 2)$ **g** $2m + mn$

   h $\frac{1}{2}(m + n)$ **i** $\dfrac{m + n}{m - n}$ **j** $n(m - 2)$ **k** $m(n - 2)$

   l $(m + 1)(n - 1)$ **m** $2mn$ **n** $2(m + n)$

3 $k = 6$ and $w = 9$. Pair off expressions with equal values:

   A $\frac{1}{2}(k + 2)$ **B** $\dfrac{k + w}{3}$ **C** $(w - k) \times 5$ **D** $2w + 2k$

   E $\dfrac{k}{3} + \dfrac{w}{3}$ **F** $\dfrac{k + 2}{2}$ **G** $5(w - k)$ **H** $2(w + k)$

Challenges

A Copy and complete this cross-number puzzle where $a = 12$, $b = 17$, $c = 8$, $m = 2$, $n = 50$, $w = 100$ and $k = 36$.

Across

1 $\dfrac{w + k}{m}$

2 $2(w + 3m)$

4 $n - (a + b)$

5 $3ab$

8 $c(a + 2b)$

11 $(b - 1)(c - m)$

12 $3n + b + m$

13 $k - (c + m)$

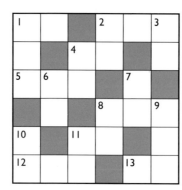

Down

1 $6(w + 2c)$

2 $(c - 1)(m + 1)$

3 $\dfrac{wm}{c}$

4 $\frac{1}{2}(c + k)$

6 $\dfrac{k}{c - 3m}$

7 $\dfrac{w}{2} + c - m$

8 $bc - w$

9 $c(w + m)$

10 $\dfrac{w}{n} + \dfrac{k}{4}$

11 $(c + 1)(a - 1)$

B In each pair of balances you have to find the values of a and b. These will be whole numbers (no fractions).

Puzzle 1

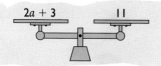
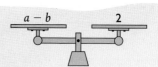

Puzzle 2

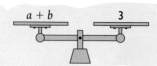
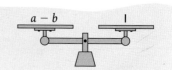

Puzzle 3

5 Repeated adding and multiplying

You should know that $8 + 8 + 8 + 8 + 8$ can be written in *short form* as 5×8 ('5 lots of 8')

Similarly $a + a + a + a$ can be shortened to $4a$ ('4 lots of a')

Now here are examples with multiplying instead of adding.

long form: $8 \times 8 \times 8 \times 8 \times 8$ *short form:* 8^5 ('8 to the power 5')
long form: $a \times a \times a \times a$ *short form:* a^4 ('a to the power 4')

Exercise 5.1

1   Write in shorter form:

   a $2 + 2 + 2$ **b** $3 + 3 + 3 + 3$ **c** $5 + 5$

   d $8 + 8 + 8 + 8 + 8 + 8$ **e** $m + m + m$ **f** $n + n + n + n$

   g $k + k$ **h** $t + t + t + t + t + t$ **i** $r + r$

   j $x + x + x + x + x$ **k** $ab + ab$ **l** $mn + mn + mn$

   m $a^2 + a^2 + a^2$ **n** $k^2 + k^2 + k^2 + k^2$ **o** $xy + xy + xy + xy$

   p $n^2 + n^2$

2   Write these in shorter form.
   For example: $3 \times 3 \times 3 \times 3 \times 3 \times 3 = 3^6$

   a 4×4 **b** $8 \times 8 \times 8$ **c** $3 \times 3 \times 3 \times 3 \times 3$

   d $m \times m \times m \times m$ **e** $n \times n \times n$ **f** $y \times y$

   g $x \times x \times x \times x \times x \times x$ **h** $a \times a$ **i** $k \times k \times k \times k \times k \times k \times k$

3   Match up the longer and shorter forms of these expressions:

   a $x + x + x$ **i** $4x$

   b $x \times x \times x$ **ii** x^2

   c $x + x$ **iii** x^3

   d $x \times x$ **iv** $2x$

   e $x + x + x + x$ **v** x^4

   f $x \times x \times x \times x$ **vi** $3x$

4   If $x = 3$ then $x^4 = 3^4 = 3 \times 3 \times 3 \times 3 = 81$.
   If $x = 3$ then $4x = 4 \times 3 = 12$.
   In a similar fashion, find the values of:

   a **i** y^3 **ii** $3y$ when $y = 3$

   b **i** m^2 **ii** $2m$ when $m = 10$

   c **i** n^4 **ii** $4n$ when $n = 2$

   d **i** x^2 **ii** $2x$ when $x = 7$

   e **i** k^5 **ii** $5k$ when $k = 2$

   f **i** w^7 **ii** $7w$ when $w = 1$

   g **i** a^5 **ii** $5a$ when $a = 10$

   h **i** c^4 **ii** $4c$ when $c = 100$

Exercise 5.2

Example 1

$2a + 3b + a - b = 3a + 2b$

Example 2

$4a \times 5a = 4 \times a \times 5 \times a = 20a^2$

1 Simplify:

a	$m \times 2m$	**b**	$m + 2m$	**c**	$a \times 2b$
d	$a + 3a - 2a$	**e**	$a \times 2a$	**f**	$k \times 2k$
g	$a + 2b + a$	**h**	$8 \times 2x$	**i**	$x^2 + x^2$
j	$2x \times x \times x$	**k**	$5m + 3m + 2m$	**l**	$5m \times 3m \times 2m$
m	$3ab + 2ab - ab$	**n**	$ab \times ab$	**o**	$a^2 \times b$
p	$5x^2 \times 3y$	**q**	$2y \times 2y \times 2y$	**r**	$k + 3k + 4k + 2k$
s	$k \times 3k \times 4k \times 2k$				

2 Match equal expressions:

a
A	$2 \times x + 2$	**i**	$x^2 - 2$
B	$2 - x \times x$	**ii**	$2 - 2x$
C	$x \times x - 2$	**iii**	$2x + 2$
D	$2 - x \times 2$	**iv**	$2 - x^2$
E	$2 + x \times x$	**v**	$x^2 + 2$

b
A	$a + b + a$	**i**	$ab + a$
B	$a \times b + a$	**ii**	$b + ab$
C	$b + a \times b$	**iii**	$a^2 b$
D	$a \times b \times a$	**iv**	$b + a^2$
E	$b + a \times a$	**v**	$2a + b$

3 $\dfrac{2a}{3} = \dfrac{2}{3} \times a = \dfrac{2}{3}a$ so $\dfrac{2a}{3} = \dfrac{2}{3}a.$

In a similar way, match up the equal fractions below.

A $\dfrac{m}{2}$ B $\dfrac{3}{2} \times m$ C $\dfrac{2m}{3}$ D $\dfrac{1}{4} \times m$ E $\dfrac{1}{3}m$

i $\dfrac{3m}{2}$ **ii** $\dfrac{1}{2}m$ **iii** $\dfrac{m}{3}$ **iv** $\dfrac{m}{4}$ **v** $\dfrac{2}{3}m$

4 Simplify:

a	$3 \times x + 2$	**b**	$5 \times m - 1$	**c**	$a \times a + 2$
d	$n \times n - 2$	**e**	$4 + 5 \times e$	**f**	$8 - 2 \times a$
g	$3 + x \times x$	**h**	$4 - c \times c$	**i**	$1 + m \times 3$
j	$t \times 3 - 2$	**k**	$8 - 3 \times m$	**l**	$4 \times p + 2$
m	$a + 2a + 2$	**n**	$4k \times k \times k$	**o**	$2a \times a + 3$
p	$m - 3m \times m$	**q**	$a \times a - a$	**r**	$4a + 2 \times a$
s	$2y + 4 \times y$	**t**	$w \times w + 3 \times w$	**u**	$6a + 3 \times 2a$
v	$4a \times 2 + a$	**w**	$8m + 3 \times 2m$	**x**	$2 \times 3m \times 2m$

6 Evaluating squares

In these examples all lengths are in centimetres.

Example 1

x ☐ Area $= x \times x = x^2$ cm^2

Example 2

Area $= x^2 + x^2 + x^2 = 3x^2$ cm^2

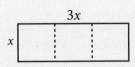

Area $= x \times 3x = 3x^2$ cm^2

Example 3

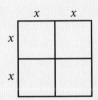

Area $= x^2 + x^2 + x^2 + x^2 = 4x^2$ cm^2

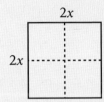

Area $= (2x)^2 = 2x \times 2x = 4x^2$ cm^2

Exercise 6.1

1 Find expressions for each area (showing working as in the examples above). All lengths are in centimetres.

a m ☐ m **b** $2n$ / $2n$ **c** n n / n n **d** t t / t **e** $2t$ / t **f** k / $3k$

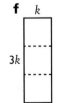

g k / k k k **h** $3x$ / $3x$ **i** x x x / x x x **j** y y / y y y **k** $2y$ / y $2y$ y

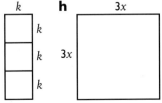
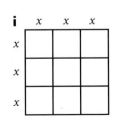
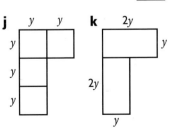

2 If $a = 2$, $b = 3$ and $c = 5$, calculate the values of:

a $2b^2$	**b** $(2b)^2$	**c** c^2	**d** $2c^2$
e $(2c)^2$	**f** $2ab$	**g** $2ab^2$	**h** $2a^2b$
i $2(ab)^2$	**j** $2a^2b^2$	**k** $3(a + b)$	**l** $(a + b)^2$
m $(b + c)^2$	**n** $(c - a)^2$	**o** $2(c - b)^2$	**p** $(2c - b)^2$
q $b(c - a)$	**r** $a(b + c)$	**s** $4(a^2 + 2)$	**t** $c(b - a)^2$
u $c^2 - a^2$	**v** $c^2 - b^2$	**w** $a^2 + c^2$	**x** $3b^2 - c^2$
y $2c^2 + 3a^2$	**z** $2(a^2 + c^2)$		

Challenges

A Compare $n(n + 1)$ with $n^2 + n$.

Let $n = 3$ $n(n + 1) = 3(3 + 1) = 3 \times 4 = 12$ and
$n^2 + n = 3^2 + 3 = 9 + 3 = 12$

Let $n = 7$ $n(n + 1) = 7(7 + 1) = 7 \times 8 = 56$ and
$n^2 + n = 7^2 + 7 = 49 + 7 = 56$

Let $n = 10$ $n(n + 1) = 10(10 + 1) = 10 \times 11 = 110$ and
$n^2 + n = 10^2 + 10 = 100 + 10 = 110$

It appears that $n(n + 1) = n^2 + n$ ... though trying values does not prove the expressions are equal!

By testing several values of n, find pairs of expressions that appear to be equal:

$n + n^2$	$n^2 + 2n$	$n^2 - 1$	$(n + 1)^2$
$(n + 1)(n - 1)$	$n(1 + n)$	$n(n + 2)$	$n^2 + 2n + 1$
$(n - 1)^2$	$n^2 - 2n + 1$		

B Copy and complete this cross-number puzzle if $m = 13$, $n = 7$, $a = 18$ and $b = 12$.

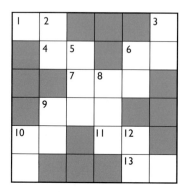

Across
1   $(m - n)^2$
4   $(m - n)(2m - a)$
6   $\dfrac{m(n + a)}{n - 2}$
7   $a^2 - b^2$
9   $(m - 1)(m + 1)$
10   $(n - 2)(b - 1)$
11   $\frac{1}{2}a(n - 4)$
13   $2n(a - b)$

Down
2   $(\frac{1}{2}a - 1)^2$
3   $am - m^2$
5   $(a + b)^2 - nb$
6   $(\frac{1}{2}a)^2 - 3n$
8   $2(a + 3)^2$
9   $\frac{1}{2}(a + b)$
10   $2m^2 - 2b^2$
12   $3a + 2b$

7 Removing brackets

Example 1   Write $3(x + 2)$ without brackets.

$$3(x + 2) = (x + 2) + (x + 2) + (x + 2)$$
$$= x + x + x + 2 + 2 + 2$$
$$= 3 \times x + 3 \times 2 = 3x + 6$$
$$3(x + 2) = 3x + 6$$

Example 2   Expand $5(y - 3)$.

$$5(y - 3) = (y - 3) + (y - 3) + (y - 3) + (y - 3) + (y - 3)$$
$$= y + y + y + y + y - 3 - 3 - 3 - 3 - 3$$
$$= 5y - 15$$
$$5(y - 3) = 5y - 15$$

In general: $a(b + c) = ab + ac$ and $a(b - c) = ab - ac$

Exercise 7.1

Write the following expressions without brackets. Use the examples to help you.

1 **a** $3(y + 2)$ **b** $2(x + 5)$ **c** $3(m - 1)$ **d** $4(k + 2)$
    e $8(w - 5)$ **f** $4(y + 7)$ **g** $9(n - 3)$ **h** $10(n - 1)$
    i $7(2 + x)$ **j** $3(1 - y)$ **k** $4(5 + a)$ **l** $8(w - 6)$
    m $2(1 + c)$ **n** $5(3 - h)$ **o** $4(1 - c)$ **p** $9(q - r)$

Example 3 $x(x + 2) = x^2 - 2x$ **Example 4** $a(y + 3) = ay + 3a$

2 **a** $m(n + 2)$ **b** $c(x - 3)$ **c** $x(y - 1)$ **d** $e(n - 5)$
    e $w(z + 3)$ **f** $a(3 + b)$ **g** $t(3 + x)$ **h** $k(2 - x)$
    i $y(4 - y)$ **j** $x(x + 2)$ **k** $x(x + y)$ **l** $m(5 - m)$
    m $3(a - b)$ **n** $y(y - 1)$ **o** $n(8 - n)$ **p** $a(a - b)$
    q $w(a - w)$ **r** $t(u + t)$ **s** $y(y - x)$

Example 5 $3(4y - 3x) = 12y - 9x$ **Example 6** $2a(a - 4b) = 2a^2 - 8ab$

3 **a** $4(2x - 1)$ **b** $2(3y - 4x)$ **c** $a(2a - b)$ **d** $2c(c - 3)$
    e $y(5y - x)$ **f** $4m(n - 3m)$ **g** $8w(2w - 3)$ **h** $17(2 - y + x)$
    i $a(a - b - c)$ **j** $2x(3x - 2y + 5z)$ **k** $5m(10 - 3m + 2n)$

Example 7   Expand and simplify $4(x + 3y) + 3(x - 2y)$

Answer: $4(x + 3y) + 3(x - 2y)$
$$= 4x + 12y + 3x - 6y$$
$$= 7x + 6y$$

Exercise 7.2

1 Remove the brackets and then **simplify** where possible:

a $3(y - 2) + 6$ b $2(m - 3) + 8$ c $12 + 3(w + 2)$

d $x + 2(3 + x)$ e $4(x + 1) + 3(x - 1)$ f $a(2a + 1) + a^2$

g $c(2 + c) + 3c$ h $x(x + 5) + 2x$ i $3(y + 2) + 2(y + 3)$

j $4(m + n) + 2(m - n)$ k $a(a + b) + b(a + b)$ l $2a(a - 1) + 3a(a + 1)$

m $a^2 + a(2 - a)$ n $2(3x + 1) + 3(2x + 3)$

o $5(5 - 2x) + 5(2x - 5)$ p $x^2(x + 1) - x^2$

2 Find an expression for the area of each rectangle

i   with brackets   ii   without brackets.

All lengths are in centimetres.

a
b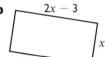
c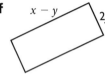

d
e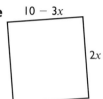
f

g
h
i

Challenges

A 1 Find the volume of water in cubic centimetres
a with brackets
b without brackets.

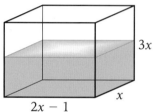

2 Check your answers to a and b are equal when $x = 2$ and $x = 3$.

B 1 Find the area of this rectangle in square centimetres
a with brackets
b without brackets.

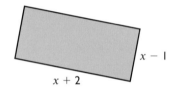

2 Check a and b are equal when $x = 3$ and $x = 4$.

8 Factorising expressions

We know that $2x(x-3) = 2x^2 - 6x$.

Could we look at $2x^2 - 6x$ and deduce that $2x^2 - 6x = 2x(x-3)$?

We first note that $2x$ is the highest common factor of $2x^2$ and $6x$.

If $\quad 2x^2 - 6x = 2x(A - B)$

$\quad$ then $\quad 2x \times A = 2x^2 \quad$ so $A = x$;

$\qquad\qquad 2x \times B = 6x \quad$ so $B = 3$.

When we reverse the process of removing brackets we are said to be **factorising**.

Example 1 Factorise $8x + 12$

Highest common factor is 4.

$8x + 12 = 4(2x + 3)$

Check by mentally removing the brackets again.

Example 2 Factorise $x^2 - x$

Highest common factor is x.

$x^2 - x = x(x - 1)$

Check by mentally removing the brackets again.

Example 3 Factorise $9xy + 12x^2$

Highest common factor is $3x$.

$9xy + 12x^2 = 3x(3y + 4x)$

Check by mentally removing the brackets again.

F

Exercise 8.1

1 Factorise, then check by mentally removing the brackets:

a $2x - 4$ **b** $5a + 10$ **c** $7y - 21$

d $8 + 32a$ **e** $x^2 + 2x$ **f** $3m - m^2$

g $ab - 2b$ **h** $8m - 4$ **i** $4 - 4n$

j $tw - t$ **k** $cd + d$ **l** $k^2 + k$

m $4ab - 6a$

2 Factorise:

a $15a^2 - 25a$ **b** $24t^2 + 18t$ **c** $14x + 18x^2$

d $28ab + 35a^2$ **e** $30m^2 - 42mn$ **f** $100x^2 - 42xy$

g $36a^2b + 27ab^2$ **h** $25ab - 30a^2b^2$ **i** $22mn^2 + 55m^2n$

j $6x^3 - 9x^2$ **k** $24y + 36y^3$ **l** $18cd^3 - 20c^3d$

m $x^3 - 3x^2 + x$ **n** $n^3 - n^2 + n$ **o** $14t - 7t^2 - 35t^3$

p $24x^2 + 16x - 4$ **q** $6m^4 - 4m^2 + 2$ **r** $pD - pd$

s $2pr^2 - 2prl$ **t** $45x^2y^3 - 72x^3y^4$

Challenge

Find expressions for the total area of these shapes in factorised form.
Remember:
- the area of a rectangle is *length × breadth*
- the area of a triangle is $\frac{1}{2}$ *base × height*.

a

b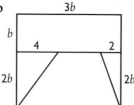

CHECK-UP

1 Evaluate:
  a $4x - 3y$ when $x = 5$ and $y = 2$
  b $50 - 3a + 2b$ when $a = 4$ and $b = 10$

2 Simplify:
  a $5m + 7 + 2n - 3m + n$ **b** $12b - 2a + 5a - 10 + b + 12$

3 If $p = 5$ and $q = 7$ calculate:
  a $40 - pq$ **b** $\dfrac{q + p}{q - p}$ **c** $q - (7 - p)$ **d** $(p - 1)(q - 1)$

4 Find the values of:
  a $2a^2$ when $a = 3$
  b $(2a)^2$ when $a = 5$
  c $3a^2 - b^2$ when $a = 4$ and $b = 6$

5 Simplify:
  a $3x \times x \times 2x$ **b** $8 + 2 \times y \times y$ **c** $8w + 4 \times 3w$

6 If $k = 2$, $t = 3$ and $w = 5$ evaluate:
  a $(2t - k)^2$ **b** $w(t + k)$ **c** $5w^2 - (k + t)^2$

7 Write without brackets and simplify where possible:
  a $3(1 - w)$ **b** $n(2n + m)$ **c** $2(x + 3) + 3(x - 2)$
  d $y(y + 3) + 2y$ **e** $c(3 - c) + c(c - 3)$

8 Factorise:
  a $8y - 10$ **b** $w^2 - 2w$ **c** $4xy + 6y$
  d $pR^2 - pR$ **e** $3a^3 - 6a^2 + 9a$

5 Information handling 1

In 1854, during the Crimean war, Florence Nightingale was sent from England to Turkey to oversee the running of nursing in the military hospitals. Conditions were very poor. A soldier was 7 times more likely to die in the hospital than in battle.

Florence collected a lot of data on the conditions, organised it and was able to use her report to get improvements made in the hospitals.

By 1855 the death rates had dropped by 20%.

Florence Nightingale

This is one of her diagrams. The outer part of a wedge shows deaths by disease. The innermost part shows deaths from wounds.

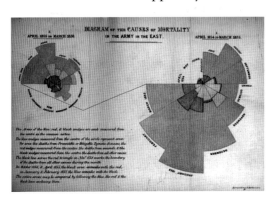

1 Looking back ◀◀

1

Number of brothers and sisters	Tally	Number of pupils
0		
1		
2		
3		
4		
Total		

'How many brothers and sisters do you have?'
Here are 33 responses to this question:

1 1 2 0 1 0 2 2 4 1 0
1 0 1 0 2 3 0 1 4 3 0
2 2 1 1 2 2 1 0 1 3 1

Organise the data using the tally chart given.
Check that your total comes to 33.

2 The school nurse measured the height and weight of a sample of pupils.

pupil	1	2	3	4	5	6	7	8	9	10	11	12
height (cm)	132	146	148	139	151	155	148	146	139	140	145	137
weight (kg)	33	33·5	38	35	38·5	45	37	38	36·5	35	37	34

a Arrange the pupils in order of height.

b Which children are taller than 145 cm?

c Which children are heavier than 37 kg?

3 In a survey of 40 teenagers, 14 girls and 16 boys said they owned a bike.
There were 22 girls in the group.

	bike	no bike	totals
girls	14		
boys			
totals			

a Copy and complete the table.

b How many boys had no bike?

c What fraction of boys had bikes?

4 a Construct the frequency table which this bar graph represents.

b How many pupils were absent for more than 10 school days?

c How many pupils were absent for fewer than 10 school days?

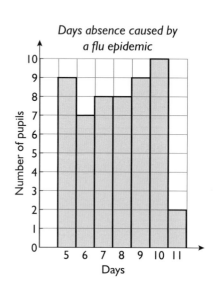

Days absence caused by a flu epidemic

2 Become a data collector

What type of school lunch is most popular? How many goals are scored by teams in the Premier League?

The answers to these, and many other questions, can be found by collecting data.

What source should I look in? How many people should be asked? What time period should the data cover?

Sometimes data can be found in newspapers, magazines or on the Internet, but often data has to be collected by direct observation, in a survey or using a questionnaire.

How much data depends on the time available and sometimes cost. Remember to choose a representative sample.

Some guidelines on questionnaire design
- Keep words and questions simple, clear and easy to understand.
- Be precise, e.g. say 'two or three times a week' rather than 'often'.
- Be polite and try not to embarrass anyone.
- Don't ask about events that took place a long time ago.

E

Example

Your class teacher would like to plan a Christmas party.
Devise a questionnaire to find out what would make a good party for your class.

At your party, which of the following would you like?   yes   no

music   ☐   ☐

food   ☐   ☐

drink   ☐   ☐

games   ☐   ☐

If your answer is yes to any of the above, say what type you would like:

music   ....

food   ....

drink   ....

games   ....

Exercise 2.1

1 Why might these questions not be suitable for a questionnaire?
   a Do you find difficulty in making friends?
   b Do you prefer not to eat non-fat yoghurt?
   c How did you spend the first weekend of last month?
   d Do you often eat chocolate?
   e If you won £1000 would you buy something for yourself or possibly save some of the money?

2 Design a questionnaire to collect information on the following topics.
   Make sure some questions have yes/no answers.
   a What is your favourite drink?
   b Which country would you like to visit on holiday?

3 How would you collect data to investigate the following questions?
   Choose any of the options given.
   Explain your choice by thinking about possible costs and time.
   a Should school uniform be changed to allow pupils to wear polo shirts?
      Data source: newspaper/magazine,   Internet,   survey
      Sample from: pupils,   parents,   local community
      Sample size: 500,   100,   30
   b Do boys dye their hair as often as girls?
      Data source: newspaper/magazine,   Internet, survey, direct observation
      Sample from: supermarket customers, school,   local community
      Sample size: 1000,   100,   10

4 Write down how you would collect data to investigate these questions.
   a How many videos are watched by 12-year-olds each week?
   b How many pictures are on the front page of daily newspapers?

3 Organising information

Raw data, which has not been organised in any way, can often look untidy and take a long time to read through. Tables can make overall results and patterns easy to spot.

Exercise 3.1

1 In an S1 maths exam, pupils were asked to measure the size of this angle.
   The results in Miss McQueen's class are given below:

   55° 54° 55° 55° 55° 54° 55° 52° 55° 54°
   53° 54° 54° 54° 54° 55° 55° 55° 55° 56°
   54° 53° 55° 54° 55° 54° 54° 54° 55° 53°
   52° 54° 55°

   Any answer between 53° and 55° was accepted as correct.
   a Organise the data into a frequency table.
   b How many pupils were marked as correct?

2 Design a table to use for collecting data to find out:

   a if one month is more popular than others for birthdays

   b how many sixes are thrown in a game with one dice

   c which number is thrown most often in a game with one dice.

3 Here are the winners of the Rugby International Championships from 1980 to 2000:

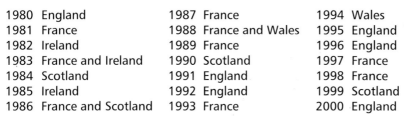

1980	England	1987	France	1994	Wales
1981	France	1988	France and Wales	1995	England
1982	Ireland	1989	France	1996	England
1983	France and Ireland	1990	Scotland	1997	France
1984	Scotland	1991	England	1998	France
1985	Ireland	1992	England	1999	Scotland
1986	France and Scotland	1993	France	2000	England

Design and complete a table in which the data can be organised to show how many times each country has either won or shared the championship.

4 For a school magazine, Su analysed which houses participated in lunchtime clubs.

In her report she said,

    'In Clyde house, 13 pupils go to Green Club, 5 go to Maths Club, 7 go to Aerobics Club and 12 go to Bridge Club.

    In Tay house, 8 pupils go to Green Club, 9 go to Maths Club, 3 go to Aerobics Club and 6 go to Bridge Club.

    In Forth house, 4 pupils go to Green Club, 2 go to Maths Club, 10 go to Aerobics Club and 4 go to Bridge Club.'

   a Construct a table which shows this information in a more organised way.

   b Find the total attendance at each club.

   c Find how many lunchtime club goers each house has.

E

5 Jack has to write a report on his team's hockey results for the season. The results of the 18 fixtures are given below. Note that the home score is given first, Jack's team's scores are in colour and his team's home matches are boxed.

4–3	2–1	3–0	2–2	1–2	4–3	5–2	1–1	3–2

0–0	2–1	3–3	2–3	2–4	3–1	2–0	0–1	6–1

Summarise Jack's team's results in this table:

hockey results 1st XI	won	draw	lost	total
home				
away				
total				

4 Summarising and comparing data: the mean

mean height

How tall is this group?

Data which can be counted or measured can be summarised by calculating a single number to represent the data set – a number whose value can be considered *typical* of the set in some way.

This kind of number is called an **average**.

One type of average is the **mean**.

$$\text{Mean} = \frac{\text{sum of the data values}}{\text{number of data values}}$$

E

Example

The number of words in the first 13 sentences of Lewis Carroll's *Alice's Adventures in Wonderland* are: 57, 55, 139, 21, 43, 34, 52, 55, 5, 13, 8, 17, 5. Calculate the mean number of words per sentence.

$$\text{mean} = \frac{57 + 55 + 139 + 21 + 43 + 34 + 52 + 55 + 5 + 13 + 8 + 17 + 5}{13}$$

$$= \frac{504}{13}$$

The calculator gives the answer 38·769 230 769.
When the mean is not an exact value it is normally rounded to one more place than the given data values, so in this case the mean = 38·8 words (to 1 decimal place).

Notes:
1 Remember units.
2 The mean is not necessarily a whole number, nor one of the data values.
3 Every member of the data set is used in calculating the mean.

Exercise 4.1

1 Calculate the mean values for the data summarised below.

    a Mean weight of a cake when 6 Dundee cakes have a total weight of 1560 g.

    b Mean cost of present when the total cost of 9 Christmas presents is £77·66.

    c Mean boy's weight when 11 boys in a football team have a weight of 693 kg.

    d Mean match score when the total score of a rugby football team is 136 in 8 matches.

2 Calculate the mean value for these samples.

    a Times to complete homework:
    31 min, 25 min, 32 min, 28 min, 22 min, 35 min,
    36 min, 27 min, 25 min, 30 min, 33 min, 40 min.

    b Numbers of pupils in S1 classes: 29, 28, 32, 31, 27, 29, 30, 31, 30.

    c Estimates of the height of a crime suspect:
    1·65 m, 1·80 m, 1·85 m, 1·70 m, 1·90 m, 1·80 m, 1·85 m.

    d Net weights of bags of sugar:
    1·020 kg, 1·050 kg, 1·100 kg, 1·010 kg, 1·040 kg, 0·980 kg, 1·060 kg,
    1·000 kg, 1·010 kg, 0·990 kg, 1·020 kg.

3 Josh takes a holiday job during the summer washing cars.
The amount he is paid depends on the number of cars he washes.
For 5 days' work he is paid £128.
Calculate his mean pay per day.

4 In a fishing competition, the weights in kilograms of all the fish caught were
(to the nearest 10 g):

1·15	0·95	0·8	2·42	1·65	2·6	2·02
2·49	1·93	1·84	2·08	2·16	1·08	1·31

How many grams above the mean weight was the largest fish caught?
(Answer to 1 d.p.)

5 Mr Buick builds conservatories. His last 9 conservatories took 5 days, 9 days, 14 days, 6 days, 10 days, 12 days, 8 days, 10 days and 25 days to complete.

    a Calculate the mean completion time to the nearest day.

    b Comment on the time taken to complete the last conservatory.

6 Alana's Autos and Clark's Cars each have several cars for sale in their forecourts.
Which of them has the cheapest cars on average?

7 The mean height in Class 1Z is 145 cm.
A new girl with a height of 160 cm joins the class, taking the number up to 30 pupils.
What is the new mean height of the class?

8 The map shows the distances of places of interest around Jody's house.
Find the mean distance in kilometres to a place of interest from Jody's house.

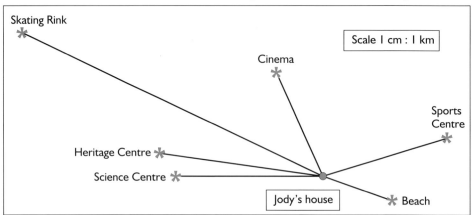

9 Three books have x pages, $2x$ pages and $(x + 20)$ pages respectively.
The mean number of pages is 240.
Find the number of pages in each book.

Finding the mean from a frequency table

When there are lots of data, the information is often organised in a frequency table. The same formula for the mean is used, with extra working shown in the frequency table.

> **Example**
>
> At Highland High School the number of pupils absent in each class on the last day of term is shown in the table. Find the mean number of absences for this day.
>
> | number of pupils absent per class | 0 | 1 | 2 | 3 | 4 | 5 | 6 |
> |---|---|---|---|---|---|---|---|
> | frequency | 6 | 7 | 5 | 7 | 3 | 1 | 1 |
>
> 3 absences in 7 classes = 3 × 7 = 21 absences
>
> Find the total number of absences in stages.
> Consider each column separately.
>
> | number of pupils absent per class | 0 | 1 | 2 | 3 | 4 | 5 | 6 | totals |
> |---|---|---|---|---|---|---|---|---|
> | frequency | 6 | 7 | 5 | 7 | 3 | 1 | 1 | 30 |
> | pupils absent per class × frequency | 0 × 6 = 0 | 1 × 7 = 7 | 2 × 5 = 10 | 3 × 7 = 21 | 4 × 3 = 12 | 5 × 1 = 5 | 6 × 1 = 6 | 61 |

$$\text{mean} = \frac{\text{sum of the data values}}{\text{number of data values}} = \frac{\textit{sum of totals for each column}}{\textit{total frequency}}$$

$$= \frac{61}{30} = 2 \cdot 033 \ldots = 2 \cdot 0 \text{ pupils}$$

Notice that if we are working without a calculator it makes sense to turn the table round:

number of pupils absent per class	frequency	pupils absent per class × frequency
0	6	$0 \times 6 = 0$
1	7	$1 \times 7 = 7$
2	5	$2 \times 5 = 10$
3	7	$3 \times 7 = 21$
4	3	$4 \times 3 = 12$
5	1	$5 \times 1 = 5$
6	1	$6 \times 1 = 6$
totals	30	61

F

Exercise 4.2

1 Calculate the mean values for the data summarised below without using a calculator.

a Mean number of peas in a pod

number of peas	3	4	5	6	7	8
frequency	1	0	3	2	4	1

b Mean test mark

mark	5	6	7	8	9	10
frequency	2	3	5	5	10	5

c Mean number of items lost property taken to the janitor's office each day of the spring term

number of lost property items	0	1	2	3	4
frequency	18	15	12	4	1

2 Calculate the mean values for the data summarised below.

a Mean score in a golf tournament

score	68	69	70	71	72	73	74	75	76
frequency	2	0	3	5	5	4	3	1	1

b Mean number of hours of sunshine in February.

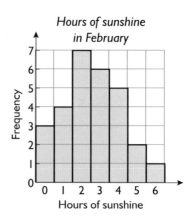

Hours of sunshine in February

3 *Dear Mrs Jones,*

My appeal for helpers with the ecoproject was successful. I had 5 days with 6 helpers, 6 days with 4 helpers, 10 days with 3 helpers, 4 days with 2 helpers and only 1 day with no helpers. Can you show our appreciation in the next newsletter please?

Yours sincerely,
Mark Black

By constructing a frequency table, calculate the mean number of helpers per day.

4 This table shows the number of pupils given detentions for lateness at Harefield Grammar School in February and March.

Number of pupils in lateness detentions	Frequencies	
	February	March
0	3	4
1	2	7
2	0	4
3	7	3
4	2	2
5	4	1
6	2	0

Find the mean number of pupils on lateness detention for each month and comment.

F

5 Summarising and comparing data: the median, mode and range

A raffle takes place with 100 prizes of £1 and one prize of £1000 000.

The mean prize $= \dfrac{1\,000\,100}{11} = £90\,918$ to the nearest pound.

However this value is misleading if it is quoted as *typical* of the size of the prize.

The mean is not always the best way of stating the *typical* score.

Other types of average value which can be more useful are the **median** and the **mode**.

- The **median** is the value which splits the data set, when ordered, into two equal halves. It is less affected than the mean by any addition of extremely large or small values to the data set.

  The median suggests the typical lottery prize is £1.

- The **mode** is the value which occurs most often.
  It is also less sensitive than the mean to changes in the data set.
  When the pieces of data are not numbers, the mode will be the only average which can be quoted. It may be that there is no score which occurs most often.

  The mode suggests the typical lottery prize is £1.

F

Example 1

The weekly wages of 7 employees in a small factory are £320, £205, £205, £280, £215, £205, £250.

Arrange the data in order.　　205　205　205　215　250　280　320

The mode is £205
(it occurs three times).

The median is £215.
It splits the set into two lists, each with three values.

Example 2

The weekly wages of 6 employees in a small factory are £320, £205, £280, £215, £205, £250.

Arrange the data in order.　　205　205　215　┆　250　280　320
　　　　　　　　　　　　　　　　　　　　middle

The mode is £205
(it occurs twice).

The median is £232·50, as
$\frac{215+250}{2} = 232{\cdot}5$
It splits the set into two lists, each with three values.

For larger data sets the centre may be harder to spot.
Halve the number of values in the set (ignoring any remainder).
This tells you how many pieces of data are on either side of the median.

(5)

Example 3

The weekly wages of 21 employees in a factory are £180, £210, £205, £220, £255, £300, £190, £230, £280, £215, £205, £250, £230, £280, £215, £205, £320, £230, £280, £215, £280.

Arrange the data in order.

180 190 205 205 205 210 215 215 215 220 | 230 | 230 230 250 255 280 280 280 280 300 320

middle

The median is £230.
$n = 21$, $\frac{21}{2} = 10\frac{1}{2}$, so 10 in each half and the eleventh value is the median.

The mode is £280 as it occurs the most often (four times).

It is often useful to know how spread out the data values are.
The **range** is a measure of spread.
It is the difference between the highest and lowest values.

In *Example 3*, the range is £140 (£320 − £180).

F

Exercise 5.1

1 Find the median, mode and range of these data sets.
Remember to put them in order.

 a 15, 10, 11, 14, 10, 11, 12, 11, 19

 b 1·4, 1·7, 1·1, 1·3, 1·4, 1·9, 1·7, 1·7

 c 98, 92, 94, 89, 92, 95, 99, 100, 90, 93, 93, 95, 90, 91, 99, 95, 96, 96, 91, 99, 95, 96, 96, 91, 90, 88, 81, 94, 93, 90, 95

 d 25, 25, 26, 23, 25, 26, 24, 24, 25, 27, 24, 25, 26, 29, 27, 25, 27, 28, 26, 28, 24, 26

2 Scott did a survey on cars parked in his neighbourhood.
He noted the cars parked outside each house in two streets.

| Ogilvie Road | 2 | 2 | 1 | 2 | 1 | 1 | 0 | 2 | |
| Stathern Road | 1 | 2 | 1 | 0 | 0 | 4 | 3 | 1 | 2 |

 a Find:
  i the median number of cars for each road
  ii the modal number of cars for each road
  iii the range in the number of cars for each road.
 b Use your answers to decide which road had more cars parked at each house on average.

3 At Ron's Rentals, staff recorded the number of videos and DVDs rented over a two-week period.

Day	M	Tu	W	Th	F	Sa	Su	M	Tu	W	Th	F	Sa	Su
Video	6	12	20	18	41	36	21	9	16	22	15	39	32	19
DVD	7	6	13	12	26	21	11	3	10	14	7	29	23	9

Compare the rentals of videos and DVDs by considering the median and range for each.

4 a If data is given in a frequency table, the mode is easy to spot. How?

   b Find the mode and range for these distributions:

   i

number of peas	3	4	5	6	7	8
frequency	1	0	3	2	4	1

   ii

mark	5	6	7	8	9	10
frequency	2	3	5	5	10	5

   iii

number of lost property items	0	1	2	3	4
frequency	18	15	12	4	1

F

Challenge

Can you find the medians for the distributions given in question 4?

---

6 Grouped frequency tables

When there is a large number of different data values, the raw data are often organised into groups.

Example

The 30 pupils of Class 1A were given a spot test out of 59. The results are shown in table 1.

All the scores from 0 to 9 were counted together (0–9) as were the scores from 10 to 19 (10–19) and so on. Each group is called a **class interval**.

Each class interval is the same size ... 10 scores in this example.

Aim for around 5 to 10 groups ... 6 groups in this example.

Table 1

23	9	27	19	27
22	23	3	24	41
17	15	27	47	50
19	24	23	33	44
25	16	20	12	32
7	40	28	26	41

The result is a **grouped frequency table** as shown in table 2.

Tally marks have been used to make the count easier.

Note that the class interval 20–29 has the highest frequency.

This is referred to as the **modal class**.

A check total is a good idea to help make sure no scores have been omitted.

Table 2

Score	Tally	Frequency
0–9	|||	3
10–19 |卌		6
20–29	卌 卌 |||	13
30–39	||	2
40–49	卌	5
50–59			1
	check total	30

Exercise 6.1

1 In an experiment, the times taken in seconds to complete a task were recorded for 30 volunteers.
Copy and complete the grouped frequency table for this distribution.

65	49	68	61	70
61	63	42	66	83
56	56	65	89	90
59	64	63	75	86
67	58	62	54	74
49	62	70	68	63

Times (s)	Tally	Frequency
40–49		
50–59		
	check total	

2 The percentage marks in a geography exam for Class 1/1 were:

45	61	93	70	71	83	54	90	80	93
66	48	62	45	49	62	53	67	60	68
98	74	62	71	51	86	79	46	72	50

Construct a grouped frequency table for these marks with class intervals of 10, starting with 40–49.

3 Drawing pins are sold in packs of 200. In a random sample of 40, checked by a quality control supervisor, the following contents were counted:

187	190	208	206	191	205	199	201	189	192
206	199	203	207	185	202	208	198	205	207
204	190	204	200	194	201	188	191	209	197
212	204	197	186	213	189	200	201	208	199

Construct a grouped frequency table for these contents with class intervals of 5.

4 Fatima was looking through her food store cupboard to collect information on food additives. She made a list of all those that she found:

E110, E250, E102, E310, E216, E131, E250, E150, E160(a), E220, E321, E224, E142, E127, E413, E320, E102, E212, E222, E413, E127, E311, E221, E407, E120, E122, E251, E120, E150, E213, E211, E102, E124, E211, E310, E320, E212.

Numbers which start with E1 are colours, E2 are preservatives, E3 are antioxidants and E4 are stabilisers.
Create a tally table showing the number in each category.

CHECK-UP

1 Say what is wrong with these questions suggested for a questionnaire on eating habits. Try to improve them.
   a What did you eat for tea last week?
   b Do you prefer not to eat non-meat dishes?
   c Do you eat sweets frequently or not?

2 Records show that a school bus arrived at the following times over several days.

08 45	08 46	08 42	08 44	08 45	08 43	08 41	08 47	08 45	08 40
08 40	08 45	08 39	08 39	08 42	08 45	08 40	08 44	08 50	08 45
08 49	08 42	08 40	08 42	08 43	08 39	08 45	08 43	08 45	08 41
08 45	08 45	08 45	08 44	08 45	08 49	08 45	08 45	08 44	08 48

   a Organise this data into a frequency table.
   b School starts at 08 50 and pupils need two minutes to get to their classrooms.
   On how many occasions were pupils on this bus late?

3 Calculate, for the data summarised below:
   a the mean score for 32 pupils in an English class when the total score is 2001
   b the mean journey time for these journeys:
   1 h 30 min, 1 h 55 min, 1 h 30 min, 1 h 8 min, 1 h 26 min, 1 h 40 min
   (Hint: change all times to minutes.)
   c the mean cost of theatre tickets when 15 are bought at £8·50, 14 at £10 and 7 at £12·50.

4 a When describing data, name three measures of average and one measure of spread.

b Which measure:

i uses all the data values?

ii uses only the highest and lowest data values?

iii ignores extreme values?

iv must be a data value?

c Say which measure is probably being used in these statements:

i The average number of children per family is 1·6.

ii The average woman's shoe size is 5.

ii 50% of wages in a factory are less than £200.

iv The difference between the maximum and minimum wage in a factory is £200.

v Mr Average has one car.

5 The ages of the prime ministers of Britain, when first elected, from Disraeli in 1868 to Blair in 1997, are as follows:

64, 59, 55, 39, 69, 56, 53, 64, 56, 58, 68, 66, 62, 58, 63, 60, 48, 54, 64, 54, 47, 43.

a Complete the table.

age when first elected	tally	count
in their 30s		
in their 40s		
in their 50s		
in their 60s		

b How many were under 50 years old when first elected?

6 Time and temperature

Measuring time

Telling the time of the year and the time of the day have always been important skills to have.

- We use a calendar to tell the time of year.
- We use a clock to tell the time of day.

The pictures show some ways used to measure time in the past.

Measuring temperature

In 1742, when Anders Celsius made his world famous Celsius thermometer, he marked the boiling point of water at 0 °C and the freezing point at 100 °C.

After his death in 1744 the scale was reversed.

Stonehenge – an ancient calendar

Sun dial

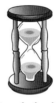

Sand clock

1 Looking back

Examples

1 7.45 a.m. = 07 45 = quarter to eight in the morning
   7.45 p.m. = 19 45 = quarter to eight in the evening

2 How long is it from:
   a 10 35 to 14 20   b 16 30 to 02 00 (next day)

a
$$
\begin{array}{r}
14.20 \\
-10.35 \\
\hline
\end{array}
$$
can't take 35 mins from 20 mins, so…
$$
\begin{array}{r}
13.80 \\
-10.35 \\
\hline
3.45 \\
\end{array}
$$

b
$$
\begin{array}{r}
02.00 \\
-16.30 \\
\hline
\end{array}
$$
2.00 the next day is 26.00
$$
\begin{array}{r}
26.00 \\
-16.30 \\
\hline
\end{array}
$$
can't take 30 mins from 00 mins, so…
$$
\begin{array}{r}
25.60 \\
-16.30 \\
\hline
9.30 \\
\end{array}
$$

Exercise 1.1

1 a Change these into 24-hour clock times.

    i 8.20 a.m.   **ii** 3.45 p.m.

    iii 12 noon   **iv** ten to eight at night

    v twenty-five past midnight

b Change these 24-hour clock times into 12-hour times.

    i 19 30   **ii** 02 15

    iii 23 50   **iv** 04 04

    v 13 35

2 Write down how long it is from:

  a 11.30 a.m. to 11.55 a.m.   **b** 6.50 p.m. to 7.15 p.m.

  c 04 20 to 05 40   **d** 10 10 to 14 55

  e 23 30 to 02 00 (next day)

3 This is part of a bus timetable.

  a When does the bus leave Glenville?

  b Write down when it gets to Brownrigg, using the 12-hour clock.

  c How long does the bus take from

    i Roberton to St Eves

    ii Glenville to Brownrigg?

Glenville	11 40
Roberton	12 05
St Eves	12 28
Brownrigg	13 10

4 a How many days are in:

    i April   **ii** October

    iii 5 weeks   **iv** 48 hours

    v a year (not a leap year)?

b How many minutes are in:

    i 4 hours   **ii** 240 seconds

    iii three and a half hours **iv** three quarters of an hour?

c How many weeks are in a year?

d How many seconds are in:

    i 2 minutes   **ii** one and a half minutes

    iii 1 hour?

5 Write these common fractions as decimal fractions:

  a $\frac{1}{2}$ **b** $\frac{1}{4}$ **c** $\frac{3}{4}$

  d $6\frac{1}{2}$ **e** $1\frac{3}{4}$ **f** $12\frac{1}{4}$

6 a Write down the digit which is in the hundredths column of these decimals:

    i 3·14   **ii** 16·98   **iii** 564·123

b Write down the number in the tenths column of these decimals:

    i 9·8   **ii** 70·52   **iii** 1·0456

2 Timetables

Timetables are essential to allow us to plan journeys.

Timetables usually show the schedule for more than one train or bus.

Each column in the table represents a different train or bus.

The table opposite shows the times of three trains going from Hilltown to Dayton, passing through other towns. The '...' means that the train does not stop at Ceeton.

Hilltown	06 22	07 22	08 22
Beeville	06 35	07 38	08 36
Ceeton	07 01	...	09 02
Dayton	07 34	08 36	09 38

Exercise 2.1

1 This timetable shows the times of buses from Rosebury to Clifton.

Rosebury	10 35	12 15	14 45	16 15
Greyling	10 57	12 37	15 07	16 36
Burn	11 03	12 44	15 13	16 43
Snowton	11 28	13 10	15 38	17 10
Clifton	12 01	13 46	16 10	17 45

a When does the second bus leave Rosebury?

b Write down, in 12-hour time, when the third bus arrives in Clifton.

c How long does the third bus take to travel from Rosebury to Clifton?

d Which bus takes the longest time for the complete journey?

e Lee lives in Burn and wants to go shopping in Clifton.
He arrives at the bus stop at five to three.
  i How long will he have to wait for the bus?
  ii When will he arrive in Clifton?
  iii How long is his bus journey?
  iv The shopping centre closes at 7 p.m.
  How long does Lee have for shopping?

f Alison is on the bus. Her watch says the time is five to one.
What town will the bus arrive at next?

g Because of bad weather, the 10 35 from Rosebury arrives in Greyling 12 minutes late.
  i At what time did it arrive in Greyling?
  By the time the bus got to Snowton it was 37 minutes late.
  ii What time did it arrive in Snowton?

E

2   Here is part of a train timetable.

Edinburgh	09 15	10 30	12 30	14 30	16 20	16 30	17 15	17 55	18 45	19 45	20 45	22 15	23 25
Haymarket	09 18	...	...	...	16 23	...	17 18	17 58	18 48	19 48	20 48	22 18	23 28
Linlithgow	...	...	...	...	...	...	17 37	...	19 05	20 08	21 06	22 32	...
Polmont	...	...	...	...	...	...	17 43	...	19 13	20 13	21 13	22 43	...
Falkirk	09 41	11 03	13 03	15 03	...	17 03	17 49	18 20	19 19	20 19	21 19	22 49	23 53
Larbert	09 58	11 08	13 08	15 08	...	17 08	17 55	...	19 25	20 25	21 25	22 55	00 01
Stirling	10 08	11 19	13 19	15 19	...	17 19	18 05	18 33	19 35	20 35	21 35	23 05	00 11
Bridge of Allan	...	11 24	13 24	15 24	...	17 24	18 10	...	19 40	20 40	21 40	23 10	...
Dunblane	...	11 31	13 31	15 31	...	17 31	18 18	18 41	19 48	20 48	21 48	23 17	00 21
Gleneagles	...	...	...	...	...	...	...	18 53	...	...	...	...	...
Perth	10 45	...	14 01	...	17 50	...	18 47	19 09	...	...	22 20	...	00 54

a   How many trains travel from
    i   Edinburgh to Perth   **ii**   Falkirk to Dunblane?

b   At which stations does the third train stop?

c **i**   When does the first train for Larbert leave Edinburgh?
    ii How long does the journey take?

d **i**   How many trains travel between Edinburgh and Linlithgow?
    ii Which one does this part of the journey the fastest?
    iii How long does it take?

e   Scott needs to be in Dunblane by 2.15 p.m. for an interview for a job.
    i   What is the latest time he can leave Falkirk?
    ii How long does the journey take?
    iii How long does he have in Dunblane to get to the offices for his interview?

3 Using stopwatches

We use stopwatches to record time intervals accurately.
In sport, stopwatches are used to record the length of a match or how fast a race is run.

To distinguish between top athletes we need to measure their times to one hundredth of a second.

minutes   seconds   tenths of   hundredths
               a second of a second

This stopwatch shows
9 minutes 38·47 seconds

Example

At the end of a race the winner's clock showed $\boxed{7:42.31}$

The runner-up clocked $\boxed{7:42.36}$

How much was she behind the winner?

minutes	seconds	
7	42·36	She was 5 hundredths of a second behind
−7	42·31	the winner.
0	0·05	

E

Exercise 3.1

1 Write down the meaning of the highlighted digits on these stopwatches.

a `2:51.22` **b** `7:35.06` **c** `12:01.85` **d** `0:44.63`

2 Write down the time which is 6 hundredths of a second after:

a 5·41 seconds   **b** 43·29 seconds

c 16·97 seconds   **d** 39·76 seconds

3 A score board showed an athlete's time to be 14·56 seconds.
Write down the time which is:

a 3 hundredths of a second earlier

b 12 hundredths of a second later

c 2 tenths of a second earlier

d 5 tenths of a second later

4 These are the times of the first three skiers in a downhill race.

F. Schmit   `1:23.68`

A. Baxter   `1:24.02`

R. Kramer   `1:23.45`

a Who won the race?

b By how many hundredths of a second did
   i the first skier beat the second
   ii the second skier beat the third?

5 In a Formula One race a record-breaking lap time of 58·37 seconds was recorded. The record was broken by 3 hundredths of a second.
What was the previous record?

6 In a cross-country competition three horses, Coco, Norseman and Spike, all achieved a clear round.
The winner is decided by looking for the fastest time for the round.
Here are the horses' individual times.

Coco `9:32.36`   Norseman `9:39.58`   Spike `9:30.72`

a Which horse won?

b A yellow rosette is awarded to the horse who came third. Who gets the yellow rosette?

c What was the difference in time between Coco and Norseman?

d How much faster was Spike than Coco?

E

7 In a cycling race the winner took 5 minutes 57·41 seconds to complete the course.
The cyclist who came in second took 14 hundredths of a second longer.
What was his time for the race?

8 Calculate the difference between each pair of times. Remember to write down the units.

a $0:11.56$ and $0:11.52$ **b** $0:09.94$ and $0:09.89$

c $0:24.35$ and $0:24.22$ **d** $3:16.04$ and $3:15.96$

e $1:53.26$ and $1:53.21$ **f** $7:32.84$ and $7:31.55$

g $2:01.04$ and $1:59.97$

9 Ela was delighted when she ran a mile in under 4 minutes.
She did it by 7 hundredths of a second.
What was Ela's time for the race?

10 The winner board at an athletics meeting showed the results of the men's 100 metre race.

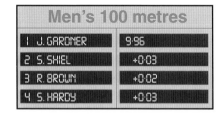

J. Gardner finished first in a time of 9·96 seconds.

Men's 100 metres	
1 J. GARDNER	9·96
2 S. SHIEL	+0·03
3 R. BROWN	+0·02
4 S. HARDY	+0·03

a Work out the times for the other three runners.

b R. Brown beat his personal best time by four hundredths of a second.
What had his personal best been?

c To get into the 4 × 100 metre relay team S. Hardy will have to run a hundred metres in 9·98 seconds.
By how much will he have to improve his time?

Practical activities

Use a stopwatch to time yourself and your friends doing various activities.
Try these.

1 A common experiment to see how fast you think.

    a Sort a pack of cards into suits.

    b Sort the cards in correct order.

Do these tasks against the clock.
Keep a record of how fast you improve.

2 **a** Measure the time taken by classmates to add ten 2-digit numbers correctly.
Compare results.
What is the record time?

    b Repeat part **a** using a calculator.
Compare your results. Write up any conclusions.

E

3 Choose a length of time between 1 and 30 seconds.
Take it in turns to try to stop a stopwatch at that time, without looking at the dial.

- The number of seconds you are out is counted as a penalty.
- The person with the lowest total number of penalty points after three rounds is the winner.

Try counting 'thousand 1, thousand 2, thousand 3, ...' to help judge seconds.

4 Calculating speed

Speed is the rate at which distance is covered in a specified time.

A car might travel at 60 mph (miles per hour).

A man might run at 9 m/s (metres per second).

A snail might crawl at 6 m/min (metres per minute).

Things move at varying speeds.
When we talk about the speed of an object we usually mean the *average* speed.
A car may speed up and slow down but if the distance covered in one hour is 60 miles, we would say its average speed was 60 mph.

Example 1

Shaun walks 15 km in 3 hours.
Calculate his average speed.

Answer: Shaun covers 15 km in 3 hours
so his average speed = 15 ÷ 3 = 5 km/hour

$$\text{average speed} = \frac{\text{distance covered}}{\text{time taken}}$$

This triangle is a memory aid.

Cover up the S and you get the formula $S = \dfrac{D}{T}$

Note: Keep the units consistent.
If distance is measured in kilometres and time is measured in hours, then speed is in kilometres per hour (km/h).

Exercise 4.1

1 Charlie drives 126 km in 3 hours.
Calculate his average speed in kilometres per hour.

2 Janice drove from Newmill to Linlithgow, a distance of 98 miles, in 2 hours.
Calculate her average speed in miles per hour.

3 Calculate the average speeds for these journeys.
(Take care with the units.)

	a	b	c	d	e
distance	225 km	56 metres	136 miles	3800 km	480 metres
time	5 hours	14 seconds	10 hours	20 hours	32 seconds

4 Four friends took part in races on a school sports day.
Derek: 200 metres in 25 seconds
Simon: 440 metres in 55 seconds
Eric: 120 metres in 16 seconds
Amir: 180 metres in 20 seconds
 a Calculate the average speed of each of the runners.
 b Which two boys ran at the same speed?

5 Morag recorded the times and distances
between towns on her delivery run.
Calculate the average speed for each part
of the journey.

156 km
2 hours
Hindley

Home

120 km
1·5 hours

165 km
3 hours
Weaver

6 Calculate the average speed for each of these journeys.
 a 384 kilometres in 6 hours
 b 158 kilometres in 4 hours
 c 1200 miles in 5 hours

7 Angela walked 2 kilometres in half an hour.
 a How far would she walk in 1 hour?
 b What is her speed in km/h?

8 Toby cycled 5 kilometres in 15 minutes.
 a How far would he cycle in
  i half an hour
  ii an hour?
 b What is his average speed in km/h?

9 It took Rosie 20 minutes to jog 4 kilometres.

   a How far would she jog in one hour?   **b** Write down her speed in km/h.

> *Remember:*
> 30 minutes = half an hour   = 0·5 hour
> 15 minutes = a quarter of an hour   = 0·25 hour
> 45 minutes = three quarters of an hour = 0·75 hour

Example 2

A journey of 63 km lasts 1 hour and 45 minutes.
Calculate the average speed of the journey.

Answer: 1 hour and 45 minutes = 1·75 hours $\text{speed} = \dfrac{D}{T} = \dfrac{63}{1 \cdot 75} = 36 \text{ km/h}$

Exercise 4.2

1 The journey to an airport takes 2 hours 30 minutes. The distance is 120 miles.
   a Write the time in hours.
   b Calculate the average speed for the journey in miles per hour.

2 Calculate the average speed for each of these journeys.

	a	b	c	d	e
distance	203 km	144 miles	299 miles	70 km	480 miles
time	3 hours 30 min	2 hours 15 min	6 hours 30 min	1 hour 45 min	2 hours 30 min

3 Neil set off from home at 1 p.m. to drive 120 km to visit his grandmother.
He arrived at 2.30 p.m.
   a How long did the journey take him?
   b Calculate his average speed for the journey.
       It took Neil an hour and fifteen minutes to
       do the return journey.

   c Calculate his average speed for his journey home.

4 3 hours 25 minutes = $3\frac{25}{60}$ hours
Express the following times in hours.
   a 2 hours 20 minutes   **b** 4 hours 12 minutes   **c** 1 hour 50 minutes
   d 3 hours 24 minutes   **e** 5 hours 5 minutes   **f** 36 minutes

5 Calculate the average speed for each of these journeys.

	a	b	c	d	e
distance	140 km	35 miles	198 miles	78 km	133 miles
time	2 hours 20 min	1 hour 10 min	4 hours 24 min	1 hour 5 min	3 hours 10 min

5 Calculating distance

> **Example 1**
>
> Ben cycled at a steady speed of 11 kilometres per hour.
> How far did he cycle in 3 hours?
>
> **Answer:**   In 1 hour he covers 11 km
>   so in 3 hours he covers 33 × 3 = 99 km
>
> | distance = average speed × time taken |
>
> Cover up the *D* and you get the formula   *D* = *ST*

Exercise 5.1

1   A bus travelled at 60 miles per hour.
How many miles did it travel in
   a   1 hour   **b**   3 hours?

2   A boy ran at 5 metres per second.
How many metres could he run in
   a   1 second   **b**   6 seconds   **c**   20 seconds?

3   Work out how far each of these would travel in the time given.
(Take care to use the correct units for distance.)
   a   Car travelling at 80 km/h for 5 hours.
   b   Aeroplane flying at 250 mph for 6 hours.
   c   Train travelling at 95 mph for 3 hours.
   d   Caterpillar moving at 6 centimetres per second for 20 seconds.
   e   Skateboard moving at 3 m/s for 7 seconds.
   f   Bicycle moving at 10 km/h for half an hour.

4   Calculate the distance travelled in each example.

	a	b	c	d	e	f
distance	50 mph	23 m/s	10 metres/min	110 km/h	16 m/s	9·8 m/s
time	7 hours	5 seconds	9·5 minutes	3 hours	20 seconds	30 seconds

5   Three girls timed themselves on a run.
Jenny ran at 8 m/s for 35 seconds.
Angela ran at 6·8 m/s for 45 seconds.
Parveen ran at 7·5 m/s for 38 seconds.
   a   Calculate how far each girl ran.
   b   What is the difference between the longest and the shortest distance run?

6   George set out from home at 14 55 and drove at an average speed of 95 km/h
on the motorway. He arrived at his destination at 17 55.
How far did he travel?

Example 2

A bus journey took 1 hour 15 minutes.
The average speed of the bus was 52 mph.
What distance was covered?

Answer: 1 hour 15 minutes = 1·25 hours

distance covered = 52 × 1·25 = 65 miles

Example 3

Another bus journey took 1 hour 10 minutes.
The average speed of the bus was 48 km/h.
What distance was covered?

Answer: 1 hour 10 minutes = $1\frac{10}{60}$ hours

distance covered = $48 \times 1\frac{10}{60}$ = 56 km

Exercise 5.2

1 A plane is flying at 200 km per hour.
How far would it fly in

   a 1 hour

   b half and hour

   c a quarter of an hour?

2 An ambulance was travelling to an emergency at an average speed of 64 mph.
It took 15 minutes to arrive at the scene of the accident.

   a What fraction of an hour is 15 minutes?

   b How far did the ambulance travel to the accident?

3 The Swanston family set off on holiday travelling at an average speed of 48 km/h.
The journey took three and a half hours.
How far did they travel?

4 Work out the distances travelled in each example.

   a Two and a half hours at 72 km/h.

   b Half an hour at 46 mph.

   c 1 hour 30 minutes at 44 km/h.

   d A quarter of an hour at 36 mph.

   e 2 hours 30 minutes at an average speed of 110 km/h.

5 Tim set off from home at 09 45 and arrived at his friend Alan's house at 11 15.
He cycled at an average speed of 12 km/h.

   a For how long was Tim cycling?

   b How far apart do Tim and Alan live?

F

6 Leah delivers medical supplies around the country.

Kirkby — 36 km/h — Rayley — 40 km/h — Hamlet — 60 km/h — Nixham
2 hours   45 minutes   3 hours 15 minutes

a Calculate the distances between the towns.

b How far is it from Rayley to Nixham?

c How far did she travel altogether?

d Check that you worked out it was 102 km from Kirkby to Hamlet. It has been entered in the distance table. Copy the table and use your answers to complete it.

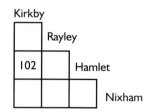

Kirkby

Rayley

102   Hamlet

Nixham

6 Calculating time

Example 1

Alastair drives 144 kilometres at an average speed of 48 km/h. How long will the journey take?

Answer: He drives 48 km in 1 hour
$144 \div 48 = 3$ ... there are three 48s in 144
So the journey takes 3 hours.

$$\text{time taken} = \frac{\text{distance covered}}{\text{average speed}}$$

Cover up the T and you get the formula $T = \dfrac{D}{S}$

Exercise 6.1

1 John walked 18 kilometres at 6 km/h.
How many hours did it take him?

2 Tessa drives 220 km at 55 km/h.
Calculate for how many hours she was driving.

3 How long would it take to travel 340 miles at 68 mph?

4 Laura can run at an average speed of 7 metres per second.
How many seconds would it take her to run 168 metres?

5 An aeroplane travels at an average speed of 200 km/h.
How many hours would it take to fly 3000 kilometres?

6 Work out how long each of these journeys would take.

	a	b	c	d	e
distance	322 m	176 m	300 km	132 miles	468 km
speed	14 m/s	10 m/s	25 km/h	22 mph	78 km/h

7 A ship sailed at an average speed of 500 miles per day. How long would it take to travel 1750 miles?

8 Sandi left home at 13 40 and drove 252 kilometres at an average speed of 84 km/h. At what time did she arrive at her destination?

9 Aleta cycled at an average speed of 12·5 km/h. She cycled for 50 kilometres. If she left home at 14 45, when would she finish her cycle run?

10 The speed limit on a motorway is 70 mph. Martin needs to drive 245 miles. If he sets out at 13 45, can he arrive at his destination by 17 00 without breaking the speed limit?
(Write down *all* the calculations you do to work this out.)

Example 2

How long does it take to cover a distance of 132 miles at a speed of 48 mph?

Answer: $T = \dfrac{D}{S} = \dfrac{132}{48} = 2\cdot75$ hours

Time taken is 2 hours and 45 minutes.

F

Exercise 6.2

1 Calculate the time taken for each journey in hours and minutes.
  a 90 miles at 36 mph **b** 80 km at 64 km/h **c** 66 miles at 24 mph
  d 315 km at 90 km/h **e** 798 miles at 152 mph

2 Kerry rode her horse at an average speed of 8 km/h. How long would it take to ride 30 kilometres?

3 A fire engine travelled at an average speed of 56 mph to a fire 14 miles away. How many minutes would it take for the engine to arrive at the scene of the fire?

4 Michael drives to town, 36 kilometres away, at an average speed of 72 km/h. How many minutes did the journey take?

5 Patricia jogs half a mile at 2 mph. How many minutes will it take her?

6 The bus travels between Ashton and Busby, a distance of 33 km, at an average speed of 44 km/h.
  a How many minutes will the journey take?
  b If the bus leaves Ashton at 11.27 a.m., when will it arrive in Busby?

7 Which formula?

$$\text{average speed} = \frac{\text{distance covered}}{\text{time taken}}$$

$$S = \frac{D}{T}$$

$$\text{distance covered} = \text{average speed} \times \text{time taken}$$

$$D = S \times T$$

$$\text{time taken} = \frac{\text{distance covered}}{\text{average speed}}$$

$$T = \frac{D}{S}$$

Exercise 7.1

1 A helicopter flies at an average speed of 85 mph for 510 miles. How long will the journey take?

2 How fast are you travelling if you cover 232 km in 4 hours?

3 A train takes three and a half hours to complete its journey. It travels at an average speed of 150 km/h. How far did it travel?

4 It takes Malik 15 minutes to walk into town. The town is 1·5 km from home. How fast is Malik walking?

5 Drew swam at 3 m/s. How long did it take him to swim 200 metres? Round your answer to the nearest second.

6 Work out the missing entries in the table. (Be careful with units.)

	a	b	c	d	e	f
distance	?	234 km	275 km	33 miles	?	0·5 km
speed	13 m/s	?	110 km/h	?	52 mph	25 m/s
time	56 s	4·5 h	?	half an hour	1 h 15 min	?

7 Fatima travels between the towns on the map delivering pottery to gift shops.
  a How long did it take Fatima to travel from Kirk Patrick to Port?
  b How long did the whole journey take?
  c Which was the fastest part of her journey?
  d How far was her whole journey?

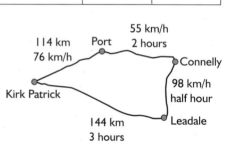

8 Distance–time graphs

Alain sets off on a cycle run.
The graph shows his progress.

Section a   In the first hour he cycled 20 km.
          So his speed was 20 km/h.
Section b   He rests for half an hour.
          So for half an hour no distance is covered.
Section c   He cycles a further 20 km.
          It takes him an hour and a half, so his
          speed was $13\frac{1}{3}$ km/h.

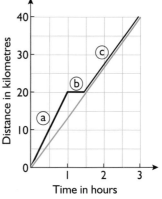

The whole journey takes 3 hours.

He cycles 40 km altogether.

Over the whole journey the *average* speed is $\frac{40}{3} = 13\frac{1}{3}$ km/h.
This is represented by the green line.

Note: The steeper the line, the faster the speed.

Exercise 8.1

1   Abby went for a walk.
     The graph illustrates her progress.
     a   How far did she walk in the first hour?
     b   What was her speed in the first hour?
     c   For how long did she stop?
     d   Did she walk quicker before or after
         her rest?
     e   What was her speed in the third hour?
     f   Use the green line and calculate the
         average speed over the whole walk.

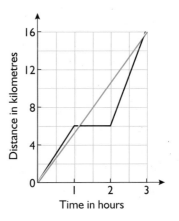

2   Liz is on a cycling holiday.
     The graph shows her journey one day.
     a   How far did Liz cycle in the first hour?
     b   What was her speed in the first part
         of her journey?
     c   For how long did she stop for lunch?
     d   How fast was she travelling between
         i   the second and third hour
         ii   the third and fourth hour?
     e   Which part of her journey was
         the fastest?
     f   Calculate her average speed for the day.

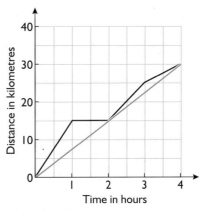

3 Ariana was driving to work. She recorded how far she had travelled every 5 minutes. The graph shows her journey.

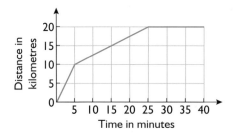

a Calculate her speed for the first part of the journey in kilometres per minute.

b How far had she travelled after 15 minutes?

c She drove onto a busier road 5 minutes from home. Calculate her average speed for this part of her journey.

d How long did it take her to get to work?

e How far does she live from where she works?

4 The graph shows the journey of an ambulance to a road accident 17 km away.

a The ambulance had to stop for a short time at roadworks. For how long was it stopped?

b Calculate the speed, in kilometres per minute, of the first part of the journey.

c How long did it take the ambulance to arrive at the scene of the accident?

d Did the ambulance travel faster before or after the roadworks?

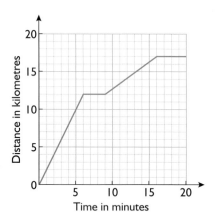

5 Jackie is standing in a shop and sees her bus in the distance. She sets off to run to the bus stop. The graph shows her run.

a How fast did she run at first?

b She stopped for a short time to catch her breath. For how long did she stop?

c How far from the shop was the bus stop?

d How long did it take her to get there?

e At one point she dropped her glove and had to go back for it. How far did she have to go back?

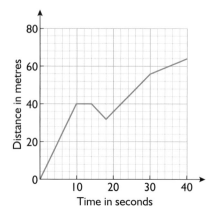

9 Drawing distance–time graphs

When drawing a distance–time graph, record

- the *time since start* on the horizontal axis
- the *distance from start* on the vertical axis.

In this example
each square in the *x*-direction represents
5 seconds,
each square in the *y*-direction represents
1 metre.

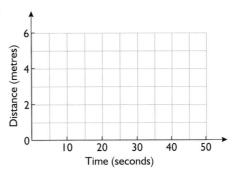

Exercise 9.1

1   Tessa leaves home and drives at a steady speed.
    She travels 70 kilometres in three hours to get
    to her office.

    a   Copy the axes opposite.

    b   Draw a straight line graph to illustrate
        Tessa's journey.

    c   Tessa's sister Maggie leaves home at the
        same time but only takes 2 hours to get to
        the same place.
        Draw another line on the same diagram
        to represent Maggie's journey.

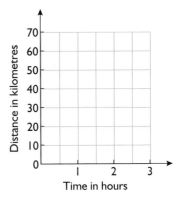

2   Megan set off from home and walked
    40 metres in 10 seconds.
    She stopped for 5 seconds, then walked a
    further 20 metres in 10 seconds.

    a   Using the axes opposite, draw a
        distance–time graph to illustrate the journey.

    b   Use the graph to help you calculate Megan's
        average speed over the whole journey.

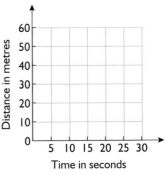

3   Kenny ran, then walked, then jogged.
    He ran for 200 metres. It took him 30 seconds.
    He took 15 seconds to walk 50 metres.
    He jogged for 15 seconds covering 100 metres.
    Draw a distance–time graph to illustrate this journey.

4   Eva drives to work each day.
    One day she took note of the distances she had travelled and the time it had
    taken her.
    - She covered the first 14 kilometres in 10 minutes.
    - She stopped for 4 minutes to buy a newspaper.
    - Finally she drove a further 12 kilometres in 15 minutes.
    Draw a distance–time graph to illustrate the journey.

F

5 Danny walked into town, stopped in a café for coffee and then walked back home.
- The walk to town lasted 25 minutes and he covered 1·4 km.
- His coffee stop lasted 20 minutes.
- His walk home was 1·4 km and took him 35 minutes.

Draw a graph to show this.

Challenge

Buses leave Edinburgh for Glasgow every half hour. The graph shows the noon bus arriving in Glasgow at 1 p.m.

Gregor left Glasgow at noon. It took him 2 hours to get to Edinburgh. How many buses passed him on the way?

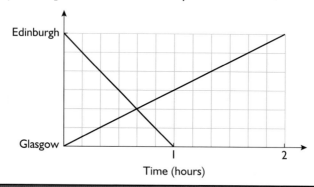

F

CHECK-UP

1 Write down the times on these digital stopwatch displays.

  a `8:25.46`   b `12:58.05`   c `0:14.69`

2 What time is 7 hundredths of a second after 1 minute 34·21 seconds?

3 These stopwatches show the times taken by two runners.

  `0:25.37`   `0:25.52`
  Russell   Daniel

  a Who won the race?   b By how much did he win?

4 A bus travels at an average speed of 54 mph for 4 hours.
  How far does it travel?

5 A plane flies at an average speed of 240 km/h.
  How long would it take to fly 600 km?

6 How fast are you running if you cover 120 metres in 15 seconds?

7 Becky leaves home at 13 45 and arrives in Carlisle at 15 15.
  a How long did the journey take her?
  b The distance from home to Carlisle is 90 kilometres.
     Calculate her average speed.

8 Ryan runs 2·5 km in 15 minutes. Calculate his speed in km/h.

9 The graph shows how Sita went from
  her home to the bus stop.

  a How far does she live from the
     bus stop?
  b How far had she gone in the first
     eight seconds?
  c She dropped her purse and stopped
     to pick it up.
     For how long did she stop?
  d Calculate her speed for the first part
     of the journey.
  e How long did it take her altogether
     to get to the bus stop?

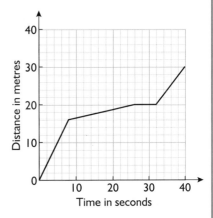

10 Dean drove 20 miles in 15 minutes, then drove a further 10 miles
   in 12 minutes.
   Draw a distance–time graph to illustrate this.

E

(7) Position and movement

People have always used maps and plans of sorts to find their position or to describe a journey.

These have not always been accurate.

After a major accident where four British warships mistook their position and were wrecked on the Scillies, the government offered a prize of £20 000 to anyone who could solve the problem. It was solved by a watchmaker, John Harrison. See what you can find out about this.

Where am I?

1 Looking back ◀◀

Exercise 1.1

1 a Which direction are you facing if you
>   **i**   face east and then turn 45° clockwise?
>   **ii** face north-west then turn 90° anti-clockwise?

  b What size of angle do you turn through
>   **i**   from west to north-east clockwise
>   **ii** from south-east to north-west anti-clockwise?

2 To go from Consett to Newcastle you go north-east.
What is the direction of travel from

  a Newcastle to Hexham
  b Durham to Sunderland
  c Newcastle to Consett
  d Whitley Bay to Morpeth?

3 On a coordinate diagram plot the points A(2, 1), B(1, 5) and C(4, 7).
  a Complete the parallelogram by plotting point D and write its coordinates.
  b On the same diagram plot point E such that ACED is a kite and write down the coordinates of E.

4 Here is a maze on a coordinate plane.
Write down the route through the maze, staying on gridlines and starting with (0, 0), (0, 2) until you get to 'out'.

5 **a** Identify the type of quadrilateral ABCD whose vertices are A(2, 0), B(4, 3), C(2, 5) and D (0, 3).
b Where do its diagonals intersect?

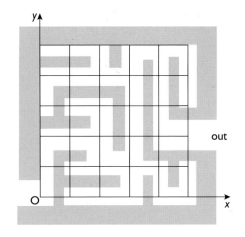

2 Bearings

In what direction should the hiker travel to reach the tree?

This direction can be described by giving the angle between it and north, measured clockwise.

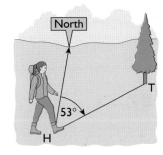

Example 1
The tree is on a bearing of 053° from the hiker.

> Bearings are measured from north in a clockwise direction.
> Bearings are given as 3 figures.

Example 2
The **back bearing** (or **return bearing**) is the bearing of the hiker from the tree.
In this case it is 53 + 180 = 233°.

> If a bearing is greater than 180°, then the return bearing is calculated by subtracting 180°.

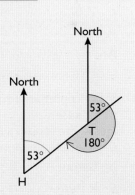

Example 3
The bearing of the hiker from the tree is 233°.
The return bearing is 233 − 180 = 053°.

E

Exercise 2.1

1 For each diagram state or calculate the bearing of **i** P from A **ii** A from P.

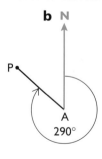

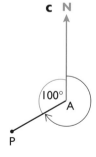

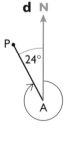

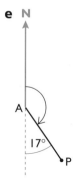

2 Each diagram gives the bearing of one point from another.
  i In each case describe the bearing.
  ii Calculate the return bearing for each diagram.

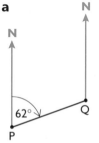

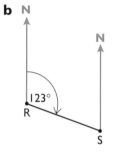

3 P is on a bearing of 030° from A and 310° from B.
Name the point which is:
  a 050° from A and 310° from B
  b 070° from A and 020° from B
  c 100° from A and 180° from B
  d 180° from A and 265° from B
  e 350° from A and 290° from B.

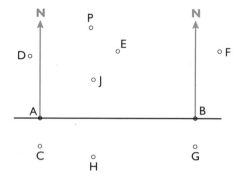

4 A site is prepared for the foundations of a house.
This is the rectangle ABCD. DA runs north.
Calculate the bearing of:
  a B from A **b** C from B
  c D from C **d** A from D.

E

5 Draw a square, PQRS, of side 10 cm with PQ running north.

    a Draw the following lines:

        i   from P on a bearing of 120°

        ii from Q on a bearing of 040°

        iii from R on a bearing of 300°

        iv from S on a bearing of 200°.

    b Calculate the size of each angle in the square.

6 **a** Measure the bearing of each link of the pitch-n-putt course.

    b What are the bearings of the diagonals of the rectangular perimeter of the course?

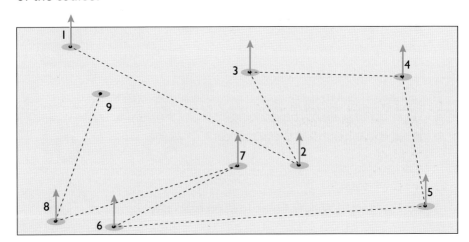

3 Scale drawings

The picture of the pitch-n-putt course is not actual size.

It is a drawing where 1 cm represents 10 m.

Example 1

The distance between hole 6 and hole 5 can be measured as 8·5 cm.
So we know the actual distance is 8·5 × 10 = 85 m.

Example 2

The actual distance between hole 8 and hole 9 is 36 metres.
So it is drawn as a 36 ÷ 10 = 3·6 cm line.

Exercise 3.1

1 This picture is drawn to a scale where 1 cm represents 25 cm.
   a How tall is the boy?
   b How big is the bin?

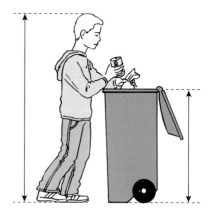

2 The actual car is 4 m long.
   a What is the scale of the drawing?
   b What is the height of the actual car?

E

3 A yacht sails from Willow Creek to Blackfriars Bay.

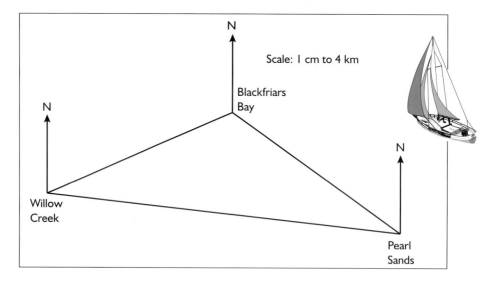

a Describe this journey by giving its bearing and distance.
b The yacht sails on to Pearl Sands.
   Find the bearing and distance for this part of the voyage.
c i What bearing would take the yacht back to Willow Creek?
  ii What distance would the yacht sail on the return journey?

4   Four marker buoys are positioned at
    sea for a race.
    The route is round B1, then B2, B3,
    B4 and then to the home port.
    Home port is 2 km due north of B4.
    This scale diagram shows the positions
    of the buoys.

    a For each leg of the race calculate
        i   the bearing
        ii the distance.

    b How long is the whole race?

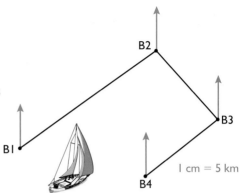

1 cm = 5 km

5   A radar screen at an airport shows aeroplanes within range.
    The distance between each circle represents 10 km.
    The airport is at the centre of the screen.
    The aeroplane at A is 30 km from the airport on a bearing of 120°.
    We can write its position like this: (30, 120°)

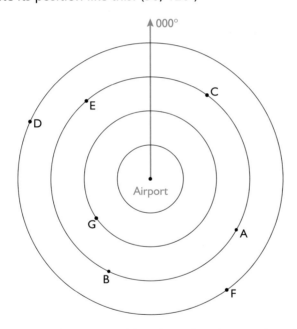

E

    a Write down the distance and bearing of each aeroplane B, C, D, E, F and G
        in the same way.

    b The aeroplane nearest to the airport is coming in to land.
        i   Which one is it?
        ii On which bearing is it flying?

    c Plane E is flying away from the airport. It is told to change its bearing to
        345°. Through what angle will the plane have to turn and in which
        direction to follow this instruction?

    d Plane B is on a flight path to the airport.
        What is the bearing from plane B to the airport?

4 Problem solving using scale drawings

Example

A TV detector van picks up a signal on a bearing of 060°.
It moves 100 m due east and takes another bearing on the signal.
This time it is 300°.

a Find the source of the signal and give its distance from the second position of the van.

b How close did the van get to the source?

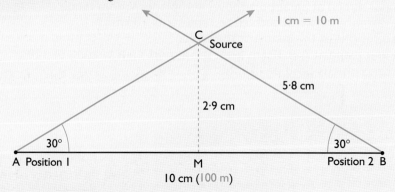

Answer: Draw a scale drawing using 1 cm = 10 m.
Thus 100 m is represented by a 10 cm line AB.
AC is on a bearing of 060°.
BC is on a bearing of 300°.

a Measure BC as 5·8 cm. So C is the source and it is 58 m from B.

b Measure CM, where ∠CMB is a right angle. It is 2·9 cm.
So the van got as close as 29 m to the source.

Exercise 4.1

1 An orienteer measures the bearing of Ben Mhor, 5 km away, as 050°.
He takes a bearing on Ben Tarsun, 4 km away, and finds it to be 135°.

a Make an accurate scale drawing of the information.

b How far apart are the two mountains?

2 A radar beam from *The Lucky Star* picks up an object on a bearing of 035°.
A second ship, *The Tempest*, 12 miles due east of *The Lucky Star*, picks up the
same object on a bearing of 315°.

a Make an accurate scale drawing of the situation.

b How far is the object from **i** *The Lucky Star* **ii** *The Tempest*?

3 A catamaran sails daily from Port Paddy to the nearby islands of Midgie and Clegg.
Midgie is 30 miles away on a bearing of 210°.
From here the catamaran sails 30 miles on a bearing of 295° to Clegg before returning to port.

a Using a scale of 1 cm to 5 miles, make an accurate scale drawing of the voyage.

b Use your drawing to find
i the bearing of the port from Clegg
ii the distance from Clegg to Port Paddy.

4 On an army exercise soldiers identify their objective 30 km away on a bearing of 120°. They walk towards their objective, but after 10 km they are forced to change direction. They walk for 15 km on a bearing of 075°.

a Make a scale drawing of the soldiers' exercise so far using a suitable scale.

b How far away are they now from their objective?

c What is the bearing which will take the soldiers to their objective?

Another way of expressing scale

On some Ordnance Survey maps you will see

> Scale 1 : 50 000
> 2 centimetres to 1 kilometre

1 : 50 000 means that 1 unit on the map *represents* 50 000 units in real life.
1 mm on the map represents 50 000 mm in real life.
1 cm on the map represents 50 000 cm in real life.
1 : 50 000 is referred to as a **ratio** or a **representative fraction**.

1 : 50 000
⇒ 1 cm : 50 000 cm
⇒ 1 cm : 500 m
⇒ 1 cm : ½ km
⇒ 2 cm : 1 km
(every 2 centimetres on the map represents 1 km)

1 : 50 000
⇒ 1 mm : 50 000 mm
⇒ 1 mm : 50 m
(each millimetre on the map represents 50 m)

Example
Express a scale where 2 cm represents 1 km as a ratio.

Answer: 2 cm represents 1 km
⇒ ratio = 2 cm : 1 km
= 2 cm : 100 000 cm
= 1 : 50 000

Exercise 4.2

1   Express each of the following scales as a ratio in its simplest form.

   a 1 cm represents 2 km   **b** 1 cm represents 5 km
   c 1 cm represents 2·5 km   **d** 5 cm represents 1 km
   e 5 cm represents 2 km   **f** 4 cm represents 5 km

2   Copy and complete this table.
   Always give your answer in the most appropriate units.

Scale	Length on diagram	Actual length
1 : 1000	5 cm	
1 : 5000	2·4 cm	
1 : 50 000	7·6 cm	
1 : 25 000	3·5 cm	

3   On a map two towns are 4·6 cm apart.
   If the scale on the map is 1 : 40 000, how far apart are the towns in kilometres?

4   A street plan has a scale of 1 : 10 000.
   On this map a bridge is 18 mm long.
   How long is the bridge in real life?

5   2 cm on a map represents 5 km on the ground.
   a Express the scale of the map in the form 1 : n.
   b How would a distance of 7 km be represented on the map?
   c What distance does 3·4 cm on the map represent?

6   On an Ordnance Survey map, 4·8 cm represents 12 km on the ground.
   Write down the scale of the map in two different forms.

F

Investigation

1   What is the smallest scale you can find?
   (Hint: generally used for whole world maps.)
2   What scale is generally used for street plans?
3   Look for large scale maps or plans and find out what their uses are.

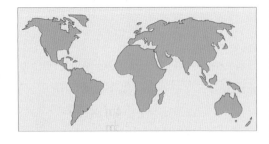

5 Coordinates in four quadrants

The x and y axes divide the coordinate plane into four parts.

The four parts are given special names: **quadrants**.

A(3, 2) lies in the first quadrant,
B(−3, 4) lies in the second,
C(−4, −3) lies in the third
and   D(5, −2) lies in the fourth.

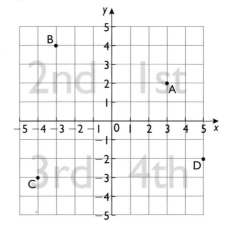

Exercise 5.1

1 Examine this list of points:
A(2, 3), B(−5, 1), C(−3, 4), D(−2, −1), E(5, −2), F(3, 3), G(0, −6), H(2, −4), I(−2, −2), J(−3, 0).

  a In which quadrant will you find   **i** A   **ii** B   **iii** D   **iv** E?

  b Between which two quadrants does G lie?

  c What is   **i** the lowest x-coordinate   **ii** the highest x-coordinate quoted?

  d What is   **i** the lowest y-coordinate   **ii** the highest y-coordinate quoted?

  e Use the answers from **c** and **d** to help you plan and draw a suitable grid for plotting all the points.

  f Plot all the points on your grid.

  g If H and I are joined by a line, what are the coordinates of the point midway between them?

  h Similarly, find the midpoint of BF.

2 This arrow is pointing along the x-axis.

  a List the coordinates of points A to G.

  b The arrow rotates through 90° anti-clockwise so that it points up the y-axis with D at (0, 5). Write down the coordinates of the new positions of A, B, C, E, F and G.

  c It is rotated again so that D now lies on (−5, 0). List the coordinates of all its vertices now.

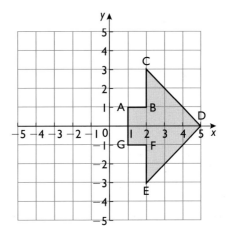

E

3 Plot the following points on a coordinate diagram and join each one to the next:
(2, 1), (1, 1), (1, 6), (−2, 6), (−4, −1), (−1, −1), (−1, −3), (1, −3), (1, −1), (2, −1), (2, 1).
Then plot: (−1, 1), (−1, 5), (−2, 1), (−1, 1).
What have you drawn?

4 On a coordinate plane, plot the points S(−2, 2), T(3, 4), U(8, 2) and join them up in order.

a Plot point V such that STUV is a rhombus and write down the coordinates of V.

b i STUW is a kite.
Give the coordinates of three possible positions of W.

ii There are infinitely many possible answers for the coordinates of W.
What is true about the coordinates of any point which fits the description?

c STUX is a V-kite.
Write down the coordinates of three possible positions for X.

5 P(−5, 0), Q(−3, 4), R(−2, 0), S(−3, −1) and T(−4, −1) are the vertices of a shape which represents a yacht on a computer screen.

a Plot the points to form the yacht.

b The computer animates the drawing by adding 2 to each x-coordinate and subtracting 1 from each y-coordinate. Draw the yacht in its new position.

6 a On a coordinate diagram, plot the points P(−4, 2), Q(2, 2), R(4, −2) and S(0, −6).

b What shape is PQRS?

c Q moves to a new position, Q'.
It moves 2 units to the left and 4 units up.
What are the coordinates of Q'?

d Name the shape PQ'RS.

e i By joining the diagonals, find the centre of PQ'RS.
ii Write down the coordinates of the centre.

7 In the coordinate diagram ABC is a triangle.

a State the coordinates of each vertex.

b ACEB is a V-kite. State the coordinates of E.

c ABCD is a plain kite.
State the coordinates of D.

d ADEF is also a kite.
State the coordinates of F.

e The area of a kite is *half the product of its diagonals*.
What is the area of ADEF?

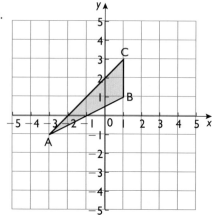

8 A helicopter is searching for
a boat in trouble.
Its flight path takes it over the
points (5, 4), (3, 3) and (1, 2).

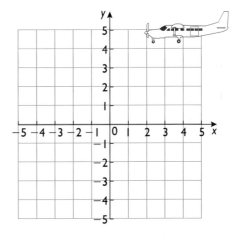

   a Name one point on this
   path which is
   i   in the second quadrant
   ii in the third quadrant
   iii between the second
        and third quadrants.
   b A second helicopter flies
   over (−3, −4) and (−1, −3).
   Name one point on this
   path which is
   i in the fourth quadrant
   ii between the first and fourth quadrants.
   c What can be said about the two flight paths?
   d The boat has broken down at the point (−3, −3).
   Which helicopter comes closest to its position?

9 A light plane leaves an airstrip
and flies in a straight line over
(4, −4) and (−4, 0).

   a Name one point in the third
   quadrant that it flies over.
   b It flies over a highway.
   This highway runs through
   (0, 3) and (−1, 1).
   Where does the plane fly
   over the highway?
   c A second plane flies on a
   course parallel to the first.
   It flies over the highway at
   the point (0, 3).
   Give the coordinates of three
   other points it flies over.

10 For a point (p, q) what can you say about p and q if the point lies:
   a in the first quadrant
   b in the second quadrant
   c in the third quadrant
   d in the fourth quadrant
   e on the x-axis, between the first and fourth quadrants
   f on the y-axis, between the third and fourth quadrants
   g between all four quadrants?

6 Sets of points

A rose bush is trained up a trellis.
One branch is tied to the points
$(2, -4)$, $(2, -3)$, $(2, -1)$, $(2, 0)$, $(2, 1)$.

Notice that all the x-coordinates are 2 and that the points all lie on the same line.

This line takes the name $x = 2$.

Similarly, the branch A lies along the line $x = 4$
the branch B lies along the line $x = -3$.

> The y-axis itself is given the name $x = 0$.

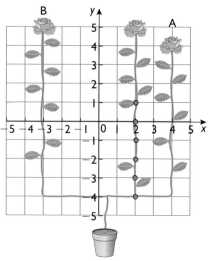

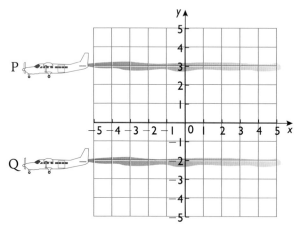

Here plane P is flying along
the line $y = 3$
and plane Q is flying along the
line $y = -2$.

> The x-axis is given the name
> $y = 0$.

Exercise 6.1

1 a Write down the names of
the labelled lines in the
diagram.

 b What kind of shape is
contained within the
four lines?

 c $x = 1$, $x = 2$, $y = 0$ and a
fourth line form a square.
What is the fourth line?

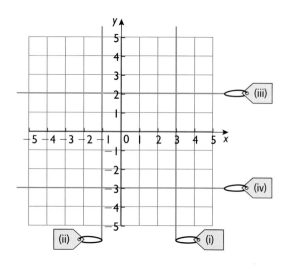

2 a On the same coordinate diagram, draw the following lines.
    i $x = 4$ **ii** $y = 3$ **iii** $x = -3$ **iv** $y = -1$
  b Write down the coordinates of the points of intersection of the lines.
  c Draw the diagonals of the rectangle formed by the four lines.
  d Name the horizontal line which passes through the point of intersection of
     these diagonals.

3 a Draw the lines $x = 5$ and $y = 2$.
  b i   Mark T, the point of intersection of the lines.
    ii   State the coordinates of T.
  c T and the point (0, 0) are opposite corners of a rectangle whose sides lie
     on the lines $x = 5$ and $y = 2$.
     Name the lines on which the other two sides lie.
  d What is the perimeter of the rectangle?

4 The sides of a rectangle are parallel to the x and y axes.
  The points (4, 1) and (5, −3) are opposite vertices.
  a Name the four lines on which its sides lie.
  b What is the area of the rectangle?

5 a i   Plot the points A(−1, 3), B(3, 3), C(3, −1) and D(−1, −1).
    ii   Draw the square ABCD.
  b Name the line which contains:
    i AB   **ii** DC   **iii** BC   **iv** AD.
  c i   Draw in the diagonals AC and BD.
    ii   Write down the coordinates of T, the point of intersection.
  d i   Draw lines through T parallel to the x and y axes.
    ii   Name both lines.

6 a i   Name the line which passes through (4, 1) and (8, 1).
    ii   Name the line parallel to this passing through (7, 6).
  b i   Name a line parallel to the x-axis passing through (4, −2)
    ii   Name a line perpendicular to this passing through (5, 1).

7 Linking y to x

The set of points $(-1, -1)$, $(0, 0)$, $(1, 1)$, $(2, 2)$,
... all have one thing in common.

In each case, the y-coordinate is the same as
the x-coordinate.

When these points are plotted we see they all
lie in a straight line. Every point on this line
shares this same property:
the y-coordinate is the same as the x-coordinate.

We give this line the name $y = x$.

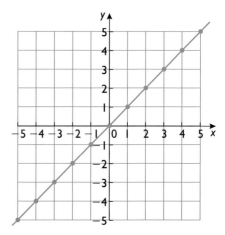

Exercise 7.1

1 a Which of these points fit the description that the y-coordinate is double the x-coordinate?
   (1, 2), (4, 2), (2, 4), (3, 6), (6, 3), (8, 4), (4, 8)
 b Plot the points that fit and draw the line.
 c Name four other points that fit the description.
 d Label the line $y = 2x$.

2 a List three points which fit the description that the y-coordinate is three times the x-coordinate.
 b Plot the points and draw the line.
 c Label the line $y = 3x$.

3 a List three points that lie on the line $y = 4x$.
 b Draw the line.
 c Name one point that is common to each of the lines $y = x$, $y = 2x$, $y = 3x$ and $y = 4x$.

4 a Plot the points (2, −2), (1, −1), (0, 0), (−1, 1), (−2, 2) and join them up.
 b This line is called $y = -x$. Find three more points on this line.
 c Give the coordinates of three points that lie on the line $y = -2x$.

5 a Which of these points fit the description that the y-coordinate is half the x-coordinate?
   (1, 2), (4, 2), (2, 4), (3, 6), (6, 3), (8, 4), (4, 8)
 b Draw each of the following lines:
   i $y = \frac{1}{2}x$
   ii $y = \frac{1}{3}x$
   iii $y = -\frac{1}{2}x$
   iv $y = -\frac{1}{3}x$

6 Name each labelled line in the diagram opposite.

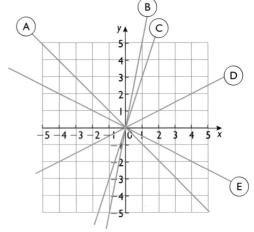

7

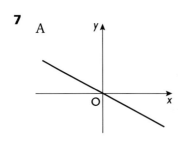

One of these is a sketch of the line $y = 3x$.
The other is a sketch of $y = -\frac{1}{2}x$.
Draw the sketches and label them correctly.

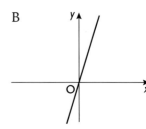

8 This is a sketch of the four lines $y = -2x$, $y = \frac{1}{3}x$, $y = 4$ and $x = 3$.
Draw the sketch and match up each label with the correct equation for the line.

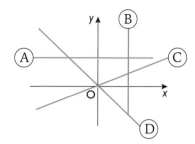

9

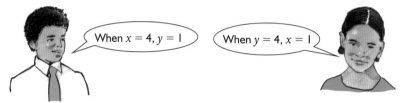

When $x = 4$, $y = 1$

When $y = 4$, $x = 1$

  a Which statement is true for which line?
$y = 4x$ or $y = \frac{1}{4}x$
  b Which line is steeper?

10 The points (1, 2), (2, 3), (3, 4) all fit the description $y = x + 1$.
  a The points $(-1, a)$, $(-2, b)$ and $(0, c)$ also fit the same description.
What are the values of a, b and c?
  b Plot the points and draw the line called $y = x + 1$.

11 a List three points which fit the description that the y-coordinate is 3 more than the x-coordinate.
  b Draw the line $y = x + 3$.
  c In a similar manner, and on the same diagram, draw the lines:
  i $y = x + 5$ **ii** $y = x + 6$
  iii $y = x - 3$ **iv** $y = x - 5$
  d In the line $y = x + a$, what effect does changing the value of a have?

12 a On the same diagram draw the lines:
  i $y = x - 2$ **ii** $y = x + 4$
  iii $y = 6 - x$ **iv** $y = 1 - x$
  b Name the shape contained within the four lines.

13 a The points (1, 3), (2, 5) and (3, 7) each fit the description $y = 2x + 1$.
Draw the line $y = 2x + 1$.
  b Draw $y = 2x$ on the same diagram.
  c What do the two lines have in common?
  d Draw the lines
  i $y = 2x + 4$ **ii** $y = 2x - 3$ **iii** $y = 2x + 6$.
Comment.

F

14 a The points (1, 4), (2, 7), (3, a), (4, b) and (5, c) each fit the description that $y = 3x + 1$. Draw the line $y = 3x + 1$.

b Which of the following points also lie on the line?
$(-3, -8)$, $(-2, -7)$, $(-1, -2)$, $(0, 0)$, $(30, 91)$

c Draw the lines **i** $y = 3x + 2$ **ii** $y = 3x - 2$ **iii** $y = 3x$.
Comment.

15 a Find three points which fit the description $y = 4x - 3$.

b Draw the line $y = 4x - 3$.

c Draw a line parallel to $y = 4x - 3$ passing through the origin.

d Name this line.

Challenge

Name each line in this diagram.

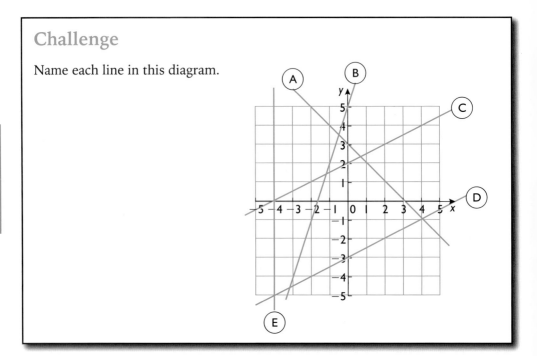

CHECK-UP

1 Calculate the bearing of P from O in each case.

a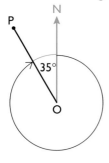

b

c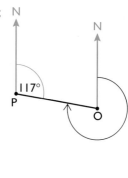

2 Spotlights are positioned on a stage to give maximum effect to the actors.
The bearing from the spotlight to Actor 1 is 205°.
He is 11 metres from the light.
The spotlight is turned to create a pool of light on another actor 7 metres to the right of Actor 1.
Here is a rough sketch of the scene.

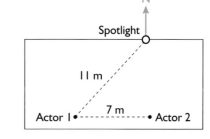

a Draw a scale diagram using a scale of 1 cm to 2 m.

b Measure the shaft of light and the bearing of Actor 2 from the spotlight.

3 ABCD is a rhombus with vertices A(−4, −1), B(−2, 2), C(0, −1) and D.

a What are the coordinates of D?

b What are the coordinates of the point of intersection of the diagonals?

c A second rhombus has coordinates P(−4, 1), Q(1, 1), R(4, −3) and S. Find the point of intersection of its diagonals.

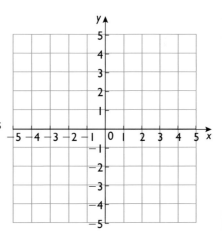

E

4 The captain of *The Star of the Sea* spots the Lone Rock Lighthouse on a bearing of 065°.
After travelling 2 km due east, another reading is taken.
Its bearing is now 035°.

   a Make a scale drawing using a scale of 1 : 50 000 to illustrate the story.

   b How close does *The Star of the Sea* get to the lighthouse?

5 a Plot the points $(1, -2)$, $(0, 0)$, $(-1, 2)$, $(-2, 4)$ and $(-3, 6)$.

   b Draw the line that passes through these points.

   c What do we call this line?

   d Write down three other points that lie on the line.

6 Draw the lines:

   a $y = x$ b $y = 2$ c $x = 3$ d $y = 3x$ e $y = 2x + 1$

F

8 Solving equations

A puzzle expert called Sam Loyd once asked:

'If a brick weighs as much as three quarters of a brick and three quarters of a kilogram, what does a brick weigh?'

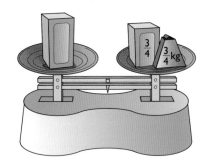

1 Looking back ◄◄

Exercise 1.1

1 Solve these equations. Give the solutions like this: $x = 3$.

   a $m + 3 = 7$ **b** $w - 2 = 5$ **c** $3x = 18$

   d $15 = y + 2$ **e** $4t - 2 = 26$ **f** $3x + 7 = 25$

2 Form an equation and solve it to answer the question under each picture.

a

How many £1 coins are in each bag?

b

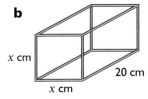

x cm

x cm

20 cm

The total length of the straws used in this model is 144 cm. What are the dimensions of the cuboid?

c

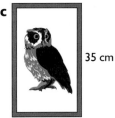

35 cm

x cm

The total length of wood used to make this frame is 94 cm. What is the width of the picture?

3 For each of these machines, form an equation and solve it to find the IN numbers.

a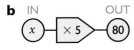

b   **c**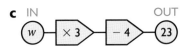

2 Covering up equations

Example

Solve the equation $\frac{1}{2}x + 2 = 6$

$\frac{1}{2}x + 2 = 6$

so $\qquad \frac{1}{2}x = 4$

so $\qquad\quad x = 8$

○ + 2 = 6
4 is covered

$\frac{1}{2}$ of ○ = 4
8 is covered

Exercise 2.1

1 Solve these equations:

a $5 - 2x = 1$ **b** $14 + 7x = 28$ **c** $\frac{1}{2}y - 2 = 3$

d $9k + 3 = 66$ **e** $20 - \frac{1}{3}y = 17$ **f** $1 = 22 - 3t$

g $57 = 9m + 12$ **h** $7 = \frac{1}{5}w - 3$ **i** $57 = 17 + 8y$

j $29 = 45 - \frac{1}{4}x$ **k** $19c - 5 = 71$ **l** $18 + \frac{1}{7}a = 21$

2 Solve this cross-number puzzle:

Across

3 $20 = \frac{1}{8}x - 11$

5 $37 - \frac{1}{5}x = 0$

7 $25 - 2m = 3$

8 $20 - \frac{1}{6}y = 3$

9 $100 = 6m - 44$

10 $\frac{1}{3}w - 50 = 33$

12 $20 = 3 + \frac{1}{25}x$

Down

1 $3y - 12 = 30$

2 $100 - 5y = 10$

3 $55 - \frac{1}{4}x = 2$

4 $\frac{1}{9}t - 1 = 90$

5 $100 = \frac{1}{4}x + 69$

6 $5 = \frac{1}{5}x - 100$

11 $20 = 100 - 2e$

13 $\frac{1}{4}n + 3 = 8$

3 Solve each of these equations by first simplifying each side:

   a $2x + 5 + x = x + 14 - x$

   b $14 + 5y + 2 + y = 2y + 46 - 2y$

   c $w + 3 + 5w - 1 = 3 + 5w + 41 - 5w$

   d $t + 18 - t = 2t + 2 + t + 1$

4 For each of these, form an equation and solve it to answer the question.

   a Total perimeter of frame is 102 cm.
      What are the dimensions of the frame?

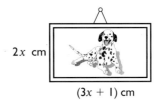

      $2x$ cm

      $(3x + 1)$ cm

   b

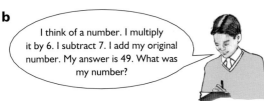

I think of a number. I multiply it by 6. I subtract 7. I add my original number. My answer is 49. What was my number?

   c The total length of straw needed to make
      this cuboid is exactly 100 cm.
      What are its dimensions?

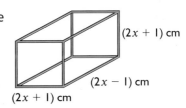

      $(2x + 1)$ cm

      $(2x - 1)$ cm

      $(2x + 1)$ cm

5 For each of the equations, one of the numbers 1, 2, 3, 4, 5 and 6 is a solution
   to the equation. Find this solution in each case.

   a $2x - 1 = x + 2$ **b** $8 - x = 2x - 1$

   c $\frac{1}{2}x + 2 = x - 1$ **d** $4x = 2x + 2$

3 Keeping your balance

When the unknown quantity appears on both sides of the equations, the *cover-up* method is not suitable.

In this case we use the **balance** method.

Imagine the equation is a balance where you can add or subtract weights.

> Golden rule: Keep the balance ... do the same action to both sides of the equation.

Example 1 Solve $4x + 1 = x + 4$

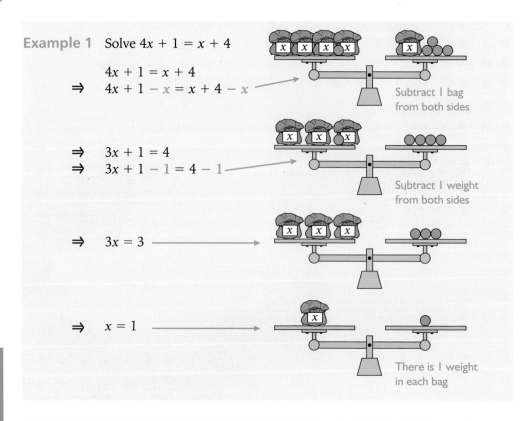

$$4x + 1 = x + 4$$
$$\Rightarrow \quad 4x + 1 - x = x + 4 - x$$

Subtract 1 bag
from both sides

$$\Rightarrow \quad 3x + 1 = 4$$
$$\Rightarrow \quad 3x + 1 - 1 = 4 - 1$$

Subtract 1 weight
from both sides

$$\Rightarrow \quad 3x = 3$$

$$\Rightarrow \quad x = 1$$

There is 1 weight
in each bag

E

Example 2 Solve $4x + 9 = 7x$

$$4x + 9 = 7x$$
$$\Rightarrow \quad 4x + 9 - 4x = 7x - 4x$$
$$\Rightarrow \quad 9 = 3x$$
$$\Rightarrow \quad 9 \div 3 = 3x \div 3$$
$$\Rightarrow \quad 3 = x$$
$$\Rightarrow \quad x = 3$$

Example 3 Solve $3x - 4 = 31 - 2x$

$$3x - 4 = 31 - 2x$$
$$\Rightarrow \quad 3x - 4 + 2x = 31 - 2x + 2x$$
$$\Rightarrow \quad 5x - 4 = 31$$
$$\Rightarrow \quad 5x - 4 + 4 = 31 + 4$$
$$\Rightarrow \quad 5x = 35$$
$$\Rightarrow \quad 5x \div 5 = 35 \div 5$$
$$\Rightarrow \quad x = 7$$

Exercise 3.1

1 Solve each equation by using the given action on both sides of the equation:

a $2x = x + 7 \ (-x)$

b $3x = 8 - x \ (+x)$

c $y + 3 = 2y \ (-y)$

d $5m = m + 12 \ (-m)$

e $n + 5 = 2n \ (-n)$

f $8 + 2k = 6k \ (-2k)$

g $w = 10 - w \ (+w)$

h $15 - a = 2a \ (+a)$

i $12 + 3x = 5x \ (-3x)$

j $5c = 24 - c \ (+c)$

k $8 - e = e \ (+e)$

l $7y = y + 48 \ (-y)$

m $3m + 32 = 7m \ (-3m)$

n $36 - h = 3h \ (+h)$

o $5t = 66 - t \ (+t)$

p $8x = 100 - 2x \ (+2x)$

2 Solve these equations:

a $3x = 2 + 2x$ **b** $4m = 3m + 3$ **c** $5u = 3u + 6$

d $n + 3 = 2n$ **e** $2k + 1 = 3k$ **f** $4 + 3x = 5x$

g $10 - y = y$ **h** $w = 6 - w$ **i** $x = 9 - 2x$

j $7a = 2a + 5$ **k** $4y = 10 - y$ **l** $3n + 4 = 5n$

m $14u = 10u + 32$ **n** $42 - 5x = 2x$ **o** $3y = 121 - 8y$

3 For each pair of straws,
  i make an equation
  ii solve it to find the length of the straws. (All lengths are in centimetres.)

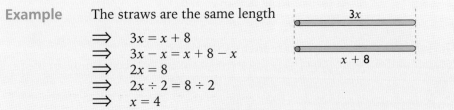

Example   The straws are the same length $3x$

$\Rightarrow$ $3x = x + 8$
$\Rightarrow$ $3x - x = x + 8 - x$
$\Rightarrow$ $2x = 8$
$\Rightarrow$ $2x \div 2 = 8 \div 2$
$\Rightarrow$ $x = 4$

$x + 8$

a $2x$ / $x + 5$ **b** $4x$ / $3x + 2$ **c** $2x + 10$ / $7x$

d $20 - 3x$ / x **e** $2x$ / $18 - x$ **f** $11x$ / $8x + 12$

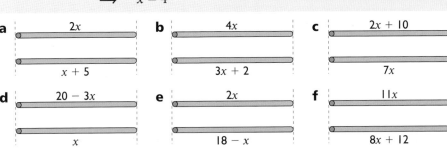

E

4 For each isosceles triangle,
  i make an equation   **ii** solve it to find x
  iii calculate the size of each angle in the triangle.

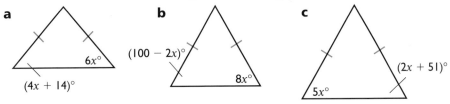

a $6x°$ / $(4x + 14)°$

b $(100 - 2x)°$ / $8x°$

c $(2x + 51)°$ / $5x°$

5 The same length of frame is required for both pictures in each pair. For each,
  i form an equation   **ii** solve to find x
  iii give the dimensions of each picture.

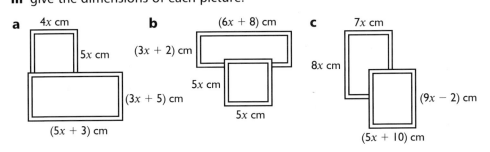

a $4x$ cm / $5x$ cm / $(5x + 3)$ cm

b $(6x + 8)$ cm / $(3x + 2)$ cm / $5x$ cm / $(3x + 5)$ cm / $5x$ cm

c $7x$ cm / $8x$ cm / $(9x - 2)$ cm / $(5x + 10)$ cm

4 Inequations

Examine this table:

Statement	Meaning	Whole number examples
$x > 2$	x is greater than 2	3, 4, 5, ...
$x \geqslant 2$	x is greater than or equal to 2	2, 3, 4, ...
$x < 2$	x is less than 2	0, 1
$x \leqslant 2$	x is less than or equal to than 2	0, 1, 2

The symbols $>$, $\geqslant$, $<$ and $\leqslant$ are **inequality** signs.
An **inequation**, or inequality, is a statement, like $x > 2$, containing an inequality sign.

Example

Solve $x \leqslant 4$ choosing from the list $\{2, 3, 4, 5, 6\}$.

Answer: $x = 2, 3$ or 4 are the only solutions.

Exercise 4.1

1   Solve each inequation, choosing only from the given list.
   a $x \geqslant 3$ {2, 3, 4, 5}   **b** $y < 4$ {1, 2, 3, 4}
   c $m \geqslant 0$ {0, 1, 2, 3}   **d** $t \leqslant 5$ {4, 5, 6, 7}
   e $c > 2$ {0, 1, 2, 3}   **f** $x < 9$ {8, 9, 10, 11}
   g $k \leqslant 2$ {0, 1, 2, 3}   **h** $y > 3$ {0, 1, 2, 3}

2   For each situation, form an inequation to describe it.
   For example; 'Don't spend more than £30.
   It's OK I only spent £x.' becomes $x \leqslant 30$.

   a Don't go faster than 30 mph.   It's OK I'm going at y mph.

   b You'll need at least £10.   That's OK I've got £x.

   c You need to be over 290 cm tall to get the job. Oh dear, I'm only h cm tall!

   d You need more than 3 kg sugar for this recipe. That's OK I've got w kg.

   e The car only holds 5 people at the most.   Oh no! That's no good, there are n people.

   f That'll be 40 pence please.   I'm sorry I've only got x pence, that's not enough.

3 Find solutions for these inequations, choosing values from {1, 2, 3, 4, 5, 6} only:

    a $3x \geqslant 15$ **b** $4y \leqslant 12$ **c** $3m + 1 > 15$

    d $8 < 3k - 1$ **e** $2 + 7n \leqslant 16$ **f** $2x + 3 \geqslant 7$

    g $3y - 2 > 2y + 2$ **h** $21 - 3x < x$ **i** $5x - 1 \leqslant 4x + 2$

    j $11 - x > 16 - 2x$ **k** $24 - 4x > 22 - 3x$ **l** $36 - 4x \leqslant 42 - 7x$

5 Solving more equations

Example 1 Solve $5x - 2 = 2x + 7$

$5x - 2 = 2x + 7$
$\Rightarrow 5x - 2 - 2x = 2x + 7 - 2x$
$\Rightarrow 3x - 2 = 7$
$\Rightarrow 3x - 2 + 2 = 7 + 2$
$\Rightarrow 3x = 9$
$ 3x \div 3 = 9 \div 3$
$ x = 3$

Example 2 Solve $2y + 3 = 8y - 33$

$2y + 3 = 8y - 33$
$\Rightarrow 2y + 3 - 2y = 8y - 33 - 2y$
$\Rightarrow 3 = 6y - 33$
$\Rightarrow 3 + 33 = 6y - 33 + 33$
$\Rightarrow 36 = 6y$
$\Rightarrow 6y \div 6 = 36 \div 6$
$\Rightarrow y = 6$

Exercise 5.1

1 Solve these equations:

    a $7x - 3 = 5x + 1$ **b** $9a + 3 = 5a + 15$ **c** $2x + 1 = x + 3$

    d $8w - 3 = 3w + 22$ **e** $n + 3 = 4n - 9$ **f** $7x + 8 = 9x + 2$

    g $7k - 3 = 5k + 11$ **h** $3x + 5 = 2x + 9$ **i** $4y - 2 = 13 - y$

    j $5k + 3 = 45 - k$ **k** $5k - 2 = 28 - 5k$ **l** $58 - y = 6y + 2$

    m $33 - 3w = 8 + 2w$ **n** $17 + 8m = 89 - m$

2 Write an equation suggested by each picture, then solve the equation.
Use your solution to answer the question.

a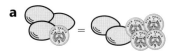

What is the cost of
1 egg?
(Let 1 egg cost x pence.)

b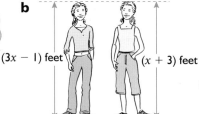

$(3x - 1)$ feet $(x + 3)$ feet

Alison and Amy are
identical twins.
How tall are they?

c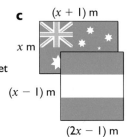

$(x + 1)$ m

x m

$(x - 1)$ m

$(2x - 1)$ m

The flags have the
same perimeter.
What are the
dimensions of
each flag?

3 Solve this cross-number puzzle:

Across
1 $3x + 2 = x + 38$
3 $6x + 79 = 29 + 11x$
4 $5x + 99 = 12x - 90$
6 $179 + x = 9x - 69$
8 $49 + 10x = 400 + 7x$
11 $1 + x = 61 - x$
12 $99 - 2x = x + 42$
13 $x + 22 = 715 - 2x$
15 $144 - x = 48 + x$
16 $201 + x = 3x + 15$
18 $15x - 54 = 45 + 6x$
19 $3x + 56 = 456 - 5x$

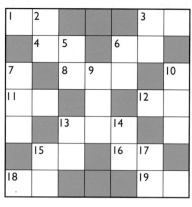

Down
2 $7x - 30 = 2x + 380$
3 $14 + 13x = 4x + 113$
5 $3x - 108 = 7x - 392$
6 $9x - 22 = 200 + 3x$
7 $10 - 2x = 241 - 3x$
9 $600 - x = 3x + 28$
10 $488 - x = 100 + x$
13 $33 - x = 173 - 6x$
14 $28 + 4x = 6x - 10$
15 $13 + 4x = 300 - 3x$
17 $155 - 2x = 2x + 15$

4 First remove the brackets, then solve the equations.
Remember $3(x - 2) = 3 \times x - 3 \times 2 = 3x - 6$

a $5(x - 1) = 3x + 7$ **b** $2(x + 5) = 5x - 2$ **c** $9x - 20 = 7(x - 2)$
d $12 - 3x = 2(x + 1)$ **e** $3(x - 2) = 15 - 4x$ **f** $5(3 - x) = x + 3$
g $8(x + 7) = 9(6 + x)$ **h** $2(3x + 1) = 4(2x - 3)$
i $5(10 - x) = 6(13 - 2x)$

Brainstormer

This is based on another puzzle by Sam Loyd.

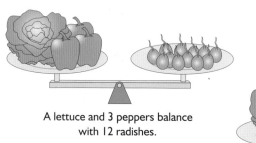

A lettuce and 3 peppers balance
with 12 radishes.

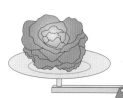

A lettuce balances with 1 pepper
and 8 radishes.

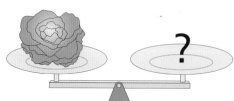

How many radishes balance with a lettuce?

F

6 Negative numbers and expressions

Example 1 The value of $10 - x$ when $x = -2$ is $10 - (-2) = 10 + 2 = 12$

Example 2 The value of $2y - 3x$ when $y = -1$ and $x = -2$ is
$2 \times (-1) - 3 \times (-2) = -2 + 6 = 4$

Example 3 The value of $\dfrac{3 - y}{4}$ when $y = 11$ is $\dfrac{3 - 11}{4} = \dfrac{-8}{4} = -2$

Example 4 The value of $-5(a - b) - 3c$ when $a = 2$, $b = -3$ and $c = -1$
is $-5(2 - (-3)) - 3 \times (-1)$
$= -5(2 + 3) + 3 = -5 \times 5 + 3 = -25 + 3 = -22$

Exercise 6.1

1 Find the value of each expression using the given values.

a $8 - y; y = -2$ **b** $2(y + 3); y = -5$

c $-3(2 + x); x = 3$ **d** $3a - 2b; a = 1, b = 5$

e $m - 3n; m = -2, n = -1$ **f** $ab + 2; a = -1, b = 3$

g $\dfrac{5 - x}{3}; x = 8$ **h** $-(w + t); w = -2, t = -3$

i $-2(a + b) + c; a = 3, b = -5, c = -3$ **j** $3x - 4y + 2; x = -5, y = 3$

k $-5(10 - x) + 2y; x = 12, y = -5$ **l** $x^2; x = -3$

m $2x^2; x = -3$ **n** $(2x)^2; x = -3$

o $(2 - x)^2; x = -3$

2 Complete this cross-number puzzle by evaluating the expressions where
$x = -7$, $y = 6$, $a = -12$, $b = -3$ and $c = -8$.

Negative answers, for example -23, are entered like this: $\boxed{-}\,\boxed{2}\,\boxed{3}$

Across
1 $x - y$
3 $2a - b$
5 $2(2a + 1)$
7 $-(y - x)$
9 $bc(y - b)$
11 xb
13 $3b$
14 $bc + x + y$
16 $c - 3a$
17 $-x(ac + y)$

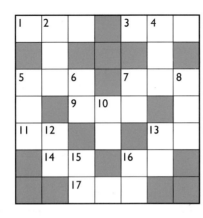

Down
2 a^2
4 $(a + b)^2 + 2a$
5 $c(c - a)$
6 $xc + c$
7 $\dfrac{a}{-y-c}$
8 $41 - abc$
10 $y - x$
12 $\dfrac{2a}{y + c}$
13 $a + b - x$
15 $ab - x - y$
16 $\dfrac{ay}{b}$

F

7 Negative numbers and equations

Example 1 Solve $-10 + x = 15$

$$-10 + x = 15$$
$$\Rightarrow \quad -10 + x + 10 = 15 + 10$$
$$\Rightarrow \quad x = 25$$

Example 2 Solve $14 - 2x = 18$

$$14 - 2x = 18$$
$$\Rightarrow \quad 14 - 2x - 14 = 18 - 14$$
$$\Rightarrow \quad -2x = 4$$
$$\Rightarrow \quad -2x \div (-2) = 4 \div (-2)$$
$$\Rightarrow \quad x = -2$$

Exercise 7.1

1 Solve these equations:

a $x + 10 = 3$ **b** $y - 3 = -6$ **c** $-2 + t = -3$

d $6 - m = 8$ **e** $2x = -4$ **f** $-3y = 9$

g $2w + 8 = 0$ **h** $5 - 2x = 1$ **i** $6 - 3x = 0$

j $12 - 4y = 4$ **k** $1 = 5 + 2x$ **l** $3t - 2 = -11$

2 Make a blank 4×4 grid.
Solve each question below.
Enter the solution in the corresponding
square in the grid.
The result is a magic square.

a	b	c	d
e	f	g	h
i	j	k	l
m	n	p	q

a $-3 - 2a = a - 27$ **b** $3b + 5 = b - 5$

c $-2c + 3 = 21 + c$ **d** $-d + 3 = -2d + 8$

e $3e - 1 = -16 - 2e$ **f** $10 - 2f = -f + 8$

g $-5g = 21 - 12g$ **h** $3h - 2 = -5h - 2$

i $7 - 3i = -2i + 6$ **j** $-3j - 8 = -6 - 2j$

k $-3 + 4k = 8k + 1$ **l** $-6l = -12 - 3l$

m $-2m - 3 = 1 - m$ **n** $16 = -2n + 30$

p $-3p - 2 = 10 - 5p$ **q** $-5 - 3q = -q + 9$

8 Brackets and equations

Example 1 Solve $3(x + 2) = 15$

$$3(x + 2) = 15$$
Get rid of $\Rightarrow$ $3x + 6 = 15$
the brackets. $\Rightarrow$ $3x + 6 - 6 = 15 - 6$
$$\Rightarrow \quad 3x = 9$$
$$\Rightarrow \quad 3x \div 3 = 9 \div 3$$
$$\Rightarrow \quad x = 3$$

Example 2 Solve $2x = 3(x - 4)$

$$2x = 3(x - 4)$$
$$\Rightarrow \quad 2x = 3x - 12$$
$$\Rightarrow \quad 2x + 12 = 3x - 12 + 12$$
$$\Rightarrow \quad 2x + 12 = 3x$$
$$\Rightarrow \quad 2x + 12 - 2x = 3x - 2x$$
$$\Rightarrow \quad 12 = x$$
$$\Rightarrow \quad x = 12$$

Exercise 8.1

1 Solve these equations by first removing the brackets:

a $2(y + 3) = 10$ 　　**b** $3(m - 2) = 15$ 　　**c** $7(n + 6) = 70$
d $9(x - 3) = 18$ 　　**e** $4(k + 3) = 5k$ 　　**f** $7(w - 2) = 5w$
g $6x = 4(x + 8)$ 　　**h** $5t = 2(t + 6)$ 　　**i** $3(y + 2) = 2(y + 5)$
j $7(c - 2) = 4(c + 1)$ 　**k** $8(n - 1) = 3(1 - n)$ 　**l** $2(12 - m) = 4(m - 6)$

2 Solve:

a $3(2x + 1) + 4 = 19$ 　**b** $5(x - 3) + 12 = 22$ 　**c** $7(x + 4) + x = 44$
d $6(y - 2) - 2y = 8$ 　**e** $2m + 3(m + 2) = 11$ 　**f** $x + 4(2x - 3) = 15$
g $x + 3(x - 2) = 2x$ 　**h** $5(2 - x) + 8x = 16$
i $3(x + 4) + 2(x - 3) = 7x$

Brainstormer

These three equations have positive whole number solutions:

$4(\boxed{}) = 2x$ 　　$3(\boxed{}) = x$ 　　$2(\boxed{}) = 3x$

　　Equation I 　　　　　　Equation 2 　　　　　　Equation 3

The three missing expressions in the brackets are:

$\boxed{x + 1}$ 　　　$\boxed{x - 1}$ 　　　$\boxed{x - 2}$

Expression A 　　Expression B 　　Expression C

Which expression goes in which equation?

F

---

9 A negative multiplier

Example 1
Expand $-2(x + 3y)$
$-2(x + 3y) = (-2) \times x + (-2) \times 3y$
$\qquad = -2x - 6y$

Example 2
Remove the brackets from $-(2m - 4)$
$-(2m - 4) = -1(2m - 4)$
$\qquad = (-1) \times 2m - (-1) \times 4$
$\qquad = -2m - (-4)$
$\qquad = -2m + 4$

Example 3
Remove the brackets from $-3(a - 2b)$
$-3(a - 2b) = (-3) \times a - (-3) \times 2b$
$\qquad = -3a - (-6b)$
$\qquad = -3a + 6b$

Example 4
Expand $8 - 3(a - 2b)$
$8 - 3(a - 2b) = 8 - 3a + 6b$

Example 5

Expand and simplify $14 - 2(x - 3)$

$14 - 2(x - 3) = 14 - 2x + 6$
$\qquad\qquad\;\; = 20 - 2x$

Example 6

Solve $12 - 3(x - 2) = 12$

$12 - 3(x - 2) = 12$
$\Rightarrow\quad 12 - 3x + 6 = 12$
$\Rightarrow\quad 18 - 3x = 12$
$\Rightarrow\quad 18 - 3x - 18 = 12 - 18$
$\Rightarrow\quad -3x = -6$
$\Rightarrow\quad -3x \div (-3) = -6 \div (-3)$
$\Rightarrow\quad x = 2$

Exercise 9.1

1 Remove the brackets:

a $-3(y + 2)$
b $-(x - 3)$
c $-2(x + 4)$
d $-3(2x + 1)$
e $-(a + b)$
f $-5(2y - 3)$
g $6 - (x - y)$
h $2 - 3(x - y)$
i $8 + 2(x - 5)$
j $14 - 3(a + b)$
k $-(p + q) + 3$
l $1 - (m - n)$
m $-7(r - 2s)$
n $12 - 3(2a - 5b)$

2 Expand and simplify:

a $18 - 2(x + 3)$
b $5x - 3(x - 2)$
c $2y - (y + 3)$
d $8 - 3(m - 2)$
e $-2 - 4(t - 2)$
f $7 - (7 - x)$
g $3(n - 2) - 2(n + 3)$
h $-(4 - x) - 2(5 - x)$
i $-5(m + 3) - 2(4 - m)$
j $7(3x - 2) - 2(4x - 3)$

3 Solve these equations. Remove the brackets and simplify first.

a $10 - 2(x - 3) = 6$
b $7 - (y + 2) = 2$
c $12x - 3(x + 2) = 3$
d $x - 4(x - 2) = -7$
e $5m = -2(m - 7)$
f $16 - 4(n + 1) = 2n$
g $7x = 16 - 2(3 - x)$
h $4w - 13 = 8 - (3 + 2w)$
i $1 - 3(c - 4) = 1$
j $5 - 2(3 - t) = 1$
k $5 - 2(2k + 1) = 5 - (k - 1)$

4 **Bar problems**

a

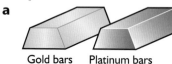

Gold bars   Platinum bars
weigh   weigh
$(x + 3)$ kg $(2x - 1)$ kg

   i Eight gold bars weigh 11 kg more than five platinum bars. Check that this leads to the equation $8(x + 3) - 5(2x - 1) = 11$

  ii Solve the equation.

 iii What is the weight of one bar of each metal?

b A lead bar weighs $(2x + 1)$ kg. A silver bar weighs $(x - 2)$ kg. If four lead bars weigh 2 kg more than ten silver bars, find the weight of each bar.

c A copper bar weighs $(3x - 4)$ kg. A brass bar weighs $(2x + 3)$ kg. If nine copper bars weigh 6 kg more than six brass bars, find the weight of each bar.

d An iron bar weighs $(20 - 2x)$ kg. A steel bar weighs $(5x - 4)$ kg. Seven iron bars weigh 10 kg more than eight steel bars. Find the weight of each type of bar.

Example 7

Solve $\dfrac{5x - 2}{3} = -9$

$\dfrac{5x - 2}{3} = -9$

$\Rightarrow \dfrac{5x - 2}{3} \times 3 = -9 \times 3$

$\Rightarrow 5x - 2 = -27$

$\Rightarrow 5x - 2 + 2 = -27 + 2$

$\Rightarrow 5x = -25$

$\Rightarrow 5x \div 5 = -25 \div 5$

$\Rightarrow x = -5$

Example 8

Solve $\dfrac{7x + 1}{3} = \dfrac{5x - 1}{2}$

$\dfrac{7x + 1}{3} = \dfrac{5x - 1}{2}$

$\Rightarrow \dfrac{7x + 1}{3} \times 6 = \dfrac{5x - 1}{2} \times 6$

$\Rightarrow 2(7x + 1) = 3(5x - 1)$

$\Rightarrow 14x + 2 = 15x - 3$

$\Rightarrow 14x + 2 - 14x = 15x - 3 - 14x$

$\Rightarrow 2 = x - 3$

$\Rightarrow 2 + 3 = x - 3 + 3$

$\Rightarrow 5 = x$

$\Rightarrow x = 5$

Exercise 9.2

Solve each of the following equations by first getting rid of the fractions.

1 $\dfrac{8x - 2}{3} = 10$

2 $9 = \dfrac{2x + 7}{3}$

3 $\dfrac{12 - 5x}{2} = x - 1$

4 $2x - 3 = \dfrac{3x - 1}{5}$

5 $32 - x = \dfrac{6x - 5}{5}$

6 $\dfrac{x + 3}{2} = \dfrac{4x - 8}{3}$

7 $\dfrac{5x + 3}{4} = \dfrac{4x}{3}$

8 $\dfrac{5 - 3x}{2} = \dfrac{2 - 9x}{5}$

9 $\dfrac{7x - 2}{5} = \dfrac{3x + 3}{2}$

10 More inequations

Example 1

From the picture we can form the inequation

$$5 + x > 12$$

$\Rightarrow \quad 5 + x - 5 > 12 - 5$

$\Rightarrow \quad x > 7$

The bar must weigh more than 7 kg.

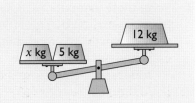

Example 2

Solve $10 - 3x > 16$

$$10 - 3x > 16$$
$$\Rightarrow \quad 10 - 3x - 10 > 16 - 10$$
$$\Rightarrow \quad -3x > 6$$
$$\Rightarrow \quad 3x < -6$$
$$\Rightarrow \quad 3x \div 3 < -6 \div 3$$
$$\Rightarrow \quad x < -2$$

Note the switching of symbols.

If $-a > -b$ then $a < b$

Look at these:
- $-2 > -4 \Rightarrow 2 < 4$

  2 is below 4 on the number line and -2 is above -4.
- $-2 < 4 \Rightarrow 2 > -4$

  -2 is below 4 on the number line and 2 is above -4.

Exercise 10.1

1 For each picture
  i form an inequation
  ii solve it
  iii make a statement about the weight of the bar.

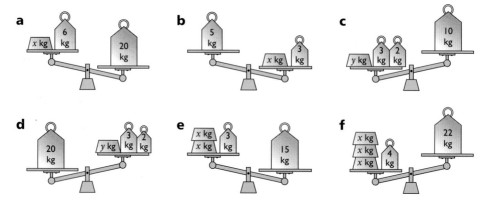

2 Rewrite each inequation to read '$x > ...$' or '$x < ...$' or '$x \leqslant ...$' or '$x \geqslant ...$'.
  a $-x > 2$ **b** $-x \leqslant 7$ **c** $-x \geqslant -3$ **d** $-x \leqslant -5$
  e $4 > x$ **f** $3 < x$ **g** $-2 \geqslant x$ **h** $-1 \leqslant x$
  i $2 > -x$ **j** $-3 \leqslant -x$ **k** $7 \geqslant -x$ **l** $-2 > x$
  m $-2 > -x$ **n** $-10 \leqslant x$ **o** $-x > 8$

3 Solve these inequations. You may need to switch the symbols.
  a $x - 3 \geqslant 5$ **b** $7 - x < 9$ **c** $2y + 1 < 7$ **d** $8 \leqslant 2x - 4$
  e $x > 2x - 3$ **f** $x + 3 \geqslant 2x - 1$ **g** $5x + 2 < x - 6$ **h** $x + 7 > 4x + 13$

CHECK-UP

1 Solve these equations, simplifying first if necessary:

  a $5m - 3 = 22$ **b** $\frac{1}{2}x + 5 = 15$ **c** $12 - 3y = 6$

  d $6 + 2w - 2 = 18$ **e** $3n + 7 - 3n = 5n - 3$

2 The total length of this frame is 154 cm.

  a Form an equation and solve it.

  b Give the dimensions of the frame.

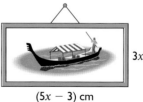

$3x$ cm

$(5x - 3)$ cm

3 Solve these equations:

  a $4x = x + 9$ **b** $3m = 2m + 4$ **c** $5t = 18 - t$

4 These buses are the same length.

  a Make an equation and solve it to find the value of x.

  b Find the length of the buses.

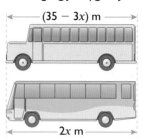

$(35 - 3x)$ m

$2x$ m

5 Find the solution for these inequations from the values {1, 2, 3, 4, 5} only:

  a $2x > 6$ **b** $20 - 3x \leqslant 8$ **c** $7 + 2x \leqslant 19 - 2x$

6 Solve these equations:

  a $5n - 2 = n + 6$ **b** $12 + 3y = 27 - 2y$ **c** $6 - k = 2k - 15$

7 The two ranks of toy cars are the same length.

  a Form an equation in x and solve it.

  b Give the length of each toy vehicle.

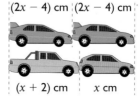

$(2x - 4)$ cm $(2x - 4)$ cm

$(x + 2)$ cm x cm

8 If $a = -1$, $b = -2$ and $c = 3$ find the value of:

  a $2a^2$ **b** $(2a)^2$ **c** $bc - a$ **d** $b(a - c)$

9 Solve these equations:

  a $3(m - 2) = 9$ **b** $5(x - 2) - 2x = 2$

  c $8 - 2(y - 1) = 2$ **d** $4n = 1 - 3(n + 5)$

10 Nine tin bars weigh 9 kg more than six aluminium bars. Find the weight of each bar.

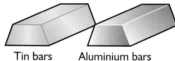

Tin bars weigh $(2x - 1)$ kg   Aluminium bars weigh $(x + 7)$ kg

11 Solve these inequations:

  a $-2 > -m$

  b $x + 3 \leqslant 2x$

  c $3y - 1 \geqslant y + 4$

(9) Measuring length

Our earliest measurements were based on parts of the body.

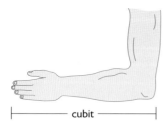

cubit

The dimensions of Noah's Ark are given in cubits in the bible.

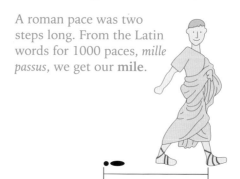

A roman pace was two steps long. From the Latin words for 1000 paces, *mille passus*, we get our **mile**.

In 1793 the French mathematician Lagrange was put in charge of a committee whose task it was to reform the measuring system. They began by inventing a new unit of length ... the **metre**. Its length was chosen so that the distance from the North Pole to the equator would be 10 000 000 metres.

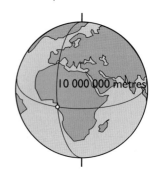

10 000 000 metres

---

1 Looking back ◀◀

Exercise 1.1

1 The Lena river is 4310 km long and the Mackenzie river is 4240 km long. How much longer is the Lena than the Mackenzie in metres?

2 In a triathlon event, Rory swims for 300 metres, cycles for 3000 metres and runs for 3000 metres.
   What is the total distance, in kilometres, covered in the event?

3 Calculate the perimeter of this poster in
   a centimetres
   b metres.

35 cm

1 m 10 cm

4 The side view of a house is a square topped by a triangle. The perimeter of this view is 16·2 metres and has some dimensions as shown.
Calculate the width of the base in

   a metres   **b** millimetres.

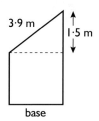

3·9 m   1·5 m

base

5 Measure the perimeter of these shapes in millimetres, then convert to centimetres.

   a    **b**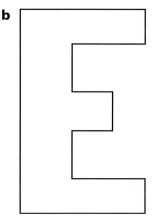

6 Sound travels 340 metres per second (approximately). How far, in kilometres, does sound travel in:

   a an hour   **b** a day?

7 In a roll of photographic film each exposure is 35 mm long. There is a 2 mm gap between each exposure and 5 cm at the beginning and end of each roll.
What is the length, in centimetres, of:

   a a 24 exposure film   **b** a 36 exposure film?

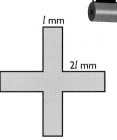

8 This cross is formed from four rectangles and a square. The perimeter of this shape is 360 mm.
Calculate the length of the sides marked

   a l **b** $2l$.

l mm

$2l$ mm

2 Reading scales

Example

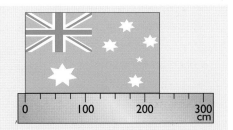

Four divisions on the ruler make 100 cm.
So one division makes $100 \div 4 = 25$ cm.
The flag is 225 cm wide.

Exercise 2.1

1 The height of a tree is recorded at various stages in its growth.

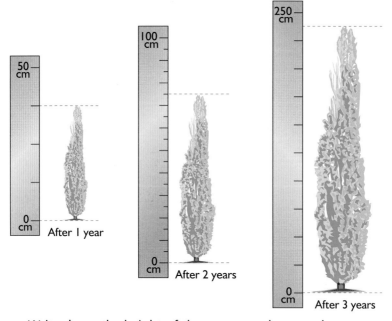

After 1 year

After 2 years

After 3 years

a Write down the height of the tree at each stage shown.
b How much does the tree grow during the second year?
c How much does the tree grow during the third year?

2 The arrows show the heights achieved by each person in the high jump.
List the entrants and say to what height each of them jumped.

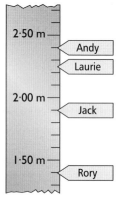

3 In a triple jump competition, some of the jumps recorded are marked with arrows.
Write down the length each person jumped.

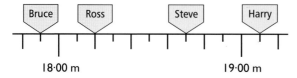

4 This is an accurate scale drawing of Tom's flat.
Above is a ruler drawn to the same scale.

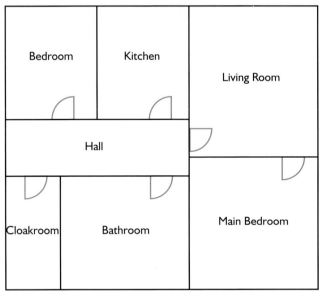

a Copy the above ruler onto paper.

b Use the ruler to help you answer the following.
  i What are the dimensions of the bathroom?
  ii What are the dimensions of the hall?

c Tom wants to put new wood flooring in the hall.
The kind he chooses comes in strips like this:
Strips are sold in packs of 15.
Work out the best way to lay the flooring and
how many packs will need to be bought.

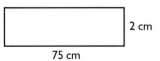

Challenge

Estimating measures

1 Choose some items to which you have easy access, for example:
a key; a pencil; a stamp; a £1 coin; a comb; an envelope; a can of juice.

Estimate the length of each item using appropriate units.

For example, you would estimate the length and breadth of a stamp in
millimetres, the height of a can of juice in centimetres, the diameter of the
£1 coin in millimetres.

2 Estimate some distances around your school.

E

3 Now, for each item, measure its length accurately.

4 Compare the estimate with the correct value.
   Work out the difference as a percentage of the actual measurement.

Example

Length of a mobile phone:
Estimate = 16 cm; actual length = 14·6 cm

$$\text{Percentage difference} = \frac{(\text{Estimate} - \text{Actual})}{\text{Actual}} \times 100$$

$$= \frac{(16 - 14\cdot6)}{14\cdot6} \times 100\%$$

$$= 9\cdot6\% \text{ (1 d.p.)}$$

5 Record your findings
   in a table like this:

Item	Estimate	Actual	Difference	% difference
Phone	16 cm	14·6 cm	1·4 cm	9·6%

6 Write a report on your results, paying particular attention to how the percentage difference varies for different units of measurement.

   ● Does estimating longer distances produce bigger percentage differences than when estimating smaller measures?
   ● Is there a significant difference between estimating vertical and horizontal measures?

3 Calculating the perimeter using rules

The perimeter P of a rectangle $= l + b + l + b = 2(l + b)$

$$P = 2(l + b)$$

b

l

Example

Calculate the perimeter of a rectangle with length 11·4 cm and breadth 3·9 cm.

$P = 2(11\cdot4 + 3\cdot9)$
$= 2 \times 15\cdot3$
$= 30\cdot6$ cm

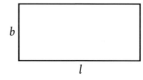

11·4 cm

3·9 cm

E
F

Exercise 3.1

1 Use the above formula to calculate the perimeter of the following rectangles.

a
41·8 mm
60·9 mm

b
108·8 mm
33·6 mm

c
47 cm
1·05 m

2 The perimeter of a rectangular floor is 60 metres.
The breadth is 2 metres wider than the length.
Using the formula for the perimeter of the rectangle,
  a write down an equation connecting the length and the breadth
  b calculate the dimensions of the floor.

3 A rectangle is such that its length is one more than five times its breadth.
Let x be the breadth of the rectangle in centimetres.
Thus its length is $(1 + 5x)$ cm.
  a Write down the perimeter of the rectangle in terms of x.
  b If the perimeter is 74 centimetres, calculate the dimensions of the rectangle.

4 The breadth of a rectangle is ten less than four times its length.
Let x be the length of the rectangle.
  a Write down the perimeter of the rectangle in terms of x.
  b If the perimeter is 75 centimetres, calculate the dimensions of the rectangle.

5 **a** What is the value of AB + CD?
  b Find an expression for FA + BC.
  c Show that the perimeter of this shape is $2(b + 5)$ cm.
  d Could you have arrived at this answer without working?
Write down your reasons (or show them in a diagram).

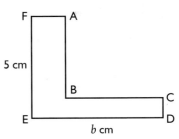

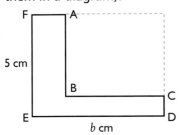

6 Calculate the perimeters of the following shapes.

a
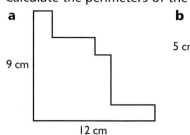
9 cm

12 cm

b
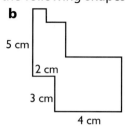
5 cm

2 cm

3 cm

4 cm

c
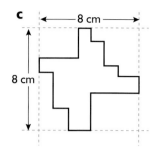
8 cm

8 cm

4 The theorem of Pythagoras

In a right-angled triangle, the side opposite the right angle is called the **hypotenuse**. This word comes from the ancient Greek language and means 'stretched under'.

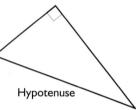
Hypotenuse

Investigation

Draw each of the following triangles accurately on centimetre squared paper. Carefully measure the hypotenuse and record your results in a table.

a
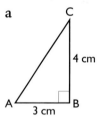
C
4 cm
A
3 cm
B

b
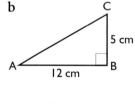
C
5 cm
A
12 cm
B

c
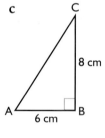
C
8 cm
A
6 cm
B

d
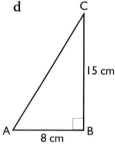
C
15 cm
A
8 cm
B

Comment on the last two columns of the table.

	AB	BC	AC	AB²	BC²	AC²	AB² + BC²
a							
b	3	4					

Around 2500 years ago a Greek mathematician called Pythagoras discovered a useful connection between the sides of a right-angled triangle.

Pythagoras

Take four copies of any right-angled triangle. They can be arranged in two ways:

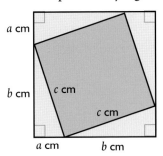

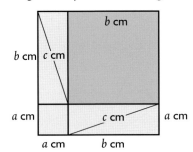

Note that the large square is the same in both cases.

Here we see the large square is made of the four triangles and a square whose side is the hypotenuse of the triangle.

Here we see the large square is made of the four triangles and two squares whose sides are the shorter sides of the triangle.

So the area of the square on the hypotenuse is equal to the sum of the areas of the squares on the other two sides.

$$c^2 = a^2 + b^2$$

This is known as Pythagoras's theorem.

When we know the area of a square we can get the length of its side by using the $\boxed{\sqrt{}}$ button on the calculator.

For example, if the area of a square is $16\,cm^2$ then its side is $\sqrt{16} = 4\,cm$.

We can use this fact and Pythagoras's theorem to find the lengths of sides in a right-angled triangle.

Given two sides we can find the third.

Example 1

Find the length of PR.

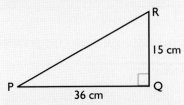

$\triangle PQR$ is right angled, so by Pythagoras's theorem

$PR^2 = PQ^2 + QR^2$
$ = 36^2 + 15^2$
$ = 1296 + 225$
$ = 1521$
$PR = \sqrt{1521}$
$PR = 39\,cm$

Example 2

Find the length of AC.

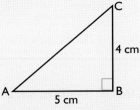

$\triangle ABC$ is right angled, so by Pythagoras's theorem

$AC^2 = AB^2 + BC^2$
$ = 5^2 + 4^2$
$ = 25 + 16$
$ = 41$
$PR = \sqrt{41}$
$PR = 6\cdot4\,cm$ (to 1 d.p.)

Exercise 4.1

1 Find the length of the hypotenuse in each of the following triangles.

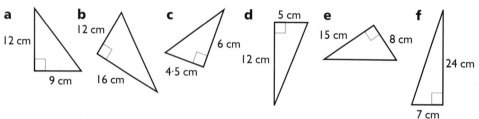

a 12 cm, 9 cm   **b** 12 cm, 16 cm   **c** 6 cm, 4·5 cm   **d** 5 cm, 12 cm   **e** 15 cm, 8 cm   **f** 24 cm, 7 cm

2 Find the length of the hypotenuse correct to 1 d.p. in each of the following.

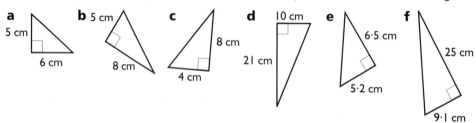

a 5 cm, 6 cm   **b** 5 cm, 8 cm   **c** 8 cm, 4 cm   **d** 10 cm, 21 cm   **e** 6·5 cm, 5·2 cm   **f** 25 cm, 9·1 cm

3 A ladder leans against a wall.
The foot of the ladder is 2 metres from the wall.
The top of the ladder touches the wall 2·1 metres from the ground.
What is the length of the ladder?

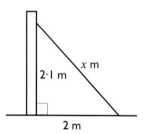

4 The *Silver Serpent* left harbour and sailed 9 km north.
It then sailed 40 km east.
How far from the harbour is it then?

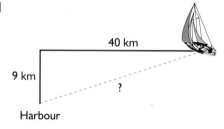

5 The Christmas tree in the town square is 6 metres tall.
It is held upright by two ropes.
One is fixed to the ground 2·4 m from the base of the tree; the other at a point 1·7 m from the base of the tree.

Calculate the length of each rope correct to 1 decimal place.

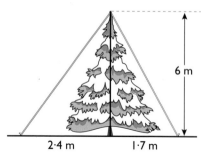

5 Finding a shorter side

Calculate the length of AB in the triangle given.

$\triangle$ABC is right angled, so by the theorem of Pythagoras:

$$AB^2 + BC^2 = AC^2$$
$$AB^2 + 8^2 = 17^2$$

Rearranging this gives:

$$AB^2 = 17^2 - 8^2$$
$$= 289 - 64$$
$$= 225$$
$$AB = \sqrt{225} = 15$$
$$AB = 15 \text{ cm}$$

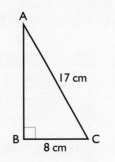

Exercise 5.1

1 Calculate the missing side in each triangle.

a 13 cm, 12 cm   **b** 17 cm   **c** 2·1 cm, 15 cm   **d** 35 cm, 37 cm   **e** 30 cm, 5·2 cm, 34 cm   **f** 4·8 cm

2 Calculate the value of x in each triangle, correct to 1 d.p.

a x cm, 12 cm, 9 cm

b x cm, 50 cm, 120 cm

c 2·5 cm, 6·5 cm, x cm

d 40 cm, 24 cm, x cm

e 10 cm, x cm, 21 cm

f 14·5 cm, 8·7 cm, x cm

3 A rectangle of length 24 cm has a diagonal of 25 cm.

  a What is the height of the rectangle?

  b A second rectangle has a length of 24 cm and a diagonal of 26 cm.
  How much taller is this rectangle?

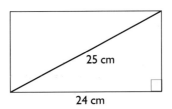

F

4 Three towns form the vertices of a triangle.
Ayton is 10 km due north of Beeton. Ceeton is due east of Beeton.
Ayton and Ceeton are 15 km apart.
  a Make a sketch to illustrate the story.
  b Calculate the distance between Beeton and Ceeton.

Exercise 5.2

1 Here are some mixed examples. Calculate the missing side in each triangle.

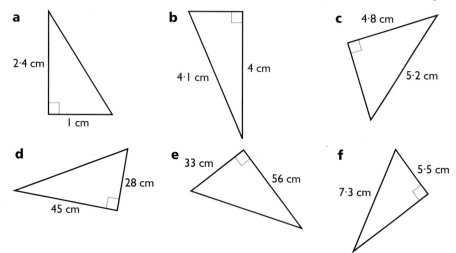

2 Calculate the value of *x* in each triangle, correct to 1 d.p.

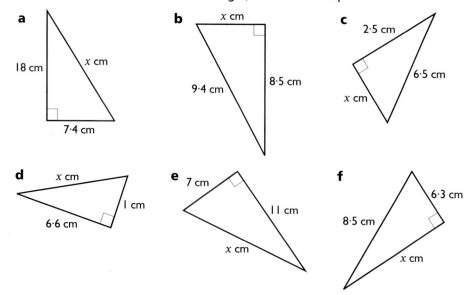

3 The diagonals of a rhombus are
AC = 25·2 cm and BD = 20·8 cm.
Calculate:
  a AM
  b BM
  c the length of a side of the rhombus.

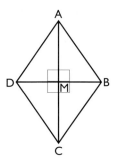

4 PQRS is a kite whose diagonals cross at T.
PT = 10·5 mm. ST = 35 mm. PQ = 25 mm.
Calculate the length of

  a QT
  b PS
  c the perimeter of the kite.

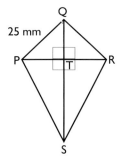

5 Two rectangles ENMH and MNFG are
joined to form a larger rectangle.
EF = 10 cm. HM = 2·6 cm. HN = 3·1 cm.

  a What is the height of the rectangle?
  b What is the length of rectangle
    MNFG?
  c Calculate the length of the diagonal NG.

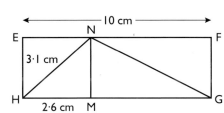

F

Challenge

In some of the examples in these exercises you will have noticed that the sides
of the triangles are all whole numbers. Such sets of numbers are called
Pythagorean triples. A famous example is the combination 3, 4, 5.

Any amount of Pythagorean triples can be found
using the following formulae:

$$a = m^2 + n^2$$
$$b = m^2 - n^2$$
$$c = 2mn$$

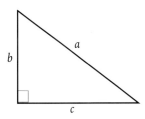

where m and n are any whole numbers with m
larger than n.

Copy and complete this table of Pythagorean triples.

Only two of the following statements are not true. Which ones?

a One of the triple is always even.

b One of the triple is always a multiple of 3.

c One of the triple is always a multiple of 4.

d One of the triple is always a multiple of 5.

e One of the triple is always a multiple of 6.

f The product of the shorter sides can always be divided by 12.

m	n	a $m^2 + n^2$	b $m^2 - n^2$	c $2mn$
2	1	5	3	4
3	1	10	8	6
3	2	13	5	12
4	1	17	15	8
4	2	20	12	16
4	3	25	7	24
5	1			
5	2			
5	3			
5	4			
6	1			

g The product of the three sides can always be divided by 60.

h The product of the larger sides can always be divided by 2.

6 The distance between two points

Example

Calculate the distance between A$(-2, 1)$ and B$(3, 4)$.

Answer:
Plot the points and construct the right-angled triangle ABC where AB is the hypotenuse and the shorter sides are parallel to the axes.
$\triangle$ABC is right angled so by the theorem of Pythagoras:

$$AB^2 = 5^2 + 3^2$$
$$AB^2 = 25 + 9 = 34$$
$$AB = \sqrt{34}$$
$$AB = 5.8 \text{ units (to 1 d.p.)}$$

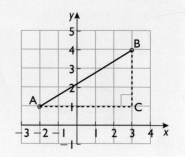

Exercise 6.1

1 Calculate the distance between each pair of points.

a P(1, 1), Q(4, 6)

b M(3, 1), N(9, 9)

c T(−4, 0), V(8, 5)

d S(0, 10), R(15, 2)

e W(−5, 8), Z(7, −8)

f D(−12, −3), E(12, 4)

2 Calculate the distance between each pair of points, correct to
1 decimal place.

a O(0, 0), A(−1, 4) **b** B(−2, −2), C(2, −5)

c D(3, −1), E(−3, 3) **d** F(−3, 6), G(4, −2)

e H(0, 7), I(7, 0) **f** J(−5, −4), K(8, 2)

3 PQRS is a rectangle with vertices P(0, 4), Q(3, 6), R(7, 0) and S(4, −2).

a Calculate **i** the length **ii** the breadth of the rectangle.

b Work out the length of a diagonal.

4 a Prove that the points A(4, 4), B(3, 5) and C(6, 0) all lie on a circle with
centre (0, 1).

b What is the radius of the circle?

5 The circle shown has a centre (4, 2).
It passes through A(4, 5) and B(7, 2).

a Calculate the length of AB.

b i What length is the radius of the circle?

ii Prove that C(2, 0) does not lie on
the circle.

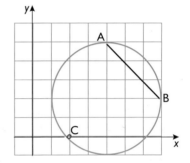

F

6 a Calculate the lengths of the diagonals of:

i the rectangle ABCD

ii the parallelogram PQRS.

b Prove that the triangle PRS is not
isosceles.

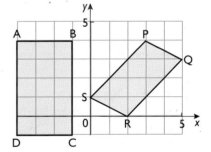

7 a Prove that the triangle with vertices O(0, 0), A(15, 20) and B(7, 24) is
isosceles.

b Prove that the shape made by joining P(−4, 3), Q(−3, 5), R(−1, 6)
and S(3, −1) is a kite.

8 A helicopter flies over three main roads
during rush hour giving early warnings
of traffic jams and accidents.
It flies in a triangle from K to L to M.
Each square has a side of 1 km.

a Calculate the longest stretch of the
circuit.

b What is the perimeter of the triangle?

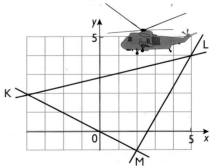

CHECK-UP

1 In a pole vault competition some of the jumps recorded are marked with arrows.
Write down the lengths recorded for each person.

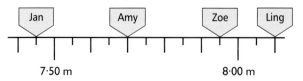

7·50 m   8·00 m

2 The base of an isosceles triangle is 5 less than 3 times the length of the equal sides.

   a Write down an expression for the perimeter of the triangle.

   b Calculate the lengths of the sides of the triangle if its perimeter is 50 cm.

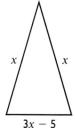

3 **a** Write an expression for the perimeter of this shape in terms of a and b.

   b Calculate the perimeter when $a = 6$ and $b = 5$.

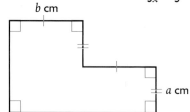

4 Calculate the value of x in each case.

  a
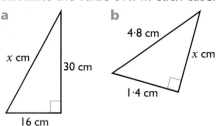

  b

  c
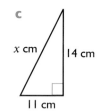

  d
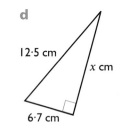

5 Calculate the distance between each pair of points.

  a A(−3, −2) and B(7, 6)   **b** P(4, −1) and Q(−2, 4)

6 Calculate the length of the diagonals of the rectangle ABCD.

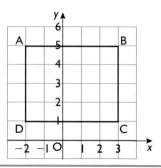

(10) Tiling and symmetry

Trace the word Hawick.
Turn the tracing paper over.
What do you notice?

HAWICK

---

1 Looking back ◀◀

Symmetry

Shapes can be changed, or **transformed**, in many ways.

When a shape looks the same after undergoing a transformation, we say the shape possesses symmetry.

Shapes may have more than one axis of symmetry.

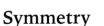

A square has 4 axes of symmetry.

A rectangle has 2 axes of symmetry.

An equilateral triangle has 3 axes of symmetry.

When a shape is reflected about a line and still looks the same, the shape is said to have **line symmetry** about that line.

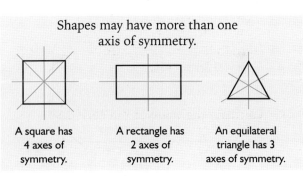

A point, A, reflects in an axis PQ.
Its **image**, A', is a point the same distance away on the other side of the axis.

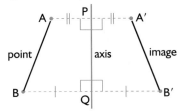

point   axis   image

Symmetrical shapes can be created by combining an object and its **reflection**.

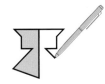

The image of the line segment joining the points A and B is a line segment joining the images A' and B'.

Tiling

We say a shape tiles when congruent copies fill space without overlapping or leaving gaps.

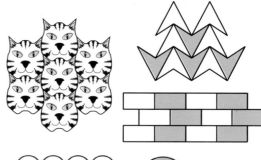

Circles don't tile but when overlapped in a regular fashion inspire new shapes which do.

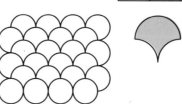

Exercise 1.1

Transform	Options
Flip Horizontally	
Flip Vertically	
Rotate 90°	
Rotate	
Zoom Out	
Zoom In	
Slide	
Stretch Horizontally	
Stretch Vertically	

1   Using a drawing package on a computer you can transform shapes quite easily. Which of the options have been used to create these transformations?

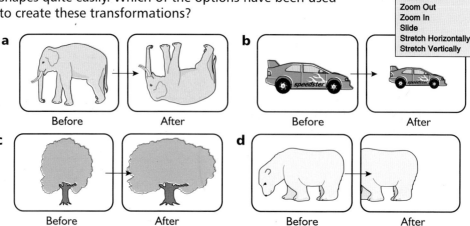

2   These transformations have been created by choosing first one option then another. State the options used.

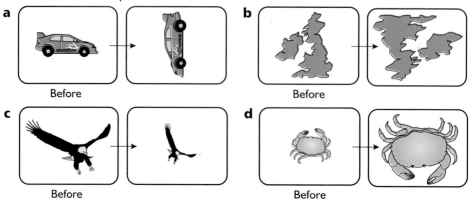

3 Copy each diagram below onto squared paper.
Use the axis indicated to create a shape with line symmetry.

a   **b**   **c**   **d**   **e**

4 Copy the diagrams below.
Shade in *as few squares as is necessary* to create a symmetrical picture in
each case.

a **b** **c** **d** **e**

5 **a** Plot the following set of points.
Join them up in the order they
are given.
(5, 0), (1, 0), (4, 1), (4, 4), (2, 4),
(1, 7), (1, 9), (5, 9)

b Plot the image of each point
reflected in the axis PQ.
Join them up to create a
symmetrical picture.

c Write down the coordinates of
the image points in order.

d Which coordinates stay the same?

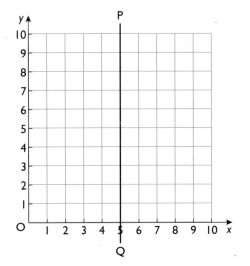

6 Shape ABCDEF is reflected in the y-axis,
such that A → A', B → B', C → C',
D → D', E → E' and F → F'.

a Copy the diagram and draw the
reflected shape.

b Which points have not moved?

c Write down the coordinates of
A', B', C', D', E' and F'.

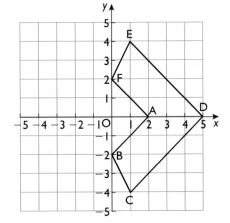

7 Triangle ABC is reflected in the *x*-axis, such that A → A′, B → B′ and C → C′.

a Copy the diagram and draw triangle A′B′C′.

b Write down the coordinates of A′, B′ and C′.

c Where do the lines and their images intersect?

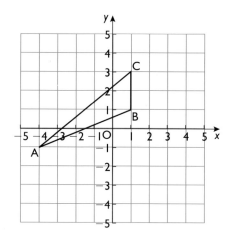

2 Rotation and rotational symmetry

A card is fixed at the point P ...

... and is turned through an angle of 100°.

We say it has undergone a rotation of 100° about P.

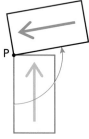

Note that the angle between any line on the object and the corresponding line on the image is 100°.
In the diagram, each angle marked by ○ is 100°

In this case a card is fixed at its centre.
After a rotation of 180° the card looks the same.

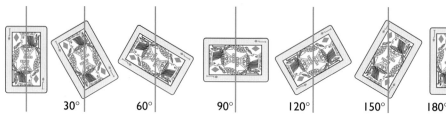

30° 60° 90° 120° 150° 180°

The card possesses half-turn symmetry, or **rotational symmetry of order 2**.

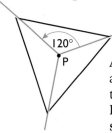

120°

P

After a rotation of 120° about P the equilateral triangle will look the same.
It possesses **rotational symmetry of order 3**.

90°

A square possesses quarter-turn symmetry or **rotational symmetry of order 4**.

Exercise 2.1

1 Use a protractor to find the size of the rotation in each case.

a

Before

After

b

c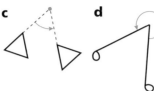

d

2 The puzzle expert Sam Loyd made a tangram puzzle which shows a man pushing a wheelbarrow. A careful look will show that the barrow is just the man having undergone a rotation. What is the size of the rotation?

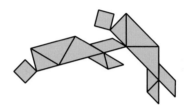

The tangram

3 **a** Which drawings below have rotational symmetry?

b For those drawings with rotational symmetry, state the order of the symmetry.

a

b

c

d

e

f

g

h

i

j

k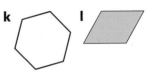

l

E

4 Use the rotational symmetry of these shapes to find the size of the lettered angles.

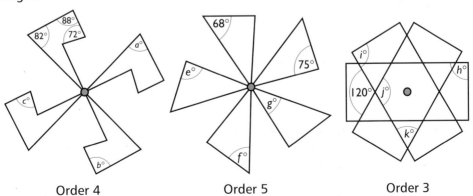

Order 4   Order 5   Order 3

5 ABCD is a parallelogram with centre of symmetry at the origin.

Point	Image
A(−4, 2)	A′(4, −2)
B	B′
C	C′
D	D′
P	P′
Q	Q′
R	R′
S	S′

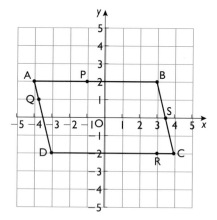

a Give the coordinates of the centre of symmetry of ABCD.
b Copy and complete the table to show the points and their images after a half turn about the centre of symmetry.
c What do you notice from the table?

6 This arrow is pointing along the x-axis.
a List the coordinates of points A to G.
b Rotate the arrow through 90° anti-clockwise about G so that it points up the y-axis.
c Write down the coordinates of the *images* of A, B, C, D, E, F and G.

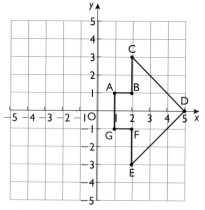

7 a Give the coordinates of the vertices of the pentagon OABCD.
b Copy the diagram.
c Using the origin as the centre of symmetry, rotate the pentagon through 90° clockwise.
d Repeat this rotation two more times to make a design with rotational symmetry of order 4.
e Make a table and record the coordinates of each image under rotation.

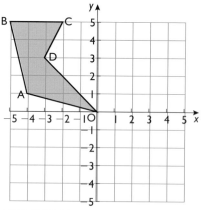

Point	Rotation 1	Rotation 2	Rotation 3
A(−4, 1)			

E

8 O is a fixed point. T(3, 3) and S(3, 1) are points on a
screen such that triangle OTS simulates a sail of a windmill
for a computer game.

   a Plot triangle OTS on a coordinate plane.

   b Draw the triangle rotated 90° anti-clockwise about O.
      What are the coordinates of the images of T and S?

   c Repeat the rotation anti-clockwise into

      i   the third

      ii the fourth quadrants.

   d Write down the coordinates of the rotated points.

9 This star has rotational symmetry.

   a Give the coordinates of the centre
of symmetry.

   b What angle of rotation was used to
create the shape?

   c The complete shape is made up of
four congruent shapes.
Name these shapes.

   d A rhombus has vertices with
coordinates (2, −3), (3, 1), (2, 5)
and (1, 1).
The centre of rotation is (2, −1).
Draw the rhombus and its image under

      i   90°

      ii 180°

      iii 270° rotation.

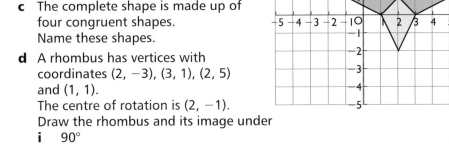

E

10 The constellation of Cassiopeia in
the night sky rotates around the
Pole Star (at the origin).

   a State the coordinates of the five
stars of Cassiopeia.

   b Draw the position of Cassiopeia
after

      i   a 90°

      ii 180° rotation.

   c If the green line represents the
horizon, which stars can still be seen
on or above the horizon after a
270° rotation?

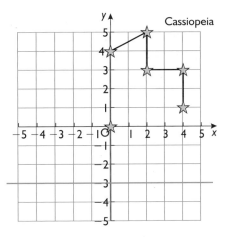

Cassiopeia

Challenge

Cut out two congruent shapes.
Glue them onto a piece of paper,
one rotated with respect to the other.

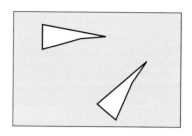

Find the centre of rotation.
Follow these instructions.

- Join a point and its image by a straight line.
- Draw the line that cuts this line in half and at right angles.
  We call this a **perpendicular bisector**.
- Repeat this with another point and its image.
- Where these two perpendicular bisectors cross is the required centre.
- Check this with a third point and its image.
- Use compasses to check that a pattern of concentric circles is formed.

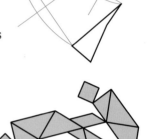

Use the technique to find the centre
of rotation of Sam Loyd's puzzle.

3 Translation and translational symmetry

When a shape is slid from one place
to another without rotation it is
said to undergo a **translation**.

Every point on the shape
moves by the same amount.

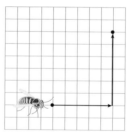

Every point on the wasp
has been moved 5 *squares*
to the right and 6 *squares up*.

Translation symmetry

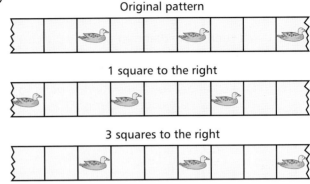

Original pattern

If we transtate this pattern by 1 square to the right, we can tell the pattern has been moved ...

1 square to the right

... but, if we transtate it by 3 squares to the right, it looks the same as the original.

Moving it 6 squares or 9 or 12 would produce the same effect.

3 squares to the right

We normally quote the *smallest* glide, or translation, which produces the symmetry. In the above example, the border repeats every **3 squares to the right**.

This is often called **the repeat** by artistic designers.

A regularly repeating pattern like this has **glide symmetry** or **translational symmetry**. This symmetry is common on wallpaper, curtain material and the outside design of buildings.

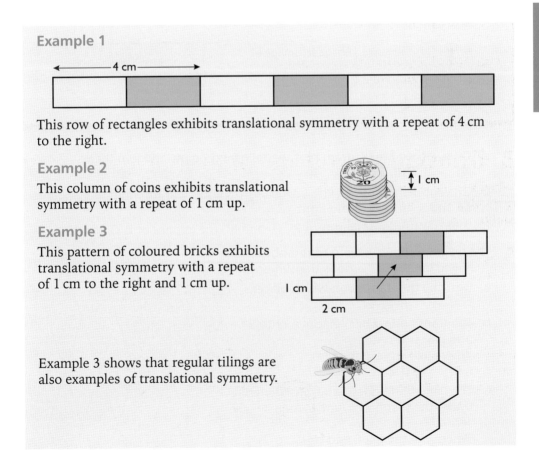

Example 1

This row of rectangles exhibits translational symmetry with a repeat of 4 cm to the right.

Example 2

This column of coins exhibits translational symmetry with a repeat of 1 cm up.

Example 3

This pattern of coloured bricks exhibits translational symmetry with a repeat of 1 cm to the right and 1 cm up.

Example 3 shows that regular tilings are also examples of translational symmetry.

E

Exercise 3.1

1 **a** On a coordinate diagram plot the points P(−4, 2), Q(2, 2), R(4, −2) and S(−2, −2).

b What shape is PQRS?

c If Q → Q′ under the translation '2 units to the left and 4 units up',
  i what are the coordinates of Q′?
  ii what are the corresponding coordinates of P′, R′ and S′?

d What kind of shape is PQ′RS?

2 ABCD is a trapezium.

a On a coordinate grid draw ABCD, then draw its image under a translation of:
  i 6 squares up
  ii 5 squares to the right
  iii 6 squares up and 5 squares to the right.

b Complete the table to show the coordinates of the vertices of ABCD and their images under each translation.

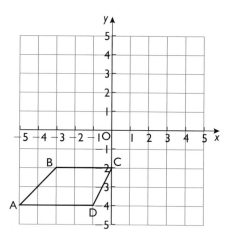

	Image i	Image ii	Image iii
A(−5, −4)	(−5, 2)		
B			
C			
D			

3 **a** On a coordinate diagram plot the following points and join them:
P(5, −2), Q(3, −5), R(1, −4).

b On your diagram show the image of PQR under a translation of 6 squares up and 5 squares to the right.

c What are the coordinates of P′, Q′ and R′, the images of P, Q and R?

4 The diagram shows a tiling of rhombuses. The tiling undergoes various translations.

a Describe the translation which places:
  i A → B **ii** A → I **iii** A → K.

b The translation which places A onto E also places D onto H.
Where will it place the tile
  i B **ii** F **iii** C?

c The tiling undergoes two translations. Under the first A → E, under the second F → G.
Where will the tile C end up?

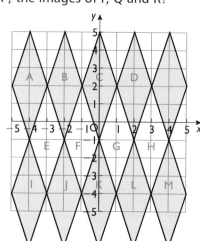

5 a Describe the translation that has produced the image A'B'C'D'.

b A further translation places an image of B' at the point B"(−1, −1). Describe this second translation.

c Write down the coordinates of A", C" and D".

d Describe the translation which would map ABCD directly to A"B"C"D".

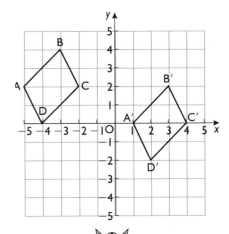

6 A tiling can be described by

- focusing on one tile
- giving a repeat to generate a column from the tile
- giving a repeat to generate the rows from the column.

Repeat tile
1 cm down

Repeat column
1 cm right
0·5 cm up

Describe the build-up of the following tilings in a similar manner.

a

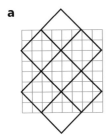

b

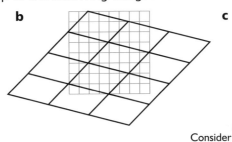

c

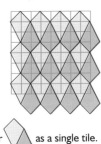

Consider ◇ as a single tile.

Investigation

Find out what you can about M.C. Escher.
There are many sites on the Internet which explore the way this artist examined transformations, especially those which produced tilings.

4 Enlargement and reduction

A shape may be *enlarged* by multiplying each
length in the shape by a fixed factor greater
than 1.

Example 1

Here a rectangle has been enlarged by a factor of 3.

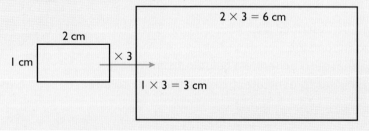

A shape may also be shrunk, or *reduced*, by multiplying each length in the shape by
a fixed factor. In this case the factor would be a proper fraction.

Example 2

Here a postage stamp has been reduced by a
factor of 2.
Each length has been multiplied by $\frac{1}{2}$.

Exercise 4.1

1 In each case the enlargement factor is given.
Work out the missing lengths.

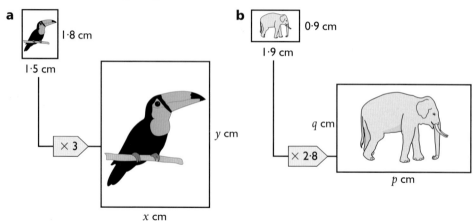

2 In each case the shape has been shrunk.
Work out the missing lengths.

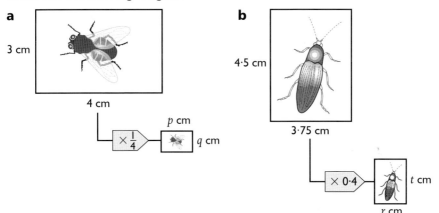

a

3 cm

4 cm

$\times \frac{1}{4}$

p cm

q cm

b

4·5 cm

3·75 cm

× 0·4

t cm

r cm

3 Work out the scale factor for each transformation.
State whether it is an enlargement or a reduction.
Calculate the missing value.

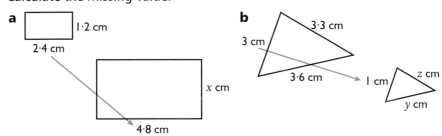

a

1·2 cm

2·4 cm

x cm

4·8 cm

b

3·3 cm

3 cm

3·6 cm

1 cm

z cm

y cm

F

4 A rectangle has vertices A(1, 1), B(1, 3), C(4, 3) and D(4, 1).
   a Draw rectangle ABCD on a coordinate grid.
   b A′ has coordinates which are 3 times the coordinates of A.
   Calculate the coordinates of A′.
   Plot A′.
   In a similar way, find and plot B′, C′ and D′.
   c What can you say about the shape A′B′C′D′?

5 A triangle has vertices P(2, 2), Q(4, 6) and R(10, 0).
   a Draw the triangle on a coordinate grid.
   b By dividing each coordinate by 2, draw a triangle half the size.
   c Use the method to draw a triangle $1\frac{1}{2}$ times the size of the original.

6 a On a coordinate diagram plot the following points and join them up in order.
   A(-4, 0), B(-1, 1), C(0, 4), D(1, 1), E(4, 0), F(1, -1), G(0, -4), H(-1, -1)
   b Draw the image of the figure using:
   i a scale factor 3
   ii a scale factor 0·5.
   c What do you notice about the centre of each shape?

7 **a** Plot the points P(3, 2), Q(5, −2), R(3, 0) and S(1, −2) to form a V-kite.
   b Multiply each coordinate by −1 to find the coordinates of P′, Q′, R′ and S′.
   c Draw the shape P′Q′R′S′ and comment.
   d Repeat this using a factor −2.

Investigations

A Other transformations

What happens if you multiply the *x*-coordinate by a different factor than the *y*-coordinate?

What happens if the *y*-coordinate stays the same but the *x*-coordinate becomes the sum of the *x* and *y* coordinates, e.g. (5, 6) becomes (11, 6)?

What other transformations can you invent? Experiment.

STRETCH

Here the word 'STRETCH' has had its *y*-coordinate multiplied by 22 and its *x*-coordinate multiplied by 2.

Search the Internet for **anamorphic projections**.

Try and find a picture of the artist Holbein's 'The Ambassadors' and study it.

B Other symmetries

Can we enlarge a picture and leave it looking the same?
A 'rep-tile' is a tile which is formed from smaller versions of itself.

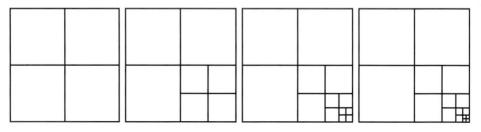

If this process is continued forever outwards as well as inwards then the pattern produced, when enlarged, will look the same. This sort of symmetry is called **self-similarity**.

Explore this idea with
  a the isosceles right-angled triangle (diagram 1)
  b the shape formed from three equilateral triangles (diagram 2).

Diagram 1

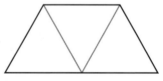

Diagram 2

F

CHECK-UP

1 Which shapes have rotational symmetry?
State the *order* of symmetry where appropriate.

a   **b**   **c** 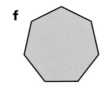 **d**

e **3** **f** ⬡ **g** FIFTY PENCE 50

2 Copy this diagram.

a Draw the image of the kite under a translation
  i 5 to the left
  ii 5 down
  iii 5 to the left and 5 down.

b State the coordinates of the vertices of the kite after the third translation.

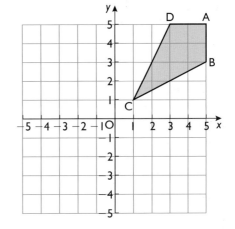

E

3 Triangle ABC is reflected in the *x*-axis, such that A → A′, B → B′ and C → C′.

a Copy the diagram and draw triangle A′B′C′.

b Write down the coordinates of A′, B′, C′.

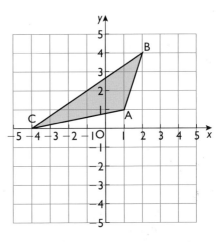

4 **a** Copy this diagram.
Draw its image after a rotation
of 90° about the centre of
symmetry O.

b Complete the diagram to produce
a shape which has quarter-turn
symmetry.

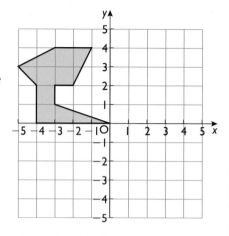

5 **a** Enlarge each diagram by scale
factor 2.

b Reduce each diagram by scale
factor 0·5.

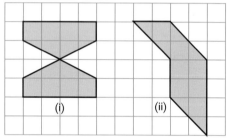

(i) (ii)

6 A triangle has vertices A(2, 2), B(4, 6) and C(4, 12).

a Multiply each coordinate by 2 to help you draw a triangle
twice as big.

b Multiply each coordinate by 0·5 to help you draw a triangle
half as big.

c What happens when you multiply by −1?

E
F

(11) Area

People have measured area throughout history for many practical purposes.

The area of a farm was once measured in **acres**. An acre was the area that a team of oxen could plough in one day.

1 Looking back ◀◀

Square centimetres (cm²) can be used to measure area.

This postage stamp has an area of roughly 5 cm².

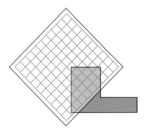

We can use a centimetre square grid to measure area.

Area of shape = 34 square centimetres

Square millimetres (mm²) can be used to measure smaller areas.

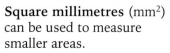

The area of a pinhead could be measured in square millimetres.

Square metres (m²) can be used to measure larger areas.

A small room might be 10 m².

173

Exercise 1.1

1 Find the area of each rectangle. **a** 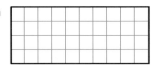 **b**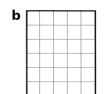

2 Find the area of
  i each rectangle
  ii each green triangle.

a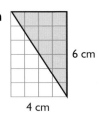
6 cm

4 cm

b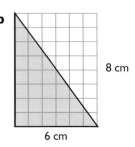
8 cm

6 cm

3 Find the area of each card by imagining a grid.

a
4 cm

12 cm

b
7 cm

6 cm

4 These shapes have been made using right-angled triangles and rectangles on a square centimetre grid. Calculate the area of the shaded part of each grid.

a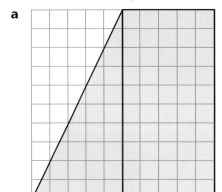

b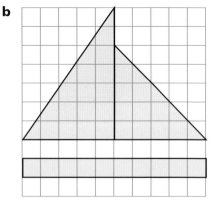

5 Which unit of area would be most appropriate to measure each of these?
  a the door of a room   **b** the sole of your foot
  c a page in your jotter   **d** a credit card
  e a coin   **f** the wings of a fly

2 Some new units

Very large areas

1 hectare

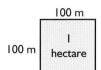

100 m

100 m | 1 hectare

Areas of land can be measured in **hectares**.

$$10\,000\ m^2 = 1\ hectare$$

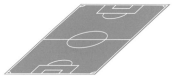

A football pitch is roughly 1 hectare.

Scotland has an area of 79 000 km²

1 square kilometre (1 km²)

1000 m

1000 m | 1 km²

The area of a country, or a forest, or the surface of an ocean could be measured in **square kilometres**.

$$1\,000\,000\ m^2 = 1\ km^2$$

E

Exercise 2.1

1 Which units would be most appropriate to measure the area of the following?

   a a hockey pitch   **b** the Cairngorm mountain range

   c a budgie feather   **d** a holiday snap

   e Loch Ness   **f** the pupil of an eye

   g a CD   **h** farmland

2 This map of a Highland picnic spot shows the area divided into squares, each of area 62 500 m².

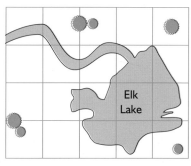

Elk Lake

   a How many square metres are represented by the whole map?

   b What is this area in

      i hectares

      ii km²?

   c Estimate the area of Elk Lake in hectares.

   d This area is part of a National Park which is 8 times bigger. What is the area of the National Park in square kilometres?

3 The table shows the area and population of different parts of the British Isles.

Country	Population	Area (km²)
Scotland	5 229 000	78 772
England	45 870 000	130 368
Ireland	3 089 000	83 937
Wales	2 724 000	20 761

a What is the area of Scotland in hectares?

b If Scotland was shared out equally among the Scots, how many hectares would each person get?

c Repeat this for the other three regions. Which region is the most densely populated? (The one with the smallest share per person.)

3 Using formulae

Count the squares   Imagine the squares   Use a formula

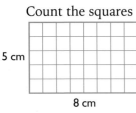    

5 cm   5 cm b cm

8 cm   8 cm l cm

8 columns of 5 squares   Area $A = 8 \times 5 = 40$ cm²   Area $A = l \times b = lb$ cm²
Area $= 8 \times 5 = 40$ cm²   When $l = 8$ and $b = 5$
                                           $\Rightarrow A = 8 \times 5 = 40$ cm²

For a rectangle   For a square

$$A = lb$$ $$A = l^2$$

Example 1

Calculate the area of a rectangle with dimensions 12·8 cm by 0·5 m.

Units must be consistent.
$A = lb$
$\Rightarrow A = 12{\cdot}8 \times 50$ (all in centimetres)
$\Rightarrow A = 640$ cm²

Example 2

Calculate the area of this shape.

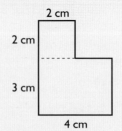

2 cm

2 cm

3 cm

4 cm

Area $=$ rectangle $+$ square
$\Rightarrow A = 3 \times 4 + 2 \times 2$
$\Rightarrow A = 16$ cm²

Exercise 3.1

1 Calculate the area of each rectangle.

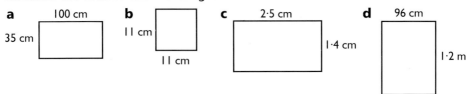

a 100 cm 35 cm

b 11 cm 11 cm

c 2·5 cm 1·4 cm

d 96 cm 1·2 m

2 Calculate the area of each shape by first breaking it up into rectangles.

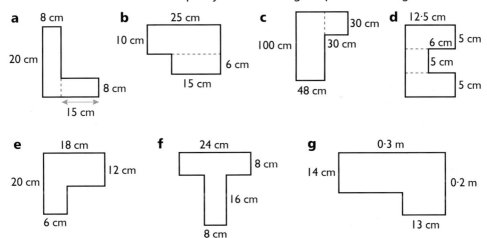

a 8 cm 20 cm 8 cm 15 cm

b 25 cm 10 cm 6 cm 15 cm

c 30 cm 100 cm 30 cm 48 cm

d 12·5 cm 6 cm 5 cm 5 cm 5 cm

e 18 cm 12 cm 20 cm 6 cm

f 24 cm 8 cm 16 cm 8 cm

g 0·3 m 14 cm 0·2 m 13 cm

3 Find the area of these rectangles.
Give your answer in the units requested.

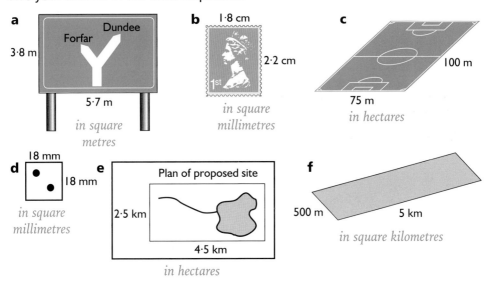

a Forfar Dundee 3·8 m 5·7 m *in square metres*

b 1·8 cm 2·2 cm 1st *in square millimetres*

c 100 m 75 m *in hectares*

d 18 mm 18 mm *in square millimetres*

e Plan of proposed site 2·5 km 4·5 km *in hectares*

f 500 m 5 km *in square kilometres*

4 Right-angled triangles

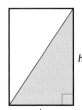

The area of the rectangle can be found using $A = bh$.

The right-angled triangle is half the rectangle.

For the right-angled triangle,

$A = \frac{1}{2}bh$

where b is the base of the triangle and h is its perpendicular height or **altitude**.

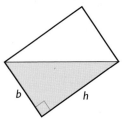

Note we use the two sides which include the right angle.

Example

Calculate the area of the triangle ABC.

Using the two sides which include the right angle, we see $b = 2 \cdot 5$ and $h = 6$.

$A = \frac{1}{2}bh$

$\Rightarrow A = \frac{1}{2} \times 2 \cdot 5 \times 6$

$\Rightarrow A = 7 \cdot 5 \text{ cm}^2$

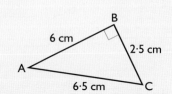

Exercise 4.1

F

1 Calculate the area of each triangle.

a
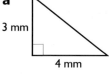

b

c
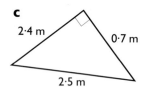

d
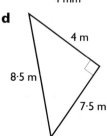

e
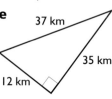

2 a Calculate the area of the triangle made by joining the points.
  i A(4, 2), B(4, 5), C(6, 2)
  ii B(4, 5), P(4, 6), R(9, 6)
  iii R(9, 6), T(9, 2), C(6, 2)
  b Calculate the area of the rectangle APRT.
  c Hence calculate the area of the triangle BCR.

3 Calculate the area of each shape by first breaking it up into suitable rectangles and triangles.

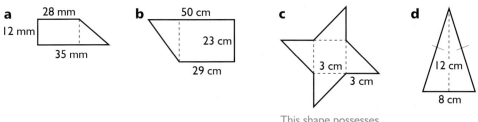

a 28 mm / 12 mm / 35 mm

b 50 cm / 23 cm / 29 cm

c 3 cm / 3 cm

This shape possesses quarter-turn symmetry.

d 12 cm / 8 cm

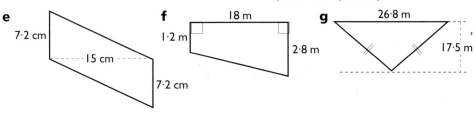

e 7·2 cm / 15 cm

f 18 m / 1·2 m / 2·8 m / 7·2 cm

g 26·8 m / 17·5 m

4 Gordon is laying out his new garden. The plan is shown opposite. The lawn and the patio are equal in area.

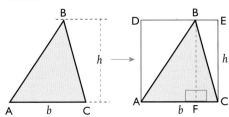

4 m
15 m
Pool
11 m
Patio
11 m
Flowerbed
Lawn
30 m

a Calculate the area of:
   i the pool
   ii the lawn
   iii the flowerbed.

b It will cost £5·45 per m² plus £250 for labour to lay the patio. How much will the finished patio cost?

5 Any triangle

Case 1

B / h / A / b / C   D / B / E / h / A / b F / C

Area of triangle ABC = △ABF + △BFC
$$= \tfrac{1}{2} \text{ rectangle ADBF} + \tfrac{1}{2} \text{ rectangle BFCE}$$
$$h = \tfrac{1}{2} \text{ rectangle ADEC.}$$
$$A = \tfrac{1}{2}bh$$

Case 2

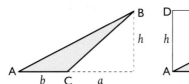 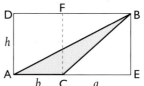

Area of triangle ABC $= \triangle$ABE $- \triangle$CBE

$= \frac{1}{2}$ rectangle ADBE $- \frac{1}{2}$ rectangle CFBE

$= \frac{1}{2}$ rectangle ADFC $+ \frac{1}{2}$ rectangle CFBE $- \frac{1}{2}$ rectangle CFBE

$= \frac{1}{2}$ rectangle ADFC

$A = \frac{1}{2}bh$

Exercise 5.1

1 Use the formula $A = \frac{1}{2}bh$ to calculate the area of each triangle.

a 20 cm, 9 cm

b 100 mm, 75 mm

c 30 cm, 65 cm

d 8 m, 12 m

e 5 cm, 4·5 cm

f 150 mm, 175 mm

g 4·9 m, 4·2 m, 3·7 m

h 29 mm, 33 mm, 35 mm

i 10·6 cm, 19·5 cm, 22·5 cm

j 3·6 m

k 8·2 m, 12 cm, 10 cm, 10 cm

l 6·5 km, 9·5 km, 2 km

2 Calculate the area of each shape, each of which involves one rectangle and one triangle.

a 50 m, 20 m, 80 m

b Hint: subtract — 17 cm, 24 cm, 2 cm

c 22·5 cm, 11 cm, 23 cm, 31·5 cm

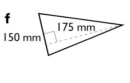
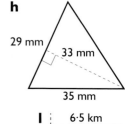
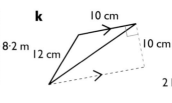
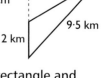
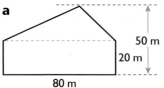
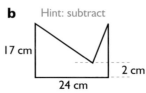
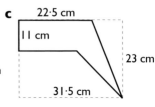

F

3 a Calculate the area of △ABC by considering AB as the base.
b i Write down an expression in x for the area by considering AC as the base.
ii Hence, calculate the value of x.

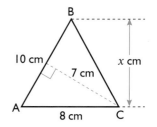

Investigation

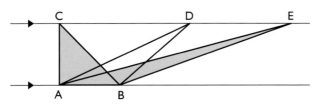

Which looks bigger, △ABC, △ABD or △ABE?
Which is bigger? Explain.

---

6 The areas of other quadrilaterals

We can make area formulae for the other quadrilaterals.

Rhombus   *Kite*

For both the rhombus and the kite we can see the area is half that of the surrounding rectangle.

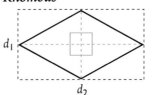 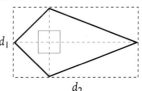

The height of the rectangle = the short diagonal, d_1
The length of the rectangle = the long diagonal, d_2

$A = \frac{1}{2}d_1d_2$ Area = half the product of the diagonals

Parallelogram
△BKC = △AED
So parallelogram DEKC = rectangle DABC
Thus

$A = bh$ Area = base times height

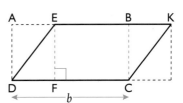

Exercise 6.1

1 Calculate the area of each rhombus and kite.

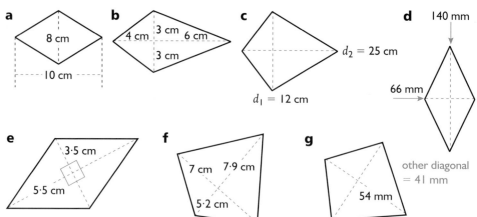

2 Find the area of each parallelogram.

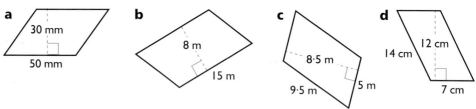

3 The flight of an arrow is made from two congruent parallelograms as shown.
Calculate the area of the flight.

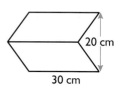

4 A diamond frame is as shown.
The outer perimeter is a rhombus with diagonals 160 mm and 100 mm.
The inner perimeter is another rhombus with diagonals 150 mm and 90 mm.
Calculate the area of the frame.

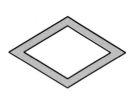

5 a A V-kite can be formed by cutting one isosceles triangle from another.
Use this idea to find the area of each of the following V-kites.

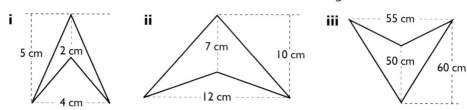

F

b Can you devise a formula for the area of a V-kite?
Use the diagram opposite.
The diagrams, a and b, are highlighted in green.

c How does your formula compare with that for the kite?

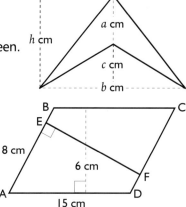

6 ABCD is a parallelogram with AD = 15 cm and AB = 8 cm.
The distance between the parallel sides AD and BC is 6 cm.
By considering the area of the parallelogram, calculate the length of EF.

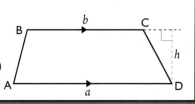

Challenge

Can you devise a formula for the area of a trapezium?
(Hint: Consider the trapezium as two triangles.)

7 Circles: circumference and diameter

A line drawn across a circle through its centre is known as a **diameter**.
The distance round a circle is known as its **circumference**.

The early mathematicians realised there was a simple connection between the circumference of a circle and its diameter.

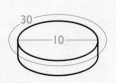

In the Old Testament 1 Kings 7:23, a description of an altar in the temple of Solomon says 'it was 10 cubits from brim to brim ... and a line of 30 cubits did compass it around.'

This suggests that at that time they thought that the circumference was 3 times the diameter.

Exercise 7.1

1 Collect some circular objects. By making suitable measurements, show that for every circle $C \approx 3 \times D$, where D is the diameter and C is the circumference measured in the same units.

2 Use the formula $C \approx 3D$ to estimate the circumference of the following circular objects.

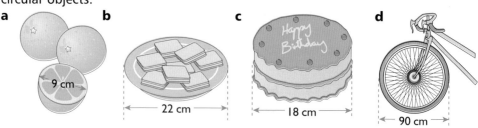

a 9 cm   **b**   22 cm   **c** 18 cm   **d** 90 cm

3 A more accurate estimate for the circumference can be found using the formula $C \approx 3 \cdot 14D$. Calculate the circumference of the following circles.

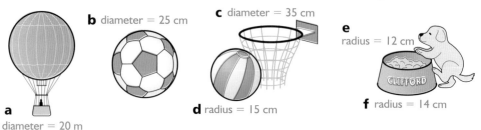

b diameter = 25 cm

c diameter = 35 cm

e radius = 12 cm

a diameter = 20 m

d radius = 15 cm

f radius = 14 cm

4 If you are working on a calculator, the $\boxed{\pi}$ button should be used.

The formula becomes $C = \pi D$. (π is a Greek letter and is pronounced 'pi'. It is the first letter of the Greek word for *perimetros* meaning 'to measure around'.)
Use $C = \pi D$ to calculate the circumference of a circle:

a with diameter   **i**   12 cm   **ii**   2·8 cm   **iii**   725 km

b with radius   **i**   4·2 mm   **ii**   10·5 cm   **iii**   17·9 cm.

5 The planet Arg goes round its sun in a circle of radius 150 million kilometres. Another planet, Tantalus, goes round in a circle of radius 108 million kilometres.
  a Calculate the distance travelled by Arg as it orbits its sun once.
  b How much further does Arg travel than Tantalus in one orbit of the sun?

8 The area of a circle

The Ancient Greeks, by 'trapping' the circle between polygons, were able to come up with better and better estimates for the area of a circle. This method eventually led to the discovery of the formula for calculating the area of a circle:

$$A = \pi r^2$$

where *r* is the radius of the circle.

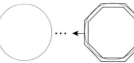

Example

Find the area of a circle of diameter 12 cm.

$D = 12 \Rightarrow r = 12 \div 2 = 6$

$A = \pi \times 6^2 = \pi \times 36$

Using the calculator button to get π, $A = 113 \cdot 1$ cm² (to 1 d.p.)

Exercise 8.1

1 Use the formula $A = \pi r^2$ to calculate the area of each circle.

a 100 mm
b 35 m
c 8 cm
d 1·5 cm
e 100 mm
f 60 m

2 Calculate the area of each circle indicated below.

a radius 1·1 m

b radius 15 cm

c diameter 6 cm

d diameter 28 cm

e diameter 64 mm

F

3 The parasol is made from a circle of cloth of radius 1·85 metres.
Calculate:
a the area of the cloth required
b the length of the fringe which goes round the circumference.

4 A metal washer is made by punching a hole of
diameter 8 mm in a disc of diameter 26 mm.
Calculate the area of:
a the original disc
b the hole
c the metal washer.

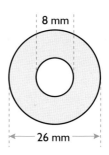
8 mm

26 mm

5 a A semicircular table stands against a wall.
Its radius is 1 metre.
Calculate the area of the semicircle
(half the area of a circle of radius 1 m).

b A semicircular tablecloth of diameter 3 metres
is made to cover it.
What area of material is used?

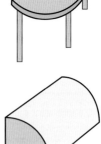

6 A breadbin has an end which is a quarter circle
of radius 36 cm.
Calculate the area of the end.

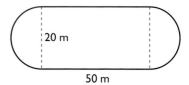

36 cm

7 A grassed area for a stadium is as shown.
It is a rectangle with two semicircular ends.
Calculate:

a the grassed area

b its perimeter.

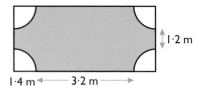

20 m

50 m

F

8 A lawn is a rectangle with congruent quarter
circles cut out of its corners as shown.
Calculate:

a the grassed area

b the amount of edging required to go
round this grass.

1·2 m

1·4 m ← 3·2 m →

CHECK-UP

1 Calculate the area of each shape.

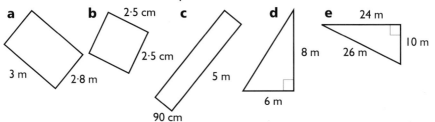

a 3 m   **b** 2·5 cm, 2·5 cm, 2·8 m   **c** 5 m, 90 cm   **d** 8 m, 6 m   **e** 24 m, 10 m, 26 m

2 **a** How many square millimetres are in a square metre?
   b How many square metres are in a square kilometre?
   c How many hectares are in a square kilometre?
   d Which units would be most appropriate for measuring the area of:
   i an ocean   **ii** a fingernail   **iii** a hockey pitch
   iv a CD   **v** the school grounds?

3 The Higgs farm is a rectangular area
3·2 km by 5·6 km.
Calculate the area of the farm in hectares.

4 Calculate the area of each triangle.

 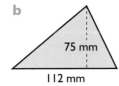 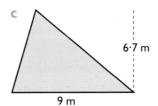

a 6 cm, 5·5 cm   **b** 75 mm, 112 mm   **c** 6·7 m, 9 m

5 Calculate the area of each quadrilateral.

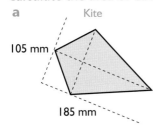 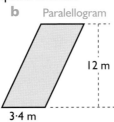 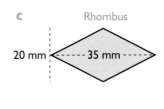

a Kite — 105 mm, 185 mm   **b** Paralellogram — 12 m, 3·4 m   **c** Rhombus — 20 mm, 35 mm

6 For each circle calculate:
   i the circumference correct to 3 significant figures
   ii the area correct to 1 decimal place.

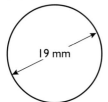 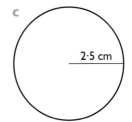

a 19 mm   **b** 5·5 m   **c** 2·5 cm

E
F

(12) Letters, numbers and sequences

Pythagoras studied numbers and found many patterns.

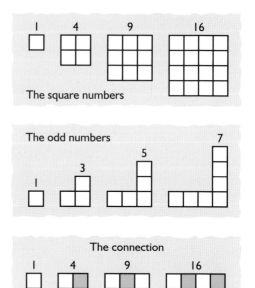

The square numbers

The odd numbers

The connection

$1 + 3$

$1 + 3 + 5$

$1 + 3 + 5 + 7$

Pythagoras

We can often spot patterns by looking at simple cases.

---

1 Looking back

Exercise 1.1

1 Find the next three terms in each sequence. Describe the rule you used.

    a 7, 13, 19, 25, ...

    b 413, 406, 399, 392, ...

    c 5, 10, 20, 40, ...

    d 4096, 1024, 256, 64, ...

2 Copy and complete this table:

$20 - x$					1
x	5	18	20		
$x + 9$			16		

3 Copy and complete this table:

Design 1   Design 2   Design 3

Design number	1	2	3	4	5		20		n
Number of dots	2								

2 The shape of numbers

To the white parallelogram, a green L-shape has been added to make a larger similar parallelogram. The Ancient Greeks referred to this added piece as a *gnomon* (from the Greek word 'to know'). It was named after the shape of the gnomon on a sundial.

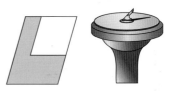

What is added to one square number to form the next were also called gnomons ... the reason why being obvious from the diagrams.

$1 = 1^2$

$4 = 2^2$
$= 1^2 + 3$

$9 = 3^2$
$= 2^2 + 5$

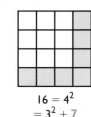
$16 = 4^2$
$= 3^2 + 7$

Note that the gnomons for square numbers 1, 4, 9, 16, ... are 1, 3, 5, 7, ..., the odd numbers.

The gnomons for triangular numbers 1, 3, 6, 10, ... are 1, 2, 3, 4, ..., the positive whole numbers.

I

3
$= 1 + 2$

6
$= 3 + 3$

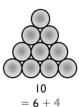
10
$= 6 + 4$

Exercise 2.1

1 Copy and complete this table of square numbers:

n	1	2	3	4	5	6	7	8	9
n^2									

2 **a** Calculate 1, $1 + 3$, $1 + 3 + 5$, $1 + 3 + 5 + 7$, $1 + 3 + 5 + 7 + 9$

b Write a sentence or two about the results of these additions, mentioning the word *gnomon*.

c What is the sum of the first 25 odd numbers?

3 Copy and complete this cross-number puzzle:

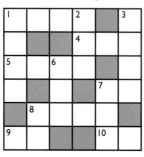

Across
3 The difference between the 8th and 14th square numbers
5 Add the 58th and 20th square numbers
7 The sum of the 45th and 27th square numbers
9 Add the 22nd and 78th square numbers
11 Subtract the 5th from the 28th square number

Down
1 The difference between the 2nd and 9th square numbers
2 Subtract the 3rd from the 16th square number
3 Sum the 22nd and 31st square numbers
4 The difference between the 14th and 48th square numbers
5 The total of the 29th and 54th square numbers
6 $73^2 + 30^2$
8 $24^2 - 3^2$
10 Subtract the 10th from the 13th square number

4 a Copy and complete this table of triangular numbers:

n	1	2	3	4	5		20		50
the nth triangular number t_n	1	3	6	10					
$2t_n$	2	6	12						
$2t_n$ factorised	1×2	2×3	3×4						

b i Use the result of **a** to describe how you would calculate the 123rd triangular number.
ii Do the calculation.

5 Copy and complete this cross-number puzzle about triangular numbers.
(Note: t_4 means the 4th triangular number, i.e. $t_4 = 10$)

Across
1 t_{81}
4 t_{27}
5 t_{91}
7 t_8
8 t_{65}
9 t_{13}
10 t_5

Down
1 t_{86}
2 t_{16}
3 t_{108}
6 t_{41}
7 t_{26}
8 t_6

E

Challenges

1 All prime numbers apart from 2 can be sorted into two types.

   Type 1:   One less than a multiple of 4, e.g. 3, 7, 11, ...
   Type 2:   One more than a multiple of 4, e.g. 5, 13, 17, ...

   A Frenchman called Albert Girard (1595–1632) noticed that all type 2 primes that he looked at could be written as the sum of two square numbers but that none of type 1 primes could be written this way. It was Pierre de Fermat (1601–65), another Frenchman, who eventually proved this result was true for all primes.
   Choose three primes of each type and check Fermat's result for your chosen primes.

2 Search the web for polygonal numbers. Write a short report.

3 The nth terms from multiples

1st term	2nd term	3rd term	4th term	...	nth term	
↓	↓	↓	↓	...	↓	
3	7	11	15	...	?	

The terms in this sequence go up by 4 each time.
This suggests comparing the sequence with the multiples of 4 since they also go up by 4 each time.

Term number (n)	1	2	3	4	...	n
Sequence	3	7	11	15	...	$4n - 1$
Multiples of 4 ($4n$)	4	8	12	16	...	$4n$

Notice that each term in the sequence is 1 less than the corresponding multiple of 4.

The nth term is $4n - 1$

Check: When $n = 1$ $4n - 1 = 4 \times 1 - 1 = 3$
           When $n = 2$ $4n - 1 = 4 \times 2 - 1 = 7$
           When $n = 3$ $4n - 1 = 4 \times 3 - 1 = 11$

So $4n - 1$ is generating the terms of the sequence.

Exercise 3.1

1 Copy and complete the tables for the given sequences.

a Sequence: 4, 7, 10, 13, ...

Term number (n)	1	2	3	4	...	n
Sequence	4	7	10	13	...	?
Multiples of 3 ($3n$)	3	6	9	12	...	$3n$

Check your formula for the nth term for $n = 1, 2, 3, 4$

b Sequence 1, 6, 11, 16, ...

Term number (n)	1	2	3	4	...	n
Sequence	1	6	11	16	...	?
Multiples of 5					...	?

Check your formula for the nth term for $n = 1, 2, 3, 4$

c Sequence: 10, 17, 24, 31, ...

Term number (n)	1	2	3	4	...	n
Sequence					...	?
Multiples of ...					...	?

Check your formula for the nth term for $n = 1, 2, 3, 4$

2 Find expressions for the nth term of each of these sequences. Make tables similar to the above.

a 1, 3, 5, 7, ...   **b** 7, 11, 15, 19, ...   **c** 1, 7, 13, 19, ...
d 4, 13, 22, 31, ...   **e** 11, 13, 15, 17, ...   **f** 1, 4, 7, 10, ...
g 12, 23, 34, 45, ...   **h** 3, 11, 19, 27, ...

Example

In the sequence 1, 5, 9, 13, ... which term is 73?

By inspection the nth term is $4n - 3$.
So we require $4n - 3 = 73$
$\Rightarrow 4n = 76$
$\Rightarrow n = 19$.
73 is the 19th term.

3 Follow the example to find which term the highlighted number is in each sequence.

a 10, 13, 16, 19, ..., 97, ...   **b** 5, 11, 17, 23, ..., 71, ...
c 8, 15, 22, 29, ..., 127, ...   **d** 5, 14, 23, 32, .., 158, ...
e 14, 19, 24, 29, ..., 129, ...   **f** 5, 13, 21, 29, ..., 213, ...
g 1, 14, 27, 40, ..., 508, ...

Example

In the sequence 40, 37, 34, 31, ... terms go *down* by 3 each time.
This suggests the multiples of −3: −3, −6, −9, −12, ...

Notice that we must add 43 to each multiple to get the required sequence.
So the *n*th term is 43 − 3*n*.

Exercise 3.2

1 Find an expression for the *n*th term of these sequences:
   a 28, 26, 24, 22, ...   **b** 37, 34, 31, 28, ...   **c** 45, 40, 35, 30, ...
   d 42, 38, 34, 30, ...   **e** 71, 65, 59, 53, ...   **f** 77, 70, 63, 56, ...

2 Here are some problem situations.
   To solve each one you must find the *n*th term of the sequence and use it to
   solve the problem.

   a

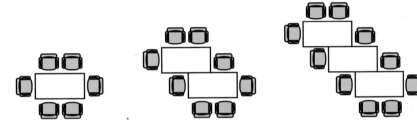

   I table with 6 chairs   2 tables with 8 chairs   3 tables with 10 chairs

   i For 47 tables how many chairs are needed?
   ii How many tables do you need for 200 chairs?

   b

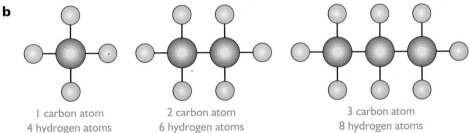

   I carbon atom   2 carbon atom   3 carbon atom
   4 hydrogen atoms   6 hydrogen atoms   8 hydrogen atoms

   i For 39 carbon atoms how many hydrogen atoms will there be?
   ii With 126 hydrogen atoms how many carbon atoms will there be?

   c

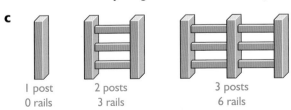

   I post   2 posts   3 posts
   0 rails   3 rails   6 rails

   i If you have 27 posts how many rails do you need?
   ii A fence has 72 rails. How many posts does it have?

d

Motorboat Hire Charges			
Hours	1	2	3
Charge	£8	£11	£14

   i If this pattern of charges continues what charge is made for a full day's hire?

   ii The charge is £56. How many hours' hire is this?

e

Hours of operation	1	2	3	4
Fuel left (litres)	238	226	214	202

The table shows the number of litres of fuel left in the tank of a water pump after various hours of operation.

   i How much fuel is left after 14 hours?

   ii How long can the pump operate until there are only 10 litres of fuel left?

Challenge

If we continue both sequences seen in the table, will the two terms ever be equal?

Sequence 1	1	8	15	22	...
Sequence 2	89	92	95	98	...

a Find the nth term of each sequence.
b Set them equal to each other.
c Solve the equation.
d Now answer the question!

4 Rule-making

Using rods and spheres from the kit we make models:

   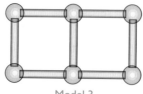 

Model I   Model 2   Model 3

Making a table we look for patterns:

Model number (n)	1	2	3	...	n
Spheres (S)	2	4	6	...	$2n$
Rods (R)	1	4	7	...	$3n-2$

By considering model number 1, 2, 3, ... in order, the rules are found by inspection.

For the spheres: $S = 2n$
For the rods: $R = 3n - 2$

With formulae for spheres and rods in terms of model number, we can answer many questions.

Example 1 Find the number of rods and spheres needed to make model number 45.

Using $S = 2n$ when $n = 45$
$$S = 2 \times 45 = 90$$

Using $R = 3n - 2$ when $n = 45$
$$R = 3 \times 45 - 2 = 135 - 2 = 133$$

So 133 rods and 90 spheres are required.

Example 2 I used 49 rods to make one of the models, what was the model number?

Using $R = 3n - 2$ you know $R = 49$
$$\Rightarrow \quad 3n - 2 = 49$$
$$\Rightarrow \quad 3n = 51$$
$$\Rightarrow \quad n = 17$$

It was model number 17.

F

Exercise 4.1

1

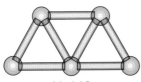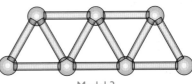

Model 1   Model 2   Model 3

a Copy and complete the table for this sequence of models.

Model number (n)	1	2	3	...	n
Spheres (S)				...	
Rods (R)				...	

b Express S and R in terms of n.

c Find the number of rods and spheres required to build model 37.

d What model am I building if I use 83 spheres?

e i Which model requires 211 rods to build?
 ii How many spheres would it need?

2

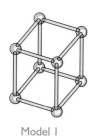 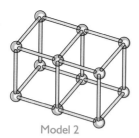 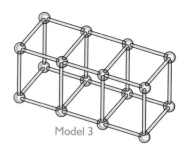

Model 1   Model 2   Model 3

a Make up a table showing the number of spheres (S) and the number of rods (R) in the first four models in this sequence.

b Give the rules for finding S and R in model n.

c You are going to build models 5 and 9.
How many spheres and rods will you need in total?

d I used 108 spheres to build one of the models.
Which model was it and how many rods did I use?

3

  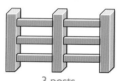

1 post   2 posts   3 posts
0 rails   3 rails   6 rails

a Copy and complete the table.

Number of posts (P)	1	2	3	4	...	P
Number of rails (R)	0	3				

b Express R in terms of P.

c How many rails does a 25 post fence require?

d I have 168 rails. How many posts do I need?

4

 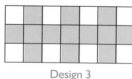

Design 1   Design 2   Design 3

This patio design sequence uses green and white slabs.

Design number (n)	1	2	3	4	...	n
Number of green (G)	5	9				
Number of white (W)	4					

a Copy and complete the table.

b Write down formulae used to find G and W given n.

c How many green and white slabs do you need for Design 45?

d I have 221 green slabs, how many white slabs do I need to complete the design?

F

5 More patio designs

  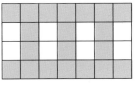

Design 1   Design 2   Design 3

a Design n uses G green slabs and W white slabs.
Find formulae to calculate G and W given n.

b I have 278 green slabs. How many white do I need?

Challenge

A spreadsheet pattern

The two numbers in row n are equal.

By finding nth term formulae for each sequence, and solving an equation, find that number.

	A	B
1	2	54
2	51	102
3	100	150
4	...	
6		
n		

F

---

5 Problem solving

Many problems can be solved using algebra.

There are usually *four steps*.

Step 1: Use a letter for the unknown quantity.
Step 2: Translate the problem into an equation.
Step 3: Solve the equation.
Step 4: Express the solution in the context of the original problem.

Example

In a triangle one angle is three times the smallest angle. The other angle is 10° more than the smallest angle.

Step 1   Let the smallest angle be $x°$.
The three angles are $x°$, $3x°$ and $(x + 10)°$

Step 2 $\Rightarrow x + 3x + x + 10 = 180$ ... the sum of the angles of a triangle = 180°
$\Rightarrow 5x + 10 = 180$
$\Rightarrow 5x = 170$

Step 3 $\Rightarrow x = 34$

Step 4   The three angles are $x° = 34°$, $3x° = 3 \times 34 = 102°$ and
$(x + 10)° = 44°$ (34°, 44° and 102° do add up to 180°)

Exercise 5.1

1 Ahmed is x years old.
  a Give the ages, in terms of x, of:
   i his mother who is 3 times his age
   ii his sister who is 6 years younger than him.
  b If the combined total of their ages is 49 years, form an equation and solve it.
  c Find the ages of Ahmed, his mother and his sister.

2 Hannah spent £x on a CD.
  a Give the costs, in terms of x, of:
   i the jacket she bought which was 5 times the cost of the CD
   ii the pack of batteries which cost her £3 less than the CD.
  b In total she spent £53 on these items. Form an equation and solve it.
  c Find the cost of each item.

3 In a triangle the largest angle is 5 times the size of the smallest angle. The third angle is 26° more than the smallest angle.
  a Let the smallest angle be $x°$ and express the sizes of the other two angles in terms of $x°$.
  b Form an equation by totalling the three angles and solve it.
  c Find the sizes of the three angles.

4 a Zoe's dad is twice her age.
   Her sister is 3 years older than her.
   If the sum of their three ages is 95 years, find their ages.
   (Hint: let Zoe's age be x years.)
  b Tom's mum is 27 years older than him.
   His sister is twice his age. Their total age is 47 years.
   Find their ages.
   (Hint: Let Tom's age be x years.)
  c The Smiths have a total age of 49 years.
   The older of the two children is twice the age of the younger.
   The mother is 19 years older and the father 20 years older than the younger child.
   Find their ages. (Hint: let the youngest be x years old.)
  d In a triangle the three angles, in size order, are each 10° apart.
   Find their sizes.
   (Hint: let the smallest be $x°$.)

e Sales at an ice-cream shop on Monday, Tuesday, Wednesday and Thursday went up by exactly 25 each day.
If the total sales for the four days were 370, how many ice creams were sold on Wednesday?
(Hint: x ice creams were sold on Monday.)

5 Ian has five more 50 pence coins than 20 pence coins in his pocket. In total he has £5·30.
How many of each coin does he have?

a Let the number of 20p coins be x.
   i Express the number of 50p coins in terms of x.
   ii Explain why the value of all the 20p coins is $20x$ pence.
   iii Write down the value of all the 50p coins in terms of x.

b Explain why $20x + 50(x + 5) = 530$.

c Solve the equation.

d State how many of each type of coin Ian has.

6 a Pete has three more 20 pence coins than 10 pence coins.
He has £2·70 in total.
How many of each coin does he have?
(Hint: he has x 10 pence coins.)

b Linzi has twice as many 10 pence coins as 5 pence coins.
She also has two more 20 pence coins than 5 pence coins.
In total she has £2·20.
How many of each coin does she have?
(Hint: she has x 5 pence coins.)

c Kerry has £6·95 in change.
It consists of three times as many 10 pence coins as 5 pence coins and two more 50 pence coins than 5 pence coins.
How many of each coin does she have?

Challenges

1 Callum notices that he can say exactly the same about the 32 coins in his change as Kerry in part **c** of question **6**, apart from what they are worth.
What are his coins worth?

2 Kim is three years older than her sister Mia.
Eight years ago Kim was twice as old as Mia.
How old is Kim?

6 Formulae and graphs

The time, t hours, taken to thaw a frozen chicken weighing w kg is given by:

$t = \frac{1}{2}(7w + 26)$ where $0 < w \leqslant 10$.

Here is a table showing some values that were calculated from this formula. (Check them!)

w	2	4	6	8	10
t	20	27	34	41	48

These pairs of values were plotted as points on the graph.

The line joining the points can then be used as a *weight/thawing time* calculator.

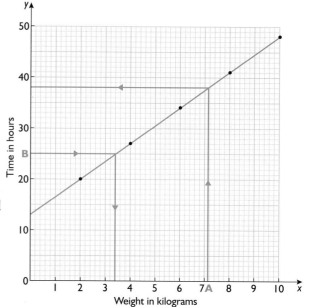

For example:

Follow trail A ... It appears from the graph that a 7·2 kg chicken takes around 38 hours to thaw.

Follow trail B ... If you only had 25 hours to thaw your chicken then the graph indicates that at most your chicken could weigh around 3·4 kg.

Exercise 6.1

1 The thawing time, t hours, for a chicken weighing w kg when it is left to thaw in the fridge is given by: $t = \frac{1}{2}(17w + 2); 0 < w \leqslant 10$.

a Copy and complete the table.

w	2	4	6	8	10
t					

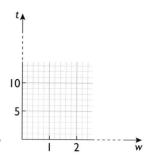

b Use the scales shown in the diagram to draw a graph for this formula with $0 \leqslant w \leqslant 10$ and $0 \leqslant t \leqslant 90$.

c From the graph estimate the time required to thaw a 4·6 kg chicken if it is left in the fridge.

d In 42 hours what weight of frozen chicken can be thawed in the fridge?

2 The roasting time, r hours, for a w kg turkey is given by:
$r = \frac{1}{2}(w + 1); 2 \leqslant w \leqslant 10.$

a Copy and complete the table.

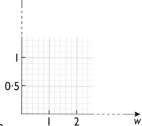

w	3	5	7	9
r				

b Using the scales indicated in the diagram, draw a graph for this formula with $0 \leqslant w \leqslant 10$ and $0 \leqslant r \leqslant 5$.

c How long should a 4·2 kg turkey be roasted for?

d I roasted my turkey for $4\frac{1}{2}$ hours. What weight was it?

3 The formula $F = \frac{1}{5}(9C + 160)$ converts temperatures measured in degrees Celsius (°C) to temperatures measured in degrees Fahrenheit (°F).

a Copy and complete the table.

C	0	10	20	30	40
F					

b Choosing suitable scales, draw a graph for this formula with $0 \leqslant C \leqslant 40$ and $0 \leqslant F \leqslant 105$.

c Estimate the temperature 15·2 °C in °F.

d From your graph, what is the normal body temperature of 98·4 °F in °C?

4 Forensic scientists use the following rule-of-thumb:
the number of hours since death, H hours, is given by $H = 66 - \frac{2}{3}T$ where T is the body temperature in °F.

a Copy and complete the table.

T	15	30	45	60	75
H					

b Choosing suitable scales, draw a graph for this formula with $0 \leqslant T \leqslant 80$.

c In a murder enquiry it was suspected the body had lain undiscovered for 20 to 30 hours.
Within what range of temperatures should the body be to confirm this suspicion?

Challenge

The 'slow' (Gas Mark 3) turkey roasting formula $r = \frac{1}{2}(w + 1)$ was given in question **2**.
There is a 'fast' (Gas Mark 8) turkey roasting formula: $r = \frac{1}{4}(w + 7)$.
By drawing graphs of these formulae on the same diagram for $0 \leqslant w \leqslant 10$, decide whether the 'fast' method really is a faster method.
Write a short account, giving details of your findings.

CHECK-UP

1 Complete this cross-number puzzle:

Across:
1 The 12th square number
3 The sum of the 7th square number
and the 2nd triangular number
5 The 5th triangular number
7 The 23rd square number

Down:
1 The 11th square number
2 The 9th triangular number
4 The sum of the 10th and 13th square numbers
6 The 10th triangular number

2 The nth term of a sequence is given by $7n - 3$. Find:
a the 4th term
b the sum of the 5th and 8th terms.

3 Find an expression for the nth terms of these sequences:
a 3, 10, 17, 24, ...
b 84, 81, 78, 75, ...

4

1 table
8 chairs

2 tables
12 chairs

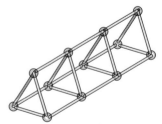
3 tables
16 chairs

a Find an expression for the number of chairs required when n tables are used.
b If 85 tables are used, how many chairs are required?
c How many tables are needed to seat 192 guests using this arrangement?

5

Model 1   Model 2   Model 3

a Copy and complete the table.

Model number (n)	1	2	3	4	...	n
Number of spheres (S)						
Number of rods (R)						

b Express S and R in terms of n.

c How many rods and spheres are required to build model 46?

d Which model requires 219 spheres to build and how many rods are required?

6 In a triangle the three angles, in order of size, are 15° apart. Find their sizes. (Hint: let the smallest angle be $x°$.)

7 Of three brothers, Amuz is the youngest, Muhab is five years older than him and Maziz is three times his age. If the total of their ages is 20 years, find their ages.

8 The average height, H cm, for a child of age A years is given by: $H = 6(A + 14); 0 \leqslant A \leqslant 10$.

a Draw a graph for this formula.

b What is the average height of a child aged 3 years 9 months?

c Thomas is 123 cm tall. If his height is average for his age, how old is he?

F

(13) The triangle

You will see examples of triangles everywhere.

They are used for symmetry, balance and strength.

Make a list of everyday objects that are triangular or contain triangles.

1 Looking back ◀◀

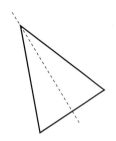

An isosceles triangle has one axis of symmetry.

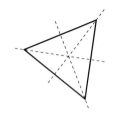

An equilateral triangle has three axes of symmetry.

Exercise 1.1

1 Decide which of the following triangles are

  a isosceles, equilateral, neither

  b acute angled, right angled, obtuse angled.

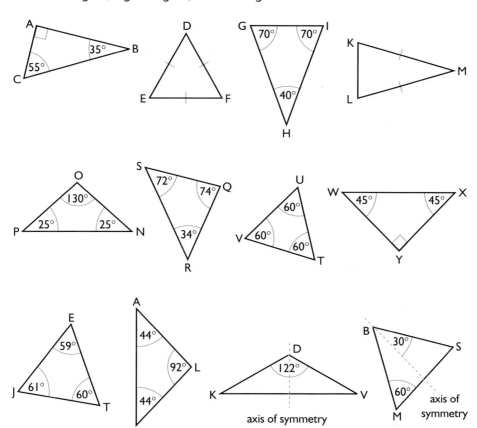

2 **a** In each diagram, name pairs of vertically opposite angles.

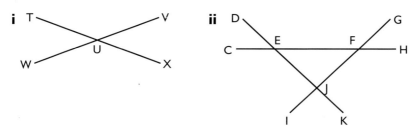

  b What is special about vertically opposite angles?

3

When the sides of two triangles are equal, then the triangles are identical in every respect. We say the triangles are **congruent**.

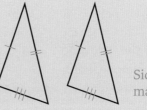

Sides with the same markings are equal.

The diagram shows part of the surface of a crystal.

Name: **a** an angle equal to ∠GIH
b three angles equal to ∠EDF
c all the angles equal to ∠DGI
d any angle equal to ∠GDI.

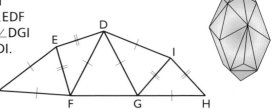

4 a On a coordinate diagram plot the points A(0, 1), B(1, 5) and C(4, 2), and join them up.

b What kind of triangle is △ABC? Give a reason for your answer.

c Write down the coordinates of three possible positions for D such that △ACD is isosceles with AC = CD.

d △PCB is isosceles with PC = PB.
If the x-coordinate of P is m, what is the y-coordinate of P?

2 The sum of the angles of a triangle

Class activities

Activity 1

a Measure the size of each angle of triangle RST.
b Calculate the sum of the three angles.

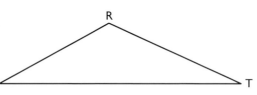

Activity 2

a Draw your own triangle.
b Measure its angles.
c Calculate the sum of the angles.
d Repeat **a**, **b** and **c** with a different triangle.
e Compare your results with others.

Activity 3

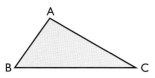

a Cut out a triangle in paper.

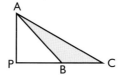

b Fold it over as shown …

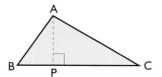

c … and open it out to form a crease perpendicular to the base of the triangle.

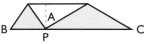

d Fold A onto P.

e Fold B onto P.

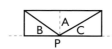

f Fold C onto P.

The three angles seem to come together to make a straight line.

Activity 4

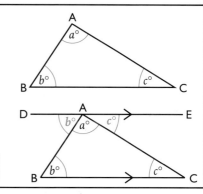

Triangle ABC has angles of size $a°$, $b°$ and $c°$.
- Draw a line DE through A parallel to BC.
- $\angle DAB = \angle ABC = b°$ (alternate angles)
- $\angle EAC = \angle ACB = c°$ (alternate angles)
- Note that $\angle DAE = 180° = b° + a° + c°$.

So $a° + b° + c° = 180°$

The sum of the angles of the triangle is 180°.

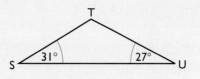

> The sum of the angles of any triangle is 180°.

E

Example 1 Calculate the size of $\angle STU$.

Answer: $\angle STU + \angle TUS + \angle TSU = 180°$
(angles of a triangle)
So $\angle STU + 27° + 31° = 180°$
So $\angle STU = 180° - 58°$
So $\angle STU = 122°$

Example 2 Find the value of: **a** x **b** y **c** z.

Answer: **a** $x + 54 + 68 = 180$ (angles of a triangle)
$\Rightarrow x + 122 = 180$
$\Rightarrow x = 58$

For $\Rightarrow$ read 'so'

b $y + x = 180$ (BDC is a straight line)
$\Rightarrow y = 180 - 58$
$\Rightarrow y = 122$

c $z + y + 25 = 180$ (angles of a triangle)
$\Rightarrow z = 180 - 147$
$\Rightarrow z = 33$

Exercise 2.1

1 Calculate the size of each lettered angle.

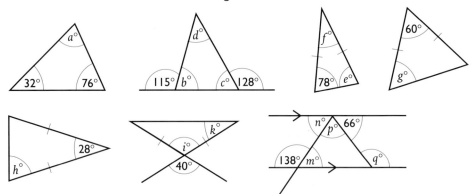

2 Which of the triangles below are isosceles? Explain your answers.

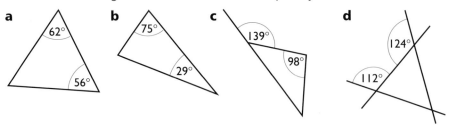

a

b

c

d

3 Copy the *triangles* in each drawing and fill in the sizes of as many angles as you can.

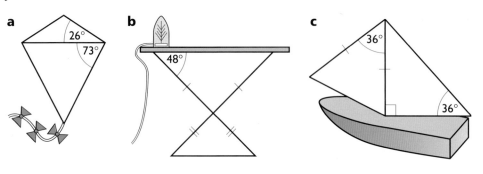

a

b

c

4 RSTU is a rectangle.
Show that the angles of △VWS are equal to the angles of △TUW.

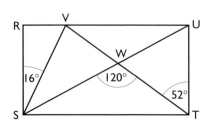

E

5 In each case calculate
  i the value of x
  ii the sizes of the angles in each triangle.

a 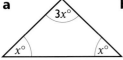 **b** 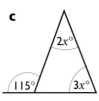 **c** 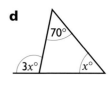 **d**

3 Drawing triangles

Class discussion

What is the least information
you need to draw a triangle?

1 the three angles
2 two angles and any side
3 one angle and one side
4 one angle and any two sides
5 one angle and two particular sides
6 the three sides

Here are two equilateral triangles.
Which of the above options do they eliminate?

E

Given one side and two angles (ASA)

Example 1

Draw the triangle PQR where PQ = 8 cm, $\angle$RPQ = 48° and $\angle$RQP = 95°.

Make a rough sketch.
It will help you plan
the steps.

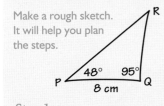

Note: we need the angles at both ends of the known side.
If one of the angles given is at R, then we will have to
work out the missing angle first.

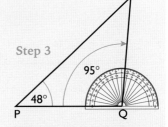

Step 1

Draw PQ 8 cm long.

Step 2

Measure and draw an angle of
48° at P.

Step 3

Measure and draw an angle of
95° at Q, identifying the
position of R.

Exercise 3.1

1 Follow the steps on page 209 to draw the triangle PQR.
Measure the third angle, ∠PRQ, and check your accuracy by calculation.

2 Draw the following triangles as accurately as you can.
Measure the third angle of each triangle, then check your accuracy by calculation.

    a Triangle KLM, with KL = 7 cm, ∠KLM = 54° and ∠LKM = 67°.

    b Triangle EFG, with EG = 9·4 cm, ∠FEG = 116° and ∠FGE = 32°.

    c Triangle TUV, with UV = 8·6 cm, ∠UVT = 83° and ∠UTV = 41°.

3 **a** Draw quadrilateral ABCD as accurately as you can.

    b Measure the angles at B and D.

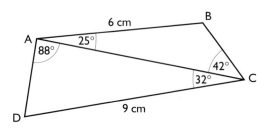

Given two sides and the angle between them (SAS)

Example 2

Draw triangle RST with RS = 8·5 cm, ST = 7·5 cm and ∠RST = 46°.

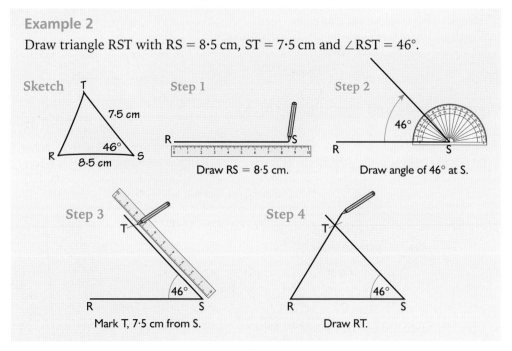

4 **a** Follow the steps above to draw the triangle RST.

    b Measure the length of side RT.

5 Draw the following triangles as accurately as you can.
In each case, measure the length of the third side of the triangle.

    a Triangle ACE, with AC = 9 cm, CE = 7·8 cm and ∠ACE = 72°.

    b Triangle NOP, with PO = 7 cm, PN = 8·8 cm and ∠NPO = 105°.

    c Triangle XYZ, with XZ = 8 cm, XY = 8 cm and ∠YXZ = 135°.

6 **a** Draw quadrilateral KLMN as accurately as you can.

    b Measure the length of side MN.

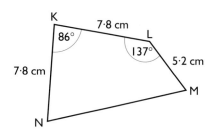

Given three sides (SSS)

Example 3

Draw triangle STU with ST = 7 cm, TU = 8 cm and SU = 9 cm.

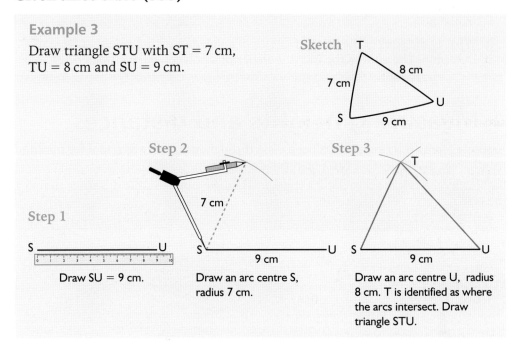

7 **a** Follow the steps above to draw the triangle STU.

    b Measure the size of ∠SUT.

8 Draw the following triangles as accurately as you can.
In each case, measure the size of the largest angle in the triangle.

    a Triangle DEF, with DE = 10 cm, EF = 6·5 cm and DF = 12 cm.

    b Triangle VWX, with VX = 8·6 cm, XW = 9·2 cm and VW = 6·5 cm.

    c Triangle KLM, with KL = LM = 7 cm and KM = 8 cm.

9 Try to draw △BDF with BF = 7 cm, BD = 12 cm and DF = 4 cm.
Comment on this task.

10 a Draw quadrilateral VWXY as accurately as you can.

b Calculate the area of VWXY.

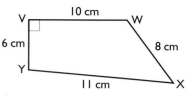

11 The diagonals of a rectangle are 10 cm long. They intersect at 40°. Find the length and breadth of the rectangle, to the nearest millimetre.

Challenge

A quadrilateral can be divided into 2 triangles. So the sum of its interior angles is equal to 4 right angles.

A pentagon can be divided into 3 triangles. So the sum of its interior angles is equal to 6 right angles.

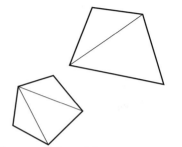

a What is the sum of the interior angles of a polygon with 8 sides?
b Determine the sum of the interior angles of a polygon with *n* sides.

---

4 Measuring heights and distances

Accurately drawn triangles have been used throughout history as a tool for finding lengths and distances that can't be measured directly.

If enough data is known to draw a triangle, then we can use scale drawings to find the rest.

Example

A diamond mine has two sloping entry shafts. One slopes at 28° to the horizontal, the other at 36°. Between the ends of these shafts is a horizontal gallery 250 metres long (BC). How deep is the mine?

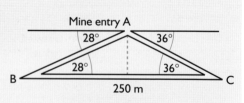

Step 1 Choose a suitable scale. If we let 1 cm represent 50 m, then the line BC, representing the length of the mine, will be 5 cm long.

Step 2 Draw the triangle to this scale. The dotted line represents the depth of the mine.

Step 3 Measure the green line. It is 1·5 cm to the nearest 0·1 cm.

Scale:
1 cm represents 50 m
or
1 : 5000

Step 4 Scale it up: 1·5 × 50 = 75 metres (to the nearest 0·1 × 50 = 5 metres)
The mine is 75 metres deep, to the nearest 5 metres.
(Note the bigger the scale, the more accurate the answer.)

Exercise 4.1

1 The diagram, not to scale, shows the position of a boat (B) in distress and two boats (R1 and R2) coming to the rescue.
Which rescue boat is nearer the boat in distress, and by how much?
(Use a scale of 1 cm to represent 200 metres.)

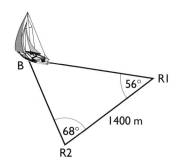

2 A helicopter is directly above a traffic jam on a straight stretch of motorway. The distance from the helicopter to the front of the traffic jam is 220 metres and to the back is 280 metres.

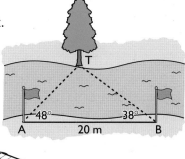

    a Choose a suitable scale and draw the triangle as accurately as possible.

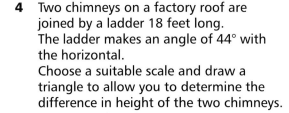

    b Find the length of the traffic jam.

    c Find the height of the helicopter.

3 Debbie wants to find the width of the river. She places two pegs, A and B, 20 metres apart. Across the river there is a tree at T. Angle TAB is measured as 48° and angle TBA as 38°.

    a Using a scale of 1 : 200, draw triangle TAB.

    b From your scale drawing find the width of the river.

4 Two chimneys on a factory roof are joined by a ladder 18 feet long. The ladder makes an angle of 44° with the horizontal. Choose a suitable scale and draw a triangle to allow you to determine the difference in height of the two chimneys.

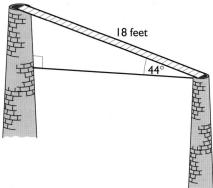

E

5 Three roads intersect as shown. Make a scale drawing and use it to determine the angles at which the roads meet.

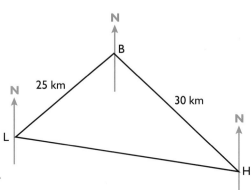

6 A boat at B is 25 km north-east of the lighthouse at L and 30 km north-west of the harbour at H.

   a Using a suitable scale draw the triangle BLH.

   b From your scale drawing find the distance between the lighthouse and the harbour.

   c Find the 3-figure bearing of the harbour from the lighthouse.

5 Drawing more triangles

Given two sides and an angle (not the included angle) (ASS)

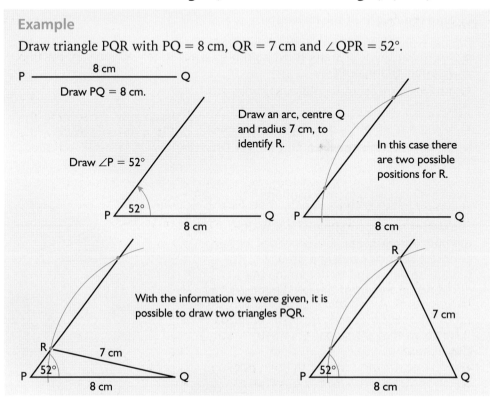

This will not always happen.
Given two sides, PQ and QR, and an angle which is not the angle between the two given sides, ∠RPQ, we may be able to draw two triangles (as above), or one triangle, when PQ ⩽ QR or ∠PRQ = 90° ...

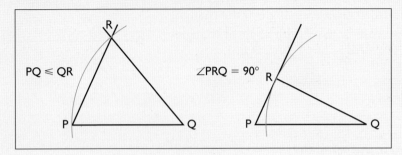

PQ ⩽ QR   ∠PRQ = 90°

or no triangles, when the given angle is bigger than or equal to 180° or QR is too short to reach PR.

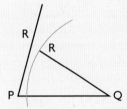

Exercise 5.1

1 a Carry out the four steps above to draw, as accurately as you can, the two possible triangles PQR.

b What are the two possible lengths of PR?

2 Attempt to draw the following triangles. In each case say whether there are two possible triangles, one possible triangle or if it is impossible to draw the triangle. Where it is possible to draw the triangle, find the length(s) of the third side.

a Triangle XYZ, with XY = 10 cm, YZ = 8 cm and ∠YXZ = 42°.

b Triangle DEF, with DE = 7 cm, EF = 6 cm and ∠DFE = 35°.

c Triangle ABC, with AB = 8 cm, BC = 9 cm and ∠CAB = 75°.

d Triangle RST, with RS = 8·5 cm, ST = 8 cm and ∠SRT = 100°.

e Triangle HIJ, with HI = 8 cm, IJ = 6 cm and ∠JHI = 47°.

3 A lifeboat at B is 800 metres due east of a harbour at H. A ship at S is in distress. It is on a bearing of 065° from the harbour. It is known that the ship is 500 metres from the lifeboat. Use a scale drawing to find the two possible distances of the ship from the harbour.

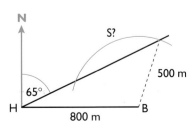

6 The exterior angles of a triangle

In triangle ABC, BA has been extended to D.
The supplement of ∠BAC is ∠CAD.

∠BAC is an *interior* angle of the triangle and
∠CAD is called an *exterior* angle of the triangle.

Similarly ∠ABF is an exterior angle of triangle
ABC, as is ∠BAE ... but ∠DAE is **not**.

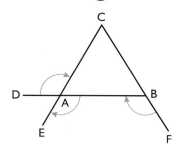

Exercise 6.1

1 **a** Copy the diagram. Mark on it all the
exterior angles of triangle RST.
(You should find six altogether.)

   b Some of the exterior angles are equal.
Which ones? How do you know
they are equal?

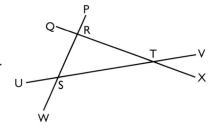

2 Calculate the lettered angles.

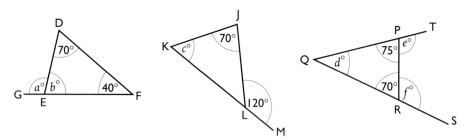

3 Calculate the lettered angle in each case and comment.

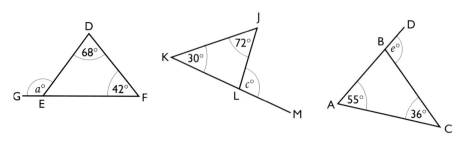

4 **a** Find an expression for the size of ∠ABC in terms of x and y.

b Find an expression for the size of ∠ABD in terms of x and y.

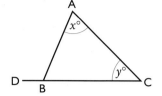

> The exterior angle of a triangle is equal to the sum of the two interior opposite angles.

5 In the diagrams below, find an expression for:

a k in terms of m

b the size of ∠EDF

c the size of ∠LKM in terms of p and q.

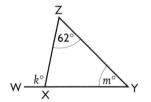 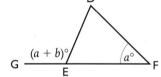 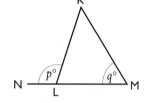

F

CHECK-UP

1 Calculate the sizes of the lettered angles in these diagrams.

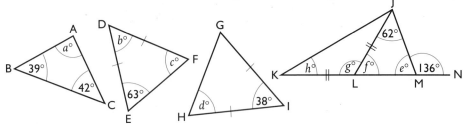

2 In each of the following, form an equation and solve it to find the size of each angle.

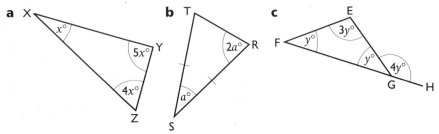

3 **a** Draw △PQR with PQ = 11 cm, QR = 10 cm and PR = 9 cm. Measure the size of ∠PQR.

    b Draw △STU with ST = 8·5 cm, TU = 7 cm and ∠STU = 57°. Measure the length of SU.

    c Draw △KLM with ∠KLM = 64°, ∠KML = 44° and LM = 8·2 cm. What is the length of KM?

4 The girders of a bridge form triangles. A section is shown opposite.

    a Using a scale of 1 : 250 make a scale drawing of △PQR.

    b From your scale drawing find h, the height of the bridge.

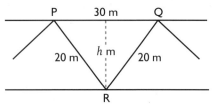

5 **a** Draw triangle FGH with FG = 9 cm, FH = 7 cm and ∠HGF = 40°.

    b What are the possible lengths of GH?

6 Express the size of angle ∠CAD in terms of a and b.

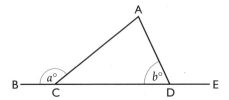

14 Ratio and proportion

It is said that over 2200 years ago a king handed over a known weight of gold to a goldsmith to make a crown. When the goldsmith produced the crown, the king was suspicious that, though the crown weighed the right amount, the goldsmith had swapped some gold for a less expensive metal. He asked the Greek mathematician Archimedes if he could solve the problem without destroying the crown. Archimedes found the solution to the problem when he stepped into a bath which was too full and watched the water spill out. He realised that if he dropped the crown into a full tank and measured the volume of the water that spilled out he would find the volume of the crown.

Archimedes realised that the weight of gold is proportional to its volume. One cubic centimetre of gold weighs 19·3 g.
Using these facts Archimedes was able to show the goldsmith was a cheat.

1 Looking back

Exercise 1.1

1   If the king had given the goldsmith 3000 g of gold, what volume would you expect the crown to be?

2   a   Share 1000 ml equally amongst   **i** 5   **ii** 10   **iii** 100 people.
    b   Divide 50 litres into 20 equal portions. Give your answer in millilitres.

3   A petrol tank holds 47 litres. In a controlled experiment, it takes a car 10 hours to go through this amount. If the fuel is used up in a regular manner, how much is used in an hour?

4 A 500 ml bottle of juice costs 20 pence.

    a What volume do you get per pence?

    b What volume would you expect for £1?

5 Using an old ruler, Jeff measured a 10 cm rod as being 4 inches.

    a What length, in inches, is 8 cm? (Give your answer to 1 d.p.)

    b How many centimetres make 12 inches?

2 Ratios

The beaker contains 50 ml of water and 150 ml of oil.
We say that the ratio of water to oil is 50 ml to 150 ml.
This ratio can be expressed as 1 part water to 3 parts oil.
We usually write

    water : oil $= 50 : 150 = 1 : 3$

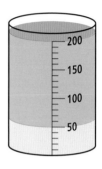

Note that once the units of both parts of the ratio are the
same then they can be dropped.
$1 : 3$ is called the **simplest form** of the ratio.

Example

A bag of sugar weighs 2 kg. A pot of jam weighs 600 g. Express the weight of
sugar to the weight of jam as a ratio in its simplest form.

  Sugar : Jam $= 2\,\text{kg} : 600\,\text{g}$
             $= 2000\,\text{g} : 600\,\text{g}$ (make units the same)
             $= 2000 : 600$ (drop units)
             $= 10 : 3$ (divide both sides by 200)

Exercise 2.1

1 Write each pair of numbers as a ratio in its simplest form.
    a $5 : 10$ **b** $6 : 2$ **c** $8 : 12$ **d** $2 : 10$ **e** $6 : 3$ **f** $15 : 20$

2 Jenna makes lime drinks by mixing
lime cordial and water.
Write the ratio of cordial : water in
its simplest form.

3 Rob and Rachel weigh their rucksacks before starting their walk.
Rob's rucksack weighs 15 kg and Rachel's weighs 9 kg.
Write the ratio of Rob's rucksack to Rachel's in its simplest form.

4 Martin takes 10 minutes to get to school.
Marie takes 8 minutes.
Find the ratio Martin's time : Marie's time in its simplest form.

5 Fast Films charge £4 to process a film. Posh Photos charge £6.
Write, in its simplest form, the ratio of the charges of Fast Films : Posh Photos.

6 When Cora drives to work it takes her 10 minutes.
On a fine day she cycles and it takes her 40 minutes.
Write the time ratio of driving : cycling in its simplest form.

7 The ratio of £1 to 20p is not 1 : 2.
The units must be the same.
What is the ratio £1 : 20p in its simplest form?

8 Jamila runs for 1 minute and then walks for 10 seconds.
Write down the ratio running time : walking time in its simplest form.

9 Write each of these ratios in its simplest form.
  a 1 mm : 1 cm   **b** 1 kg : 1 tonne
  c 1 minute : 1 hour **d** 1 ml : 1 litre
  e 1 m : 1 cm   **f** 1 hour : 1 day

10 Write the ratios, A : B, of the weights and volumes below in their simplest forms.

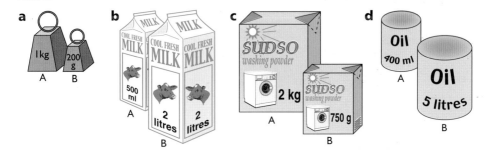

Challenge

Question: How many pairs of coins can you find whose values are in the ratio 1 : 20?

Answer: 1p : 20p   5p : £1   10p : £2

Repeat the question for the ratios:
a 1 : 2   **b** 1 : 4   **c** 1 : 5   **d** 1 : 10.

E

3 Unitary ratios

When the first part of a ratio is 1, the ratio is often referred to as a **unitary ratio**. This is a handy form for solving problems.

Example 1   Express the following as unitary ratios: a 2 : 6   b 4 : 9.

a 2 : 6
= 2 ÷ 2 : 6 ÷ 2
= 1 : 3

b 4 : 9
= 4 ÷ 4 : 9 ÷ 4
= 1 : 2·25

Example 2   The ratio of adults to children on a bus is 1 : 5.
There are 3 adults. How many children are there?

adult : children = 1 : 5
= 1 × 3 : 5 × 3 (to make number of adults 3)
= 3 : 15
So there are 15 children.

Example 3   The ratio of boys to girls in a class is 4 : 9.
There are 12 boys. How many girls are there?

boys : girls = 4 : 9
= 4 ÷ 4 : 9 ÷ 4 (to get unitary ratio of 1 boy)
= 1 : 2·25
= 1 × 12 : 2·25 × 12 (to make number of boys 12)
= 12 : 27
So there are 27 girls.

Exercise 3.1

1   Express each of the following as unitary ratios.
   a 2 : 8   b 4 : 12   c 5 : 30   d 5 : 32   e 10 : 12

2   The order of the numbers in a ratio is important. 2 : 1 is not the same as 1 : 2. Which of these could be correct?
   a age of father : age of son = 1 : 3
   b height of car : height of bus = 1 : 4
   c £1 : 10p = 1 : 10
   d population of USA : population of UK = 5 : 1

3   The ratio of Hannah's age to her sister Ruth is 1 : 3.
   Hannah is 4 years old.
   How old is Ruth? (Hint: multiply both sides by 4.)

4 a Laura is making orange drink for a party.
 She has 5 litres of juice.
   i Express the ratio juice : water as a unitary ratio.
   ii How many litres of water should be mixed with the juice?
 b How much juice is needed to mix with 12 litres of water?

ORANGE JUICE

DILUTE 1 PART
JUICE TO 4
PARTS WATER

5 Bronze is made from 2 parts copper and 1 part tin.
 a Copy and complete: tin : copper = … : …
 b How much copper is needed to mix with 10 kg of tin?
 c i Copy and complete: copper : tin = … : …
   ii Make this a unitary ratio (1 : …)
   iii How much tin is needed to mix with 8 kg of copper?

6 The Crazy Circus ticket price ratio is child : adult = 1 : 3.
 a A child pays £3·50 for a back seat.
 What will an adult pay?
 b A child pays £4·00 for a front seat.
 How much more does an adult pay for a front seat
 than a back seat?

7 A garden centre mixes fertiliser and soil in a ratio of 1 : 20.
 a How much soil is mixed with 100 kg of fertiliser?
 b Express the ratio of soil : fertiliser in the form 1 : …
 c How much fertiliser is needed to mix with 500 kg of soil?

8 The ratio of music time to advertisement time on a radio station is 10 : 1.
 If there are 20 hours of music, how long is spent on adverts?

9 A perfume company makes full-size bottles and miniatures.
 The ratio of their volumes is 50 : 1.
 a Express this in the form 1 : …
 b Calculate the volume of a miniature, in millilitres, when the full-size bottle
 holds 1 litre.

10 The ratio of a catering-size tin of baked beans to the medium-size tin is 5 : 2.
 A catering size tin weighs 2·2 kg.
 a Express 5 : 2 as a unitary ratio.
 b Calculate the weight of a medium-size tin in grams.

11 A liquid soap manufacturer produces full-size bottles and smaller free
 samples. The ratio of their volumes is 50 : 3.
 Calculate the volume of the free sample, in millilitres, when the full-size bottle
 holds 1 litre.

E

4 Sharing

Example 1

Karen and Ken distribute leaflets. Karen delivers 5 boxes and Ken delivers 3 boxes. They are paid a total of £32. To be fair they share it in the ratio 5 : 3. How much should each receive?

Answer: 5 shares for Karen and 3 for Ken make a total of 8 shares. Each share is worth £32 ÷ 8 = £4. Karen gets £4 × 5 = £20. Ken gets £4 × 3 = £12.

Example 2

Khalid wants to make 15 litres of juice for a party.
He does this by mixing concentrate and water in the ratio 2 : 3.
How much **i** concentrate **ii** water is needed?

Answer: The mixture is 2 parts concentrate and 3 parts water, making a total of 5 parts.
Each part is worth 15 litres ÷ 5 = 3 litres.
Khalid needs 2 × 3 = 6 litres of concentrate and 3 × 3 = 9 litres of water.

Exercise 4.1

1 Jane and Jake are paid £20 for gardening.
Jane works for 3 hours and Jake for 2 hours.

   a What is the ratio of Jane's work : Jake's work?

   b If they share the £20 fairly, how many shares will there be?

   c What is one share worth?

   d How should they share the £20?

2 Linda makes 12 litres of orange drink.
She mixes orange juice and water in the ratio of 1 : 3.

   a How many *parts* are involved?

   b How many litres are in one part?

   c How many litres of   **i** juice   **ii** water does she need?

3 Split:

   a £30 in the ratio 5 : 1   **b** 70 kg of bricks in the ratio 2 : 5

   c 48 metres of rope in the ratio 1 : 7   **d** 50 litres of oil in the ratio 7 : 3

   e 1024 g in the ratio 7 : 9   **f** 49 hours in the ratio 3 : 4

   g 36 tonnes in the ratio 1 : 8   **h** 420 ml in the ratio 3 : 11

4 Tom reckons the 24 hours in his day are split between sleeping and waking in the ratio 1 : 2. How many hours does he spend

   a asleep   **b** awake?

F

5   A weatherman reckons the ratio of dry to wet days in
    February (28 days) was 3 : 4. Calculate the number of

    a dry   **b** wet days in February.

6   Bronze is made from copper and tin mixed in the ratio of 1 : 2.
    Calculate the amount of
    a copper   **b** tin in a bronze church bell that weighs 240 kg.

7   In Salima's computer survey the ratio of PC owners to laptop owners is 7 : 5.
    To draw a pie chart of the data work out how many degrees represent
    a PC owners   **b** laptop owners.

8   Lee is making apple crumble, using butter, sugar and flour in the ratio 1 : 1 : 2.
    a How many *parts* are involved?
    b What weight of each ingredient is needed for 500 g of crumble?

9   Four people pay the following amounts into a weekly lottery syndicate:
    Mr Green £1, Mr Smith £2, Mrs Parker £3 and Miss Yates £4.
    How much should each receive if they win a jackpot of £8 000 000?

Challenge

Allan, Brenda and Charlie share £52. Allan's share : Brenda's share = 1 : 2
Brenda's share : Charlie's share = 3 : 2
How much money does each person get?

F

---

5 Direct proportion

4 rows of bricks
make a wall 32 cm tall.

Ratio of rows = 4 : 5

5 rows of bricks
make a wall 40 cm tall.

Ratio of heights = 32 : 40
= 4 : 5

When two quantities change in the same ratio, the quantities are said to be
directly proportional.

The number of rows of bricks in a wall is directly proportional to the height of the
wall.

This can be used to solve problems.

Example 1

A wall with 4 rows of bricks is 32 cm high.
How high is a wall with 7 rows of bricks?

Answer: 4 rows   →   32 cm

          $4 \div 4 = 1$ row   → $32 \div 4 = 8$ cm

          $1 \times 7 = 7$ rows   → $8 \times 7 = 56$ cm

> Whatever steps we take to turn 4 rows into 7 rows, we repeat with the height, 32 cm.

Example 2

A packet of 4 biscuits costs 90p.
A packet of 6 biscuits costs 130p.
Is the number of biscuits directly proportional to the cost?

Answer:
Number of biscuits in 1st line : Number of biscuits in 2nd line $= 4 : 6 = 2 : 3$
Cost in 1st line : Cost in 2nd line $= 90 : 130 = 9 : 13$
Since $2 : 3 \neq 9 : 13$ we do not have direct proportion.

Exercise 5.1

1 Which of the following could be directly proportional?
    a   5 books cost £60
        8 books cost £96
    b   3 apples weigh 27 g
        2 apples weigh 20 g
    c   after 4 minutes the tea's temperature is 80 °C
        after 5 minutes the tea's temperature is 64 °C
    d   2 coins make a stack of height 16 mm
        7 coins make a stack of height 56 mm
    e   the car travelled 5 miles in 10 minutes
        the car travelled 30 miles in an hour

In each of the following, assume the quantities are in direct proportion.

2 Margaret buys 7 books for £56.
    a   How much will it cost her for 9 of the same books?
    b   How many books will she get for £96?

3 The caterers make 60 sandwiches when they expect
    15 people.
    a   How many sandwiches will they make when they cater
        for 23 people?
    b   If they make 28 sandwiches, how many people are they expecting?

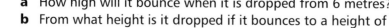

4 When a ball is dropped from a height of 4 metres it bounces to a height of
    3 metres.
    a   How high will it bounce when it is dropped from 6 metres?
    b   From what height is it dropped if it bounces to a height of 12 metres?

5 When a 50 g weight is hung on an elastic band, the band stretches by 4 cm.
  a By how much will it stretch if a 60 g weight is hung on it?
  b What weight will make it stretch by 6 cm?

6 2 litres of soup weigh 3 kg.
  a What will 5 litres of soup weigh?
  b What volume has 15 kg of soup?

6 Graphing direct proportion

Look again at the brick wall …

Number of rows of bricks	0	1	2	3	4	5
Height of wall (cm)	0	8	16	24	32	40

If the height of the wall is graphed against the number of rows of bricks, a straight line is produced.

Since a wall with 0 rows will have 0 height, the straight line will pass through the origin.

This is another test for direct proportion.

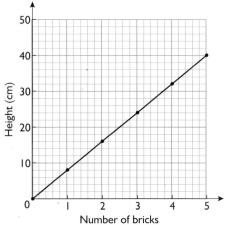

If two quantities are graphed, and a straight line passing through the origin is produced, then the two quantities are in direct proportion.

F

Exercise 6.1

1 **a** Copy and complete the table.

Number of copies	0	1	2	3	4	5
Cost (pence)						

Photocopies 5p a sheet

  b Draw a graph to illustrate the table.
  c How can you tell that the cost is directly proportional to the number of copies made?

2 Weights are hung on a spring and the stretch of the spring is measured.

Weight (kg)	0	1	2	3	4	5
Stretch (cm)	0	1·4	2·8	4·2	5·6	7·0

  a Draw a graph to illustrate the table.
  b What can be said about the weight on a spring and the amount the spring stretches?
  c How far would you expect the spring to stretch when 7 kg is hung on it?

1 kg

3 The table shows the charges made by a taxi service.

Distance (km)	5	6	7	8	9	10
Cost (£)	7	8	9	10	11	12

  a Draw a graph to illustrate the table.
  b Is it a straight line graph?
  c Is the cost directly proportional to the distance?
  d What feature of the graph is used to help you make your decision?

4 Buy four get one extra free! This special offer was printed on the side of cola cans. A can of cola costs £1.
  a Make a table to show the cost of 1 to 10 cans of cola.
  b Draw a graph to illustrate the table.
  c Say, with reasons, whether or not the cost is directly proportional to the number of cans.

5 Every 10 grams of margarine contain 8 grams of fat.
  a Make a table to show the fat content of
    i 0 g   **ii** 10 g   **iii** 20 g
    iv 30 g   **v** 40 g of margarine.
  b Make a graph of the table.
  c What is the fat content of 35 g of margarine? How do you feel justified in giving this answer?

7 Inverse proportion

If 4 people share a lottery jackpot they each get £250 000.
If 8 people share the jackpot they each get £125 000.

Ratio of people = 4 : 8   Ratio of shares = 250 000 : 125 000
            = 1 : 2   = 2 : 1

National Lottery
JACKPOT
£1 000 000

As the number of people doubles, the share halves.

When this happens we say the two quantities are in **inverse proportion**.

The share of the jackpot is inversely proportional to the number of winners.

Example

Caterers have provided enough sandwiches so that if 15 people turn up they can have 4 each.
However, 20 people turn up.
How many sandwiches can they each have?

15 people → 4 sandwiches each
1 person   → $4 \times 15 = 60$ sandwiches to himself
20 people → $60 \div 20 = 3$ sandwiches each

Exercise 7.1

1 A soft drink manufacturer makes a batch of lemonade.
   If he chooses to bottle it in 440 ml portions he will use 100 bottles.

   a How much lemonade has he made?

   b If he chooses instead to put it in 500 ml bottles, how many bottles will he need?

   c A batch of tomato juice is made and if put in 240 ml portions, 200 bottles will be required. How many bottles would be needed if it is made up in 300 ml portions instead?

2 A batch of square tiles can be used to cover a rectangle which is 40 tiles wide by 90 tiles long.

   a The batch will also make a rectangle which is 30 tiles wide.
   How long is this rectangle?

   b How wide would the rectangle be which is 60 tiles long and made from the same batch of tiles?

3 A music producer has calculated that if she uses tracks which are 3 minutes long then she can expect to get 16 tracks onto a CD.
   How many tracks of 4 minutes long can she expect to get on the CD?

4 Nick is putting a fence round his garden. He has calculated that if he buys 3 metre lengths he will need 14 such sections.
   How many sections will he need for the job if he buys 2 metre lengths instead?

5 At £10 a book, the maths teacher has enough money for 30 books. How many books can he buy if the cost of a book goes up by £2?

6 With six workers, the foreman has worked out he needs 90 hours to do a job. How many more workers will he need to enlist if he wants the job done in 60 hours?

8 Mixed examples

Example 1

Direct proportion

A keyboard operator types 200 words in 5 minutes.
How many words will he type in 8 minutes?

5 minutes   →   200 words
1 minute   → $200 \div 5 = 40$ words
8 minutes   → $40 \times 8 = 320$ words

Example 2

Inverse proportion
At 4 km/h it takes Jo 30 minutes to walk to work.
How long would it take if she walked at 6 km/h?

4 km/h	→	30 minutes
1 km/h	→	$30 \times 4 = 120$ minutes
6 km/h	→	$120 \div 6 = 20$ minutes

Note:
In direct proportion, if one quantity doubles the other quantity doubles.
With indirect proportion, if one doubles the other halves.

Exercise 8.1

1 Say whether each is an example of direct or of inverse proportion.
 a The number of workers and the time taken for a task.
 b The time taken to knit scarfs of different lengths.
 c The number of dollars that can be bought for different amounts of pounds.
 d The share of a lottery first prize and the number of winners.
 e The distance walked and the time taken (at the same speed).
 f The speed on the trip to school and the time taken.

2 If 3 kg of potatoes cost 60p, how much will 5 kg cost?

3 Six painters take 10 days to decorate the school building. How long would five take?

4 Five students share the school lottery prize and receive £16 each.
 a If there was only one winner how much would he or she receive?
 b How much would **i** 2 **ii** 8 winners receive?

5 At the travel agency, Theresa exchanges £20 and receives €36.
How much would she receive for £50?

6 Jack takes 20 minutes to cycle to school at 12 km/h.
How long would it take in a bus travelling at 30 km/h?

7 Eunice knits 400 stitches in 15 minutes.
At the same speed:
 a how long would it take to knit 600 stitches?
 b how many stitches would she knit in 24 minutes?

8 Organisers of a mountaineering expedition have bought enough supplies to last 12 people 20 days. Using the supplies at the same rate:
 a how long would the supplies last 16 people?
 b how many people could go on an expedition lasting 24 days?

CHECK-UP

1 Write these ratios in their simplest form.

   a 6 : 18   **b** £2 : 40p   **c** 1 cm : 8 mm   **d** 750 g : 1 kg

2 At a party, the ratio of old favourites to new sounds played by the DJ is 5 : 2. How many

   a new sound records should he mix with 15 old favourites

   b old favourites should he play with 8 new sound records?

3 Bernie the long distance runner can keep a steady pace for a long time. The table shows the distance Bernie has run every 10 minutes since she started the race.

Time (min)	0	10	20	30	40
Distance (km)	0	2	4	6	8

   a Draw a graph of distance against time.
      Explain how the graph shows that this is an example of direct proportion.

   b At this speed
      i how far has she run after 35 minutes
      ii how long will it take her to run 12 km?

4 To make purple paint Miss Davies mixes red and blue paint in the ratio 4 : 3.
Calculate the amount of

   a red   **b** blue paint
needed to make 140 ml of purple paint.

5 Mrs Kenyon buys eight calculators for £38·40.
How much would five calculators cost?

6 It takes four lorries 15 trips each to carry the stone needed for some road repairs. If five lorries were used, how many trips would each one have to make?

7 At Riverbank High the rule for school trips is that the ratio of staff to students should not be less than 1 : 8.

   a What is the minimum number of staff required for 56 students?

   b What is the maximum number of students that could go with nine staff?

E
F

15 Fractions and percentages

The Rhind Papyrus shows that Egyptians were using fractions as early as 2000 BC.

They only used unit fractions such as one half, one third and one quarter.

Many people now call such fractions Egyptian fractions.

The symbol ⌒ written above a number meant 1 divided by that number.

In hieroglyphics $\frac{1}{4}$ is shown as and $\frac{1}{8}$ as ⌒ |||| ||||

There was one exception and that was $\frac{2}{3}$, which was shown as ⊕

This idea lasted around the Mediterranean for about 2000 years.

1 Looking back ◄◄

Exercise 1.1

1 $\frac{1}{10}$ of an iceberg is supposed to be above the surface. What fraction should be below?

2 Calculate:

   a $\frac{1}{3}$ of 60 g   b $\frac{1}{4}$ of 20 litres   c $\frac{1}{5}$ of 35 m

   d $\frac{1}{10}$ of 300 ml   e $\frac{1}{20}$ of 400 tonnes   f $\frac{1}{100}$ of £3000

   g $\frac{1}{7}$ of 77 km   h $\frac{1}{50}$ of 200 kg

3 Write these percentages as decimals:

   a 1%   b 8%   c 10%

   d 25%   e 60%   f 250%

4 $\frac{1}{5} = 1 \div 5 = 0{\cdot}2 = 0{\cdot}2 \times 100\% = 20\%$.
In a similar way, express the following
   i as a decimal fraction   **ii** as a percentage.

   a $\frac{3}{100}$ **b** $\frac{3}{20}$ **c** $\frac{3}{4}$ **d** $\frac{2}{5}$ **e** $1\frac{1}{2}$ **f** $2\frac{1}{4}$

5 $\frac{3}{8}$ of a company's work force are women. There are 32 employees.
How many are

   a women   **b** men?

6 A supermarket's records show that $\frac{1}{100}$ of its customers are dissatisfied with its service. Out of 600 customers how many would you expect to be dissatisfied?

7 At the Cosmic Car factory $\frac{1}{20}$ of their output goes to the USA.
In a month when they make 800 cars, how many are sold in the USA?

2 Finding a fraction of an amount

Example 1

Calculate   **a** $\frac{1}{8}$ of £72   **b** $\frac{7}{8}$ of £72

a $\frac{1}{8}$ of £72 = £72 ÷ 8 = £9

b $\frac{7}{8}$ of £72 = (£72 ÷ 8) × 7 = £9 × 7 = £63

Example 2

Calculate $\frac{5}{9}$ of 54

$\frac{5}{9}$ of 54 = (54 ÷ 9) × 5 = 6 × 5 = 30

Exercise 2.1

1 Calculate:

   a $\frac{1}{2}$ of £9   **b** $\frac{1}{4}$ of £50   **c** $\frac{3}{4}$ of £60   **d** $\frac{4}{5}$ of £150

   e $\frac{3}{10}$ of £5   **f** $\frac{5}{8}$ of £120   **g** $\frac{2}{3}$ of £6000   **h** $\frac{5}{6}$ of £1800

   i $\frac{3}{20}$ of £6000   **j** $\frac{11}{12}$ of £360   **k** $\frac{-7}{100}$ of £50 000.

2 Mrs Flower plants 400 tulip bulbs. $\frac{7}{8}$ of these grow. How many is this?

3 Approximately $\frac{9}{10}$ of the population are right-handed.
Estimate the number of right-handed people in

   a a class of 30   **b** a school of 1200 students.

4 Amy is reading a book which has 240 pages.
Calculate the number of pages read when she is

   a $\frac{3}{10}$ **b** $\frac{5}{8}$ **c** $\frac{3}{4}$ through the book.

5 The pie chart shows that $\frac{2}{3}$ of the earth's surface is water and $\frac{1}{3}$ is land.
There are 360° in a circle.
What size of angle is needed to represent

a   the water

b   the land?

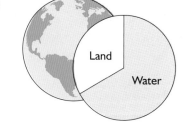

Land

Water

6 A maternity hospital's records show that $\frac{51}{100}$ of births are boys.

a   What fraction of births are girls?

b   Calculate the number of
   i   boys
   ii   girls they should expect out of 6400 births.

7 A video tape lasts for 180 minutes. A film is recorded on $\frac{7}{12}$ of it.
Calculate

a   the length of the film

b   the time left free for further recording.

8 Which of these is greater?

a $\frac{3}{5}$ of 450 or $\frac{5}{8}$ of 480

b $\frac{4}{7}$ of 420 or $\frac{5}{12}$ of 600

c $\frac{9}{10}$ of 800 or $\frac{5}{6}$ of 900

9 a   Which is greater, $\frac{5}{7}$ or $\frac{7}{9}$? (Hint: consider $\frac{5}{7}$ of 63 and $\frac{7}{9}$ of 63.)

b   Which is greater,
   i $\frac{8}{11}$ or $\frac{7}{10}$
   ii $\frac{11}{12}$ or $\frac{37}{40}$?

10 Gordon pays $\frac{3}{20}$ of his wages in tax.
Calculate the amount of tax he pays in

a   a week when he earns £475

b   a month when he earns £2640

c   a year when he earns £28 650.

11 Mrs Henderson has lectured for 33 years.
Her yearly pension is $\frac{33}{80}$ of £28 000.
Calculate her   a yearly   b monthly pension.

12 Mr Yates works for a shipping company, earns £30 000 and is about to retire.

a   He will receive a payment of $\frac{7}{20}$ of £30 000 when he retires.

b   He also gets a yearly pension which is $\frac{23}{50}$ of £30 000.
Calculate these amounts.

E

3 Calculating a percentage of an amount

Example 1   Find 16% of £45.

10% of £45 = £4·50 ($\frac{1}{10}$ of 100%)
5% of £45 = £2·25 ($\frac{1}{2}$ of 10%)
1% of £45 = £0·45 ($\frac{1}{10}$ of 10%)
──────────────────────────
16% of £45 = £7·20 (10% + 5% + 1%)

$16 \div 100 \times 45 = 7 \cdot 20$
16% of £45 = £7·20

Example 2   Find 45% of £60.

50% of £60 = £30·00 ($\frac{1}{2}$ of 100%)
5% of £60 = £3·00 ($\frac{1}{10}$ of 50%)
──────────────────────────
45% of £60 = £27·00 (50% − 5%)

$45 \div 100 \times 60 = 27$
45% of £45 = £27·00

Example 3   Find $17\frac{1}{2}$% of £560.

10% of £560 = £56·00 ($\frac{1}{10}$ of 100%)
5% of £560 = £28·00 ($\frac{1}{2}$ of 10%)
$2\frac{1}{2}$% of £560 = £14·00 ($\frac{1}{2}$ of 5%)
──────────────────────────
$17\frac{1}{2}$% of £560 = £98·00 (10% + 5% + $2\frac{1}{2}$%)

$17 \cdot 5 \div 100 \times 560 = 98$
17·5% of £560 = £98·00

Exercise 3.1

E

1 Find 10% of
  a £40   **b** £7   **c** £250   **d** £9600   **e** £6·50   **f** £0·60.

2 Write down
  i 10%   **ii** 20%   **iii** 5%   **iv** 15%   **v** 25%   **vi** 75%   **vii** 35%
  of   **a** £60   **b** £300   **c** £8.

3 1% of £1 is 1p. Find:
  a 1% of £7   **b** 1% of £35   **c** 4% of £1
  d 4% of £9   **e** 1% of 500 kg   **f** 1% of 8000 litres
  g 2% of 600 m   **h** 2% of 4000 tonnes.

4 Sharon is paid £480 for a week's work. Of this 10% goes on fares and lunches. 25% is to pay her rent. 30% pays for food and bills. She saves 15% and the rest she spends on entertainment. Calculate how much Sharon spends on each item.

5 Pat and Tim play tennis.

Player	Total no. of first serves	% of good first serves
Pat	140	65%
Tim	160	60%

  a Work out the number of good first serves for each player to find who was better at these.
  b Find the difference between the number of good serves.

6 The table compares the weekly performance of two train companies.

Company	Total no. of trains	% on time
Rotten Rail	840	45%
Terrible Trains	700	52%

  a Calculate the number of trains that are on time for each company.

  b Which company has the better performance? Explain.

7 Shane carries out a survey of 400 people to find their favourite type of book. The table shows his results.

Type of book	Percentage
Horror	10%
Travel	5%
Romance	30%
Crime	35%
Other	20%

Calculate the number of people in the survey who prefer each type.

8 Len manages a forest of 4000 trees. Of these 60% are fir trees, 15% are oak, 20% are beech and the remaining 5% are lime trees. Calculate the number of each type of tree.

9 Mrs Wilson pays 5% tax on her fuel bills.
Calculate the tax on her
  a gas bill of £124   **b** electric bill of £94.

10 In a sale, prices are reduced by $12\frac{1}{2}$%.
Calculate **i** the amount saved   **ii** the price to pay on these goods:
  a a toaster costing £18
  b a fridge priced at £370
  c an electric hob at £165.

11 The Dragons basketball team play 40 matches in the season.
They win 55%, draw 22·5% and lose the rest.
Calculate the number of   **a** wins   **b** draws   **c** losses.

12 The table shows the amount of carbohydrates and fat in a bag of crisps.
Calculate the weight of
  a carbohydrate   **b** fat
in a 40 g bag.

Typical values	Content
Carbohydrate	48·7%
Fat	34·8%

E

4 Using percentages

Marie earns £300 a week.
She receives a pay rise of 4%.
Calculate her new weekly wage.

Pay rise = 4% of £300 = £12 (4 ÷ 100 × 300)
New pay = £300 + £12 = £312

A shop offers a discount of 8% on a computer system priced at £1200.
What is the discounted price?

Discount = 8% of £1200 = £96 (8 ÷ 100 × 1200)
New price = £1200 − £96 = £1104

Exercise 4.1

1 Tanya's weekly wage is £200. She is given a rise of 5%.
   Calculate

   a the extra amount she receives each week

   b her new weekly wage.

2 In the sales, the cost of a pair of jeans is dropped by 20%.
   The normal price is £45.
   Calculate   a the discount   b the sale price.

3 There are 240 houses in the Green Forest estate. Another 15% are built.
   Calculate   a the number of new houses   b the new total of houses.

4 Mrs Baker invests £4000 in a savings account which earns 10% interest a year.

   a What is 10% of £4000?

   b What is the total amount in her account at the end of the year?
      (Total = £4000 + interest)

5 Mr Page invests £5000 in a bank account which pays 4% a year interest.

   a Calculate the interest earned in one year.

   b He leaves the interest in his account, so it is added to his £5000.
      How much is in his account at the end of the year?

   c Calculate the interest his money will earn in the second year.

6 Cara's old car is valued at £720.
   Each year its value drops by 10%.
   Calculate the value of her car after
   a 1 year   b 2 years   c 3 years.

F

7 A greengrocer bought potatoes at 95p per kilogram.

    a What should he sell them at if he wants to make 20% profit?

    b He buys carrots at £1·24 per kilogram.
       What should he set the selling price at to make an 18% profit?
       (Give your answer correct to the nearest penny.)

8 A jacket is sold in a sale for £123·20. The discount was 12%.
What was the original price? Do the following to find out.

    a With a discount of 12%, the sale price is 88% of the original cost. Why?

    b To calculate 88% of the original price we could use this number machine:

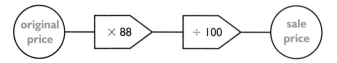

    Reverse the machine to find the original cost from the sale price.
    Draw this reversed machine.

    c Calculate the original price.

9 Mrs James bought a diamond brooch a year ago.
It has increased in value by 15% to £460.

    a Why is the value now 115% of the original cost?

    b How much did she pay for it?

10 Mr Penny collects rare stamps.
The one he bought a year ago has decreased in value by 40% and is now
worth £120.

    a What percentage of the original value is the stamp worth now?

    b How much did he pay for it?

11 House prices in the last year have risen by 5%.
The Grants' house is now valued at £94 500.
Calculate its value one year ago.

12 The population of the village of New Bush has increased
by 2·5% in the last year. It is now 656.
Calculate the population one year ago.

Example 3

A pen is bought for £2·00 and sold for £3·50.
Calculate the profit as a *percentage* of the cost price.

Profit = 3·50 − 2·00 = 1·50

$$\text{Percentage profit} = \frac{1\cdot50}{2\cdot00} \times 100 = 75\%$$

Example 4

A book is bought for £12·50 and sold at a sale for £8·25.
Calculate the loss as a *percentage* of the cost price.

Loss = 12·50 − 8·25 = 4·25

Percentage loss = $\dfrac{4·25}{12·50} \times 100 = 34\%$

Exercise 4.2

1 In each case express the first number as a percentage of the second.
   a 5; 20   **b** 4; 80   **c** 12; 300   **d** 26; 50   **e** 9; 25

2 Last year there were 1200 students at a school. This year there are only 1140.
   a Calculate the drop in population.
   b Express this drop as a percentage of last year's school population.

3 Last year James earned £790 a week.
   This year, after a pay rise, he is earning £853·20 a week.
   a What is his wage increase?
   b Express this rise as a percentage of last year's wage.

4 At the sweets factory, a rectangular slab of toffee 12 cm by 25 cm is passed through rollers.
   When it comes out it is a rectangle 24 cm by 55 cm.
   a Calculate the area of the slab
     i before   **ii** after passing through the rollers.
   b Calculate the increase in area.
   c Express this as a percentage of the original area.

5 A shrub was 54 cm high when first planted.
   A year later its height was measured as 62 cm.
   Calculate the percentage increase in height based on the height when planted.
   Give your answer correct to 1 decimal place.

6 A block of ice is weighed every hour.
   Start 500 g, 1st hour 450 g, 2nd hour 405 g, 3rd hour 324 g, 4th hour 162 g.
   a Calculate the percentage loss of weight based on the weight at the start of each hour for
     i the 1st hour   **ii** the 2nd hour   **iii** the 3rd hour   **iv** the 4th hour.
   b Is the percentage weight loss a constant?
   c Calculate the percentage weight loss over the whole period based on the weight at the start.

F

Investigation

Barbara buys a vase for £100. In the first year its value increases by 10%.
In the next year its value decreases by 10%.
Is the vase back to its original value of £100?
Show all working.

5 Rational numbers

When a number can be expressed as a common fraction it is called **rational**.

$\frac{3}{4}$ is rational since it is $\frac{3}{4}$; 6 is rational since it is $\frac{6}{1}$;

0·4 is rational since it is $\frac{4}{10}$; 0·123 is $\frac{123}{1000}$; 0·000 349 is $\frac{349}{1\,000\,000}$

When the digits of a decimal fraction repeat forever, the number is called a
recurring decimal. All recurring decimals are rational.

Example

Express: a   0·444 444 4 ...   b   0·414 141 4 ... as a common fraction.

a $x = 0·444\,444\,4\,...$
$\Rightarrow x = 0·4 + 0·044\,444\,44\,...$
$\Rightarrow 10x = 4 + 0·444\,444\,4\,...$
$\Rightarrow 10x = 4 + x$
$\Rightarrow 9x = 4$
$\Rightarrow x = \frac{4}{9}$
$0·444\,444\,4\,... = \frac{4}{9}$

b $x = 0·414\,141\,4\,...$
$\Rightarrow x = 0·41 + 0·004\,141\,41\,...$
$\Rightarrow 100x = 41 + 0·414\,141\,...$
$\Rightarrow 100x = 41 + x$
$\Rightarrow 99x = 41$
$\Rightarrow x = \frac{41}{99}$
$0·414\,141\,4\,... = \frac{41}{99}$

Exercise 5.1

1 Show that the following are rational numbers by expressing them as common
fractions.

   a 7   **b** 0·6   **c** 0·72   **d** 0·05

   e 0·172   **f** 0·0981   **g** 7·3   **h** 0·009

   i 2·5   **j** 100   **k** 0·001 01

2 Express the following recurring fractions as common fractions.

   a 0·222 222 ...   **b** 0·777 777 7 ...   **c** 0·121 212 1 ...

   d 0·545 454 54 ...   **e** 0·123 123 ...   **f** 0·022 022 0 ...

   g 0·007 007 0 ...   **h** 0·405 405 4 ...   **i** 0·123 412 34 ...

   j 0·000 900 090 0 ...

3 Write these common fractions as decimal fractions.

a $\frac{1}{10}$ b $\frac{9}{10}$ c $\frac{1}{100}$ d $\frac{23}{100}$

e $\frac{30}{100}$ f $\frac{3}{1000}$ g $\frac{13}{1000}$ h $\frac{201}{1000}$

i $\frac{59}{1000}$ j $\frac{70}{1000}$

> **Reminder**
>
> $\frac{3}{10} = 3 \div 10 = 0{\cdot}3$

4 Change each common fraction to an equivalent decimal fraction by division.

a $\frac{1}{2}$ $(= 1 \div 2)$ b $\frac{1}{4}$ $(= 1 \div 4)$ c $\frac{3}{5}$ $(= 3 \div 5)$

d $\frac{4}{5}$ e $\frac{1}{8}$ f $\frac{3}{8}$ g $\frac{7}{8}$

5 Write each decimal fraction as a common fraction.

a $0{\cdot}1$ b $0{\cdot}7$ c $0{\cdot}9$

d $0{\cdot}01$ e $0{\cdot}09$ f $0{\cdot}17$

g $0{\cdot}59$ h $0{\cdot}009$ i $0{\cdot}201$

j $0{\cdot}017$ k $0{\cdot}57$ l $0{\cdot}07$

> **Reminders**
>
> $0{\cdot}3 = \frac{3}{10}$
>
> $0{\cdot}03 = \frac{3}{100}$
>
> $0{\cdot}23 = \frac{23}{100}$
>
> $0{\cdot}023 = \frac{23}{1000}$
>
> $0{\cdot}25 = \frac{25}{100}$
> $= \frac{1 \times 25}{4 \times 25} = \frac{1}{4}$

6 Write as common fractions *in their simplest form*.

a $0{\cdot}2$ b $0{\cdot}6$ c $0{\cdot}5$

d $0{\cdot}02$ e $0{\cdot}8$ f $0{\cdot}14$

g $0{\cdot}35$ h $0{\cdot}006$ i $0{\cdot}018$

j $0{\cdot}055$ k $0{\cdot}035$ l $0{\cdot}105$

m $0{\cdot}614$ n $0{\cdot}25$ o $0{\cdot}16$

p $0{\cdot}24$ q $0{\cdot}40$ r $0{\cdot}64$

7 Copy the table and fill in the blanks.
(Write the common fractions in their simplest form.)

Decimals	0·5	0·75		0·3		0·15		0·48
Fractions	$\frac{1}{2}$		$\frac{6}{10}$		$\frac{3}{100}$		$\frac{2}{5}$	

Decimals	0·8		0·125		0·84		0·175	
Fractions		$\frac{5}{8}$		$\frac{19}{1000}$		$\frac{13}{20}$		$\frac{1}{50}$

8 In each pair, which rational number is greater?

a $\frac{1}{4}$ or $0{\cdot}2$ b $\frac{3}{10}$ or $0{\cdot}04$ c $\frac{7}{100}$ or $0{\cdot}08$ d $\frac{3}{5}$ or $0{\cdot}6$

e $0{\cdot}008$ or $\frac{1}{100}$ f $0{\cdot}045$ or $\frac{1}{20}$ g $0{\cdot}85$ or $\frac{7}{8}$ h $0{\cdot}380$ or $\frac{3}{8}$

9 For each pair of numbers
  i express each in decimal form
  ii add the numbers together and divide by 2
  iii express your answer as a common fraction to give you a fraction halfway between the two.

a $\frac{1}{2}, \frac{1}{4}$ b $\frac{1}{3}, \frac{1}{9}$ c $\frac{2}{5}, \frac{1}{8}$

d $\frac{1}{2}, \frac{1}{6}$ e $\frac{3}{4}, \frac{2}{5}$ f $\frac{5}{6}, \frac{5}{90}$

F

6 Equivalent fractions and mixed numbers

$$1 \div 4 = 2 \div 8 = 3 \div 12 = 0 \cdot 25 \text{ so } \tfrac{1}{4} = \tfrac{2}{8} = \tfrac{3}{12} = 0 \cdot 25$$

When fractions are worth the same we say they are **equivalent**.
We can find a fraction equivalent to a given fraction by multiplying both numerator and denominator by the same number.

Example 1

Find four fractions equivalent to $\frac{3}{4}$.

$$\frac{3 \times 5}{4 \times 5} = \frac{15}{20} \qquad \frac{3 \times 2}{4 \times 2} = \frac{6}{8} \qquad \frac{3 \times 12}{4 \times 12} = \frac{36}{48} \qquad \frac{3 \times 15}{4 \times 15} = \frac{45}{60}$$

Example 2

Express   **a** $\dfrac{5}{6}$ **b** 7 as 24ths

a $\dfrac{5 \times 4}{6 \times 4} = \dfrac{20}{24}$ **b** $7 = \dfrac{7}{1} = \dfrac{7 \times 24}{1 \times 24} = \dfrac{168}{24}$

When the numerator is smaller than the denominator, the fraction is called a **proper** fraction.

When the numerator is larger than the denominator, the fraction is called an **improper** fraction.

When a number is made up of a whole number part and a fractional part it is called a **mixed number**.

Example 3

Express $4\frac{2}{3}$ as an improper fraction.

$4\frac{2}{3} = 4 + \frac{2}{3} = \frac{4}{1} + \frac{2}{3} = \frac{4 \times 3}{1 \times 3} + \frac{2}{3} = \frac{12}{3} + \frac{2}{3} = \frac{14}{3}$

4 and 2 thirds = 14 thirds

Example 4

Express $\frac{26}{7}$ as a mixed number.

$\frac{26}{7} = 26 \div 7 = 3$ remainder $5 = 3\frac{5}{7}$

Exercise 6.1

1 Find three fractions that equal   **a** $\frac{1}{2}$ **b** $\frac{2}{3}$ **c** $\frac{3}{10}$.

2 Write in their simplest form:

  a $\frac{15}{20}$ **b** $\frac{2}{20}$ **c** $\frac{6}{10}$ **d** $\frac{5}{15}$ **e** $\frac{3}{12}$

  f $\frac{8}{20}$ **g** $\frac{8}{12}$ **h** $\frac{25}{40}$ **i** $\frac{24}{40}$ **j** $\frac{16}{24}$

  k $\frac{18}{24}$ **l** $\frac{9}{27}$ **m** $\frac{4}{100}$ **n** $\frac{10}{100}$ **o** $\frac{50}{100}$

  p $\frac{60}{100}$ **q** $\frac{25}{100}$ **r** $\frac{90}{100}$ **s** $\frac{75}{100}$ **t** $\frac{85}{100}$

3 Write the following as fractions in their simplest form.

  a 20 out of 30 days in June are workdays.

  b 35 out of 100 customers at the clothes shop are men.

  c 24 out of 30 trees in the park are oak.

  d 16 out of 40 students fail their maths test.

  e 64 out of 80 teachers have no sense of humour.

4 **a** Express as twentieths: **i** $\frac{1}{4}$ **ii** $\frac{2}{5}$ **iii** $\frac{7}{10}$ **iv** $\frac{1}{2}$

  b Express as twelfths: **i** $\frac{3}{4}$ **ii** $\frac{1}{6}$ **iii** $\frac{2}{3}$ **iv** $\frac{1}{2}$

  c Express as thirty-fifths: **i** $\frac{2}{7}$ **ii** $\frac{1}{5}$ **iii** $\frac{4}{5}$ **iv** $\frac{6}{7}$

5 By first expressing each as twenty-fourths, arrange these fractions in order, lowest first.

   $\frac{1}{2}$ $\frac{3}{4}$ $\frac{5}{8}$ $\frac{5}{12}$ $\frac{11}{24}$ $\frac{3}{8}$ $\frac{2}{3}$

6 Use equivalent fractions to express each pair with a common denominator. For example, with $\frac{3}{8}$ and $\frac{2}{3}$ we can write $\frac{9}{24}$ and $\frac{16}{24}$.

  a $\frac{2}{5}$ and $\frac{4}{7}$ **b** $\frac{2}{3}$ and $\frac{4}{5}$ **c** $\frac{1}{2}$ and $\frac{7}{9}$

  d $\frac{5}{8}$ and $\frac{3}{4}$ **e** $\frac{1}{3}$ and $\frac{7}{18}$ **f** $\frac{5}{9}$ and $\frac{2}{45}$

7 Express each of these improper fractions as a mixed number.

  a $\frac{11}{5}$ **b** $\frac{9}{7}$ **c** $\frac{21}{4}$ **d** $\frac{56}{9}$

  e $\frac{75}{7}$ **f** $\frac{26}{3}$ **g** $\frac{21}{2}$ **h** $\frac{113}{12}$

8 Change each of these mixed numbers to an improper fraction.

  a $4\frac{2}{5}$ **b** $6\frac{1}{7}$ **c** $3\frac{3}{4}$ **d** $4\frac{5}{9}$

  e $8\frac{2}{7}$ **f** $12\frac{1}{3}$ **g** $23\frac{1}{2}$ **h** $9\frac{4}{5}$

F

7 Adding and subtracting common fractions

To add or subtract common fractions we make sure they have a **common denominator**.

Using the **lowest common denominator** you can find keeps things simple.

Example 1

$$\frac{1}{5} + \frac{3}{5} = \frac{4}{5} \dots 1 \text{ fifth plus 3 fifths gives 4 fifths.}$$

Example 2

$$\frac{7}{8} - \frac{3}{8} = \frac{4}{8} = \frac{1}{2} \dots 7 \text{ eighths minus 3 eighths gives 4 eighths or a half.}$$

Example 3

$$\frac{1}{3} + \frac{2}{5} = \frac{1 \times 5}{3 \times 5} + \frac{2 \times 3}{5 \times 3} = \frac{5}{15} + \frac{6}{15} = \frac{11}{15} \dots \text{ the lowest common denominator is 15.}$$

Example 4

$$\frac{3}{4} - \frac{1}{8} = \frac{3 \times 2}{4 \times 2} - \frac{1}{8} = \frac{6}{8} - \frac{1}{8} = \frac{5}{8} \dots \text{ the lowest common denominator is 8.}$$

Exercise 7.1

1 Calculate and simplify your answer if possible.

a $\frac{1}{4} + \frac{1}{4}$ b $\frac{1}{8} + \frac{3}{8}$ c $\frac{1}{8} + \frac{5}{8}$ d $\frac{2}{5} + \frac{1}{5}$

e $\frac{2}{10} + \frac{3}{10}$ f $\frac{3}{5} + \frac{2}{5}$ g $\frac{4}{9} + \frac{2}{9}$ h $\frac{2}{7} + \frac{3}{7}$

i $\frac{5}{18} + \frac{1}{18}$ j $\frac{5}{21} + \frac{2}{21}$ k $\frac{3}{4} - \frac{1}{4}$ l $\frac{4}{5} - \frac{1}{5}$

m $\frac{7}{8} - \frac{1}{8}$ n $\frac{5}{6} - \frac{1}{6}$ o $\frac{9}{10} - \frac{3}{10}$ p $\frac{6}{7} - \frac{4}{7}$

q $\frac{7}{38} - \frac{3}{38}$ r $\frac{7}{9} - \frac{2}{9}$ s $\frac{7}{12} - \frac{1}{12}$ t $\frac{9}{22} - \frac{7}{22}$

2 Evaluate, making use of the lowest common denominator in each case.

a $\frac{1}{2} + \frac{1}{4}$ b $\frac{1}{2} + \frac{1}{3}$ c $\frac{1}{4} + \frac{1}{8}$ d $\frac{1}{5} + \frac{1}{4}$

e $\frac{1}{2} + \frac{1}{8}$ f $\frac{3}{5} + \frac{2}{7}$ g $\frac{5}{9} + \frac{2}{5}$ h $\frac{6}{7} + \frac{4}{11}$

i $\frac{5}{8} + \frac{1}{2}$ j $\frac{5}{6} + \frac{3}{8}$ k $\frac{1}{2} - \frac{1}{4}$ l $\frac{1}{2} - \frac{1}{3}$

m $\frac{1}{2} - \frac{1}{8}$ n $\frac{1}{3} - \frac{1}{4}$ o $\frac{1}{4} - \frac{1}{6}$ p $\frac{8}{9} - \frac{2}{3}$

q $\frac{5}{12} - \frac{1}{4}$ r $\frac{3}{9} - \frac{2}{5}$ s $\frac{7}{8} - \frac{2}{5}$ t $\frac{15}{18} - \frac{2}{3}$

3 Mr Cook lists his overtime. What is his total for the week?

Day	Mon	Tues	Wed	Thur	Fri
Hours	1	$\frac{3}{4}$	$\frac{1}{2}$	$\frac{3}{4}$	$\frac{3}{4}$

4 At Oldport Station one day, $\frac{2}{3}$ of the trains arrive early, $\frac{1}{5}$ of the remainder arrive exactly on time and the rest are late.

    a What fraction are either on time or early?

    b What fraction are late?

5 Meg's garden is $\frac{1}{2}$ lawn, $\frac{3}{8}$ flower beds and the rest is for vegetables.

    a What fraction is used for vegetables?

    b Express as a fraction the difference between the ground given to lawn and to flowers.

6 The table shows the fractions of different colour crocuses in a park.

    a What fraction are purple?

    b As a fraction, how many more are white than yellow?

Crocuses

White	$\frac{2}{5}$
Yellow	$\frac{1}{4}$
Purple	the rest

Working with mixed numbers

Example 1

$\frac{3}{4} + \frac{5}{6}$

$= \frac{9}{12} + \frac{10}{12}$

$= \frac{19}{12}$

$= 1\frac{7}{12}$

Example 2

$2\frac{2}{5} + 3\frac{3}{4}$

$= 2 + \frac{2}{5} + 3 + \frac{3}{4}$

$= 5 + \frac{8}{20} + \frac{15}{20}$

$= 5 + \frac{23}{20}$

$= 5 + 1 + \frac{3}{20}$

$= 6\frac{3}{20}$

Example 3

$7\frac{3}{7} - 3\frac{1}{5}$

$= 7 + \frac{3}{7} - 3 - \frac{1}{5}$

$= 4 + \frac{15}{35} - \frac{7}{35}$

$= 4 + \frac{8}{35}$

$= 4\frac{8}{35}$

Example 4

$6\frac{2}{5} - 3\frac{2}{3}$

$= 6 + \frac{2}{5} - 3 - \frac{2}{3}$

$= 3 + \frac{6}{15} - \frac{10}{15}$

$= 3 - \frac{4}{15}$

$= 2\frac{11}{15}$

F

Exercise 7.2

1 Evaluate:

    a $\frac{3}{4} + \frac{3}{4}$ **b** $\frac{5}{8} + \frac{7}{8}$ **c** $1\frac{3}{4} + 2\frac{3}{4}$ **d** $3\frac{2}{3} + 5\frac{2}{3}$ **e** $4\frac{7}{10} + 2\frac{9}{10}$

    f $7\frac{2}{7} + 3\frac{3}{7}$ **g** $8\frac{3}{4} + 2\frac{1}{4}$ **h** $4\frac{5}{8} + 7\frac{3}{8}$ **i** $\frac{4}{7} + 4\frac{6}{7}$ **j** $6\frac{6}{9} + 8\frac{7}{9}$

    k $1\frac{1}{4} - \frac{3}{4}$ **l** $2\frac{1}{3} - \frac{2}{3}$ **m** $3\frac{1}{5} - 1\frac{4}{5}$ **n** $5\frac{3}{8} - 1\frac{7}{8}$ **o** $4\frac{3}{10} - 3\frac{7}{10}$

    p $7\frac{1}{5} - 3\frac{3}{5}$ **q** $5\frac{3}{7} - 3\frac{4}{7}$ **r** $8\frac{1}{9} - \frac{7}{9}$ **s** $10\frac{1}{8} - 6\frac{7}{8}$ **t** $2\frac{3}{8} - 1\frac{7}{8}$

2 Evaluate:

    a $1\frac{1}{2} + \frac{1}{4}$ **b** $2\frac{1}{3} + \frac{1}{2}$ **c** $3\frac{1}{4} + 1\frac{1}{3}$ **d** $2\frac{1}{5} + 4\frac{1}{4}$ **e** $3\frac{1}{8} + 4\frac{1}{16}$

    f $8\frac{3}{7} + 9\frac{2}{5}$ **g** $1\frac{4}{9} + 2\frac{2}{7}$ **h** $3\frac{7}{11} + 2\frac{5}{8}$ **i** $\frac{4}{5} + 9\frac{2}{3}$ **j** $2\frac{5}{7} + 9\frac{6}{11}$

    k $1\frac{3}{4} - \frac{1}{2}$ **l** $1\frac{1}{8} - \frac{7}{9}$ **m** $4\frac{1}{3} - 1\frac{4}{5}$ **n** $3\frac{1}{2} - 1\frac{1}{8}$ **o** $5\frac{1}{3} - 3\frac{3}{8}$

    p $6\frac{1}{9} - 2\frac{3}{7}$ **q** $10\frac{3}{8} - 3\frac{4}{5}$ **r** $7\frac{1}{4} - \frac{7}{11}$ **s** $9\frac{3}{10} - 6\frac{5}{9}$ **t** $3\frac{3}{7} - \frac{4}{5}$

3 Evaluate:

a $1\frac{1}{3} + \frac{1}{5} + 2\frac{2}{7}$ b $2\frac{1}{7} + \frac{1}{2} + 4\frac{2}{3}$ c $2\frac{1}{4} + 7\frac{2}{3} + 5\frac{1}{8}$ d $2\frac{1}{2} + 3\frac{1}{3} + 4\frac{1}{4}$

e $\frac{3}{5} + 2\frac{1}{10} + 1\frac{1}{7}$ f $3\frac{1}{8} + 2\frac{1}{4} + \frac{1}{2}$ g $4\frac{2}{3} + 1\frac{3}{8} + 7\frac{7}{9}$ h $\frac{2}{3} + 4\frac{1}{4} + \frac{5}{6}$

i $\frac{1}{3} + 1\frac{3}{4} - \frac{1}{2}$ j $3\frac{1}{2} + 1\frac{1}{4} - \frac{3}{5}$ k $1\frac{3}{5} + 2\frac{1}{2} - 1\frac{4}{7}$ l $5\frac{3}{4} + 1\frac{1}{3} - 1\frac{1}{4}$

m $4\frac{1}{9} - 1\frac{2}{7} + 3\frac{1}{2}$ n $6\frac{1}{8} - 4\frac{4}{5} + \frac{1}{3}$ o $5\frac{1}{12} - \frac{3}{4} + 4\frac{3}{8}$ p $7\frac{5}{6} - 3\frac{5}{9} + 2\frac{2}{3}$

4 Vic has two video tapes.
One lasts for $1\frac{1}{2}$ hours, the other for $2\frac{3}{4}$ hours.
What is the total time of the tapes?

5 Mel's racing bike tyre is $1\frac{1}{4}$ inches wide.
His mountain bike tyre is $1\frac{7}{8}$ inches wide.
Calculate the difference in width.

6 Calculate:

a the total weight of the suitcases.

b the difference in weight.

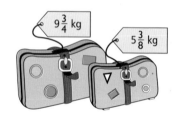

$9\frac{3}{4}$ kg $5\frac{3}{8}$ kg

7 Calculate the perimeter of each of these shapes.

a

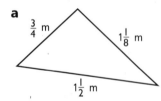

$\frac{3}{4}$ m $1\frac{1}{8}$ m $1\frac{1}{2}$ m

b

$1\frac{1}{5}$ m $2\frac{7}{10}$ m

Challenge

Start at the top and move from circle
to circle by going to a smaller fraction
each time.

List the fractions on your route in order.
Can you find a different route?

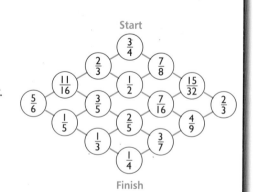

Start

$\frac{3}{4}$

$\frac{2}{3}$ $\frac{7}{8}$

$\frac{11}{16}$ $\frac{1}{2}$ $\frac{15}{32}$

$\frac{5}{6}$ $\frac{3}{5}$ $\frac{7}{16}$ $\frac{2}{3}$

$\frac{1}{5}$ $\frac{2}{5}$ $\frac{4}{9}$

$\frac{1}{3}$ $\frac{3}{7}$

$\frac{1}{4}$

Finish

8 Multiplying fractions

A square is split into thirds horizontally and into quarters vertically.

It is thus split into twelfths.

The shaded portion has an area of $\frac{6}{12}$ (by counting).
If we use the formula $A = lb$, then we get

$\frac{2}{3} \times \frac{3}{4} = \frac{6}{12}$

Similarly

  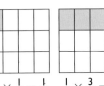

$\frac{1}{3} \times \frac{2}{4} = \frac{2}{12}$ $\frac{1}{3} \times \frac{1}{4} = \frac{1}{12}$ $\frac{1}{3} \times \frac{3}{4} = \frac{3}{12}$ $\frac{2}{3} \times \frac{4}{4} = \frac{8}{12}$

Exercise 8.1

1 The grid illustrates the product $\frac{3}{4} \times \frac{4}{5} = \frac{12}{20}$.
   Draw similar grids to illustrate:

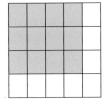

   a $\frac{1}{4} \times \frac{2}{5}$ **b** $\frac{2}{4} \times \frac{3}{5}$ **c** $\frac{3}{4} \times \frac{2}{5}$
   d $\frac{1}{4} \times \frac{1}{5}$ **e** $\frac{3}{4} \times \frac{5}{5}$

2 Draw grids to illustrate:

   a $\frac{1}{5} \times \frac{2}{3}$ **b** $\frac{2}{3} \times \frac{3}{7}$ **c** $\frac{1}{4} \times \frac{1}{6}$ **d** $\frac{1}{2} \times \frac{3}{7}$ **e** $\frac{3}{4} \times \frac{3}{4}$

> Note that we multiply the numerators to get the numerator of the product and multiply the denominators to get the denominator of the product.

3 Calculate each product, simplifying your answer where possible.

   a $\frac{1}{2} \times \frac{2}{3}$ **b** $\frac{3}{4} \times \frac{2}{3}$ **c** $\frac{1}{8} \times \frac{2}{3}$ **d** $\frac{3}{10} \times \frac{2}{3}$ **e** $\frac{4}{5} \times \frac{1}{2}$
   f $\frac{1}{4} \times \frac{2}{5}$ **g** $\frac{3}{5} \times \frac{5}{6}$ **h** $\frac{5}{8} \times \frac{4}{5}$ **i** $\frac{2}{5} \times \frac{3}{8}$ **j** $\frac{9}{10} \times \frac{1}{3}$
   k $\frac{5}{7} \times \frac{3}{4}$ **l** $\frac{8}{9} \times \frac{4}{7}$ **m** $\frac{5}{12} \times \frac{6}{15}$ **n** $\frac{9}{10} \times \frac{5}{6}$ **o** $\frac{6}{7} \times \frac{14}{15}$

4 A new pot of jam had $\frac{1}{2}$ kg of jam. It is now only $\frac{1}{4}$ full.
   What weight of jam is in the pot now?

5 In a wood, $\frac{2}{3}$ of the trees are broad leaved. Of these $\frac{9}{10}$ are oak trees.
   By considering a product, calculate the fraction of trees in the wood that are oak.

To multiply mixed numbers we must first express them as improper fractions.

Example 1

$2\frac{1}{4} \times 1\frac{2}{3}$

$= \frac{9}{4} \times \frac{5}{3}$

$= \frac{45}{12}$

$= \frac{15}{4}$

$= 3\frac{3}{4}$

Example 2

$(1\frac{3}{5})^2$

$= 1\frac{3}{5} \times 1\frac{3}{5}$

$= \frac{8}{5} \times \frac{8}{5}$

$= \frac{64}{25}$

$= 2\frac{14}{25}$

Exercise 8.2

1 Calculate each product and simplify where possible.

a $3\frac{1}{3} \times \frac{2}{5}$ **b** $\frac{3}{4} \times 1\frac{2}{3}$ **c** $2\frac{1}{2} \times 1\frac{1}{5}$ **d** $2\frac{2}{5} \times \frac{5}{8}$ **e** $3\frac{1}{3} \times 1\frac{1}{5}$

f $4\frac{1}{2} \times 1\frac{1}{3}$ **g** $1\frac{7}{8} \times 2\frac{2}{5}$ **h** $2\frac{2}{3} \times 2\frac{5}{8}$ **i** $2\frac{1}{4} \times 4\frac{2}{3}$ **j** $7\frac{1}{2} \times 1\frac{1}{5}$

k $5\frac{2}{5} \times 2\frac{1}{7}$ **l** $4\frac{2}{5} \times 1\frac{1}{8}$ **m** $1\frac{1}{6} \times 3\frac{1}{2}$ **n** $8\frac{1}{2} \times 3\frac{1}{2}$ **o** $6\frac{2}{3} \times 2\frac{3}{4}$

p $(3\frac{2}{3})^2$ **q** $(1\frac{4}{5})^2$ **r** $(2\frac{1}{7})^2$ **s** $(1\frac{1}{2})^3$ **t** $(2\frac{1}{4})^3$

2 a Tape passes through a cassette recorder at $3\frac{3}{4}$ cm per second. How much tape has passed through after $3\frac{1}{3}$ seconds?

   b James is travelling at a steady $4\frac{2}{5}$ kilometres per hour. How far will he have travelled in $2\frac{3}{5}$ hours?

3 Calculate the area of each shop window.

a

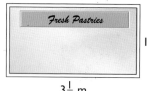

$3\frac{1}{2}$ m $1\frac{1}{2}$ m

b

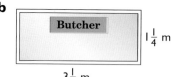

$3\frac{1}{5}$ m $1\frac{1}{4}$ m

9 Division

Examine the following cases:

A $\frac{3}{4} \times \frac{1}{5} = \frac{3}{20}$

$\Rightarrow \frac{3}{20} \div \frac{1}{5} = \frac{3}{4}$

Note that $\frac{3}{20} \times \frac{5}{1} = \frac{15}{20} = \frac{3}{4}$

B $\frac{2}{7} \times \frac{3}{4} = \frac{6}{28} = \frac{3}{14}$

$\Rightarrow \frac{3}{14} \div \frac{3}{4} = \frac{2}{7}$

Note that $\frac{3}{14} \times \frac{4}{3} = \frac{12}{42} = \frac{2}{7}$

C $\frac{11}{6} \times \frac{3}{2} = \frac{33}{12}$

$\Rightarrow \frac{33}{12} \div \frac{3}{2} = \frac{11}{6}$

Note that $\frac{33}{12} \times \frac{2}{3} = \frac{66}{36} = \frac{11}{6}$

We can change any division for an equivalent multiplication.

$$\frac{a}{b} \div \frac{c}{d} = \frac{a}{b} \times \frac{d}{c}$$

F

Example 1

$\frac{1}{2} \div \frac{1}{4}$

$= \frac{1}{2} \times \frac{4}{1}$

$= \frac{4}{2}$

$= 2$

Example 2

$\frac{2}{3} \div \frac{5}{6}$

$= \frac{2}{3} \times \frac{6}{5}$

$= \frac{12}{15}$

$= \frac{4}{5}$

Example 3

$2\frac{2}{3} \div 1\frac{5}{6}$

$= \frac{8}{3} \div \frac{11}{6}$

$= \frac{8}{3} \times \frac{6}{11}$

$= \frac{48}{33}$

$= 1\frac{15}{33}$

$= 1\frac{5}{11}$

Exercise 9.1

1 Evaluate the following, simplifying where possible.

a $\frac{1}{4} \div \frac{1}{2}$ **b** $\frac{1}{8} \div \frac{1}{2}$ **c** $\frac{1}{2} \div \frac{1}{8}$ **d** $\frac{1}{6} \div \frac{1}{2}$ **e** $\frac{2}{3} \div \frac{2}{5}$

f $\frac{2}{3} \div \frac{1}{6}$ **g** $\frac{3}{10} \div \frac{3}{5}$ **h** $\frac{2}{3} \div \frac{5}{6}$ **i** $\frac{9}{10} \div \frac{3}{4}$ **j** $\frac{3}{20} \div \frac{3}{5}$

k $\frac{5}{6} \div \frac{2}{9}$ **l** $\frac{6}{7} \div \frac{3}{8}$ **m** $\frac{4}{7} \div \frac{3}{5}$ **n** $\frac{6}{11} \div \frac{22}{25}$ **o** $\frac{14}{23} \div \frac{7}{9}$

2 Calculate the following, expressing your answer as a mixed number where appropriate.

a $1\frac{1}{2} \div \frac{3}{4}$ **b** $2\frac{2}{3} \div \frac{1}{6}$ **c** $1\frac{1}{8} \div 1\frac{1}{2}$ **d** $1\frac{1}{4} \div \frac{5}{6}$ **e** $1\frac{1}{7} \div 2\frac{1}{2}$

f $3\frac{1}{5} \div 1\frac{1}{5}$ **g** $2\frac{1}{2} \div 3\frac{1}{3}$ **h** $1\frac{1}{8} \div 4\frac{1}{2}$ **i** $3\frac{1}{3} \div 3\frac{3}{4}$ **j** $3\frac{3}{5} \div 2\frac{7}{10}$

k $3\frac{3}{5} \div 1\frac{1}{4}$ **l** $5\frac{2}{3} \div 2\frac{5}{8}$ **m** $6\frac{1}{2} \div 1\frac{4}{7}$ **n** $5\frac{4}{9} \div 1\frac{1}{6}$ **o** $4\frac{1}{2} \div 4\frac{1}{3}$

3 A jug contains $\frac{3}{4}$ of a litre of water.
A glass can hold $\frac{1}{8}$ of a litre.
How many glasses can be filled from the jug?

4 Stan has $\frac{7}{10}$ of a tonne of sand to move.
His wheelbarrow will take $\frac{1}{20}$ of a tonne.
How many full loads will be needed?

5 How many $\frac{1}{2}$ kg packets of sugar can be filled from a $5\frac{1}{2}$ kg container?

6 How many $1\frac{1}{4}$ metres of wire can be cut from a drum holding $17\frac{1}{2}$ metres?

7 Calculate the height of each rectangle.

a $3\frac{1}{7}$ cm

Area = $6\frac{2}{3}$ cm²

b $5\frac{2}{3}$ cm

Area = $9\frac{1}{5}$ cm²

c $4\frac{2}{5}$ cm

Area = $8\frac{2}{5}$ cm²

F

CHECK-UP

1 Find:

   a $\frac{3}{5}$ of £1   **b** $\frac{7}{10}$ of 600 g   **c** $\frac{11}{20}$ of 80 m

   d $\frac{9}{50}$ of 250 litres   **e** $\frac{3}{100}$ of 2000 tonnes   **f** 10% of £7

   g 30% of 400 ml   **h** 75% of 52 weeks   **i** 15% of 90 kg

   j 4% of 5000 km

2 Copy and complete the table. Write fractions in their simplest form.

Fraction	$\frac{7}{10}$		$1\frac{3}{4}$		$\frac{9}{20}$
Decimal		0·14		0·09	

3 **a** Increase £365 by 9%.   **b**   Decrease £620 by 8%.

4 **a** Express £4 as a percentage of £32.

   b A book was bought for £12 and sold for £15.
      Express the profit as a percentage of the cost price.

   c In a sale, a pair of jeans is sold for £24 instead of £30.
      Express the discount as a percentage of the original cost.

5 **a** When it is reduced by 10%, a coat costs £117.
      What is the original cost?

   b TV coverage of a football match is extended by 25%.
      The coverage lasts for 3 hours.
      For how long was it originally timetabled?

6 Calculate:

   a $\frac{4}{5} + \frac{7}{10}$ **b** $3\frac{1}{3} - 1\frac{3}{5}$ **c** $\frac{9}{10} \times \frac{3}{4}$

   d $\frac{9}{10} \div \frac{3}{4}$ **e** $3\frac{3}{5} \div 2\frac{1}{4}$ **f** $3\frac{1}{2} \times 1\frac{2}{7}$

(16) Two-dimensional shapes

The study of shape is called **geometry**, and the word comes from two Greek words: *ge* (earth) and *metron* (measure).

The Ancient Egyptians and Greeks were among the first people to study shape.

Euclid (300 BC) wrote all that was then known about geometry in a work known as *The Elements*.

One problem the Ancient Greeks could never solve was known as 'squaring the circle'. See if you can find out more about it.

1 Looking back ◀◀

Exercise 1.1

1 A mineralogist studies minerals and their crystal forms.
   Give a name to each of the highlighted faces on these crystals.

a  b 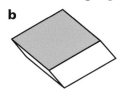 c 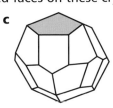 d

2 Copy and continue the tiling.

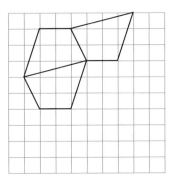

3 Name all the triangles in the diagram.

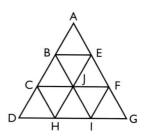

4 **a** Draw a square and its four axes of symmetry.

b Draw a rectangle and its axes of symmetry.

5 Make a drawing of a circle and label it to identify:

a its centre **b** its diameter **c** its radius **d** its circumference.

2 The square and rectangle

A **square** is a quadrilateral with four axes of symmetry.
A **rectangle** is a quadrilateral with two axes of symmetry which pass through its sides.

These definitions allow us to make deductions about the properties of the shapes.

Example 1 Look at the square ABCD with axis of symmetry MN.
Reflecting in the axis we see that:

A → B (A *goes to* B)
D → C (D *goes to* C)

and so AD → BC (AD *goes to* BC)
so AD = BC

Example 2 Again reflecting in the axis MN, we see that:

B → A   A → B   D → C

and so ∠BAD → ∠ABC
so ∠BAD = ∠ABC

Example 3 In the square ABCD, prove AD = AB.
Reflecting in the axis PQ:

A → A (A *goes to* A)
D → B

and so AD → AB
so AD = AB

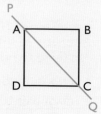

Exercise 2.1

1 Given that a square has four axes of symmetry as shown opposite, prove:
   a AB = DC   **b** BC = DC   **c** AB = BC

2 **a**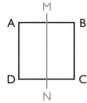

Prove ∠ADC = ∠BCD

      b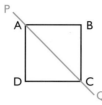

Prove ∠ADC = ∠ABC

      c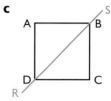

Prove ∠DAB = ∠DCB

   d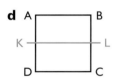

Prove ∠DAB = ∠ADC

   e

Prove the sum of the angles of a square is 360°.

   f Prove each of the angles of a square is 90°.

3 AC and BD are the diagonals of the square.
They intersect at E.
E lies on the axis of symmetry as shown.

   a Prove: **i**   AC = BD   **ii**   AE = EB
              iii DE = EC   **iv**   DE = AE
              v   AE = EC   **vi** the diagonals bisect each other.

   b Prove: **i**   ∠AED = ∠BEC   **ii**   ∠AEB = ∠DEC
              iii ∠AED = ∠AEB   **iv** the diagonals bisect at right angles.

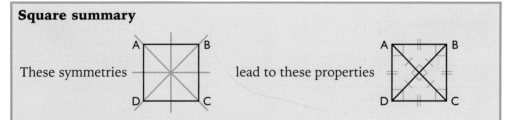

Square summary

These symmetries   lead to these properties

4 The rectangle has two axes of symmetry as shown.
Use these to prove that:

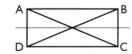

   a opposite sides are equal   **b** diagonals are equal
   c diagonals bisect each other   **d** all angles are equal
   e all angles are right angles.

5 Use symmetry to prove that:

  a the four angles marked x are equal

  b the four angles marked y are equal.

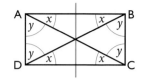

6 Copy each rectangle and find the size of each angle.

a 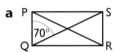 **b** 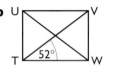 **c**   **d**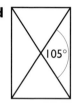

7 Which of these shapes is definitely not a rectangle?

a 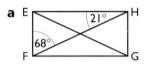 **b** 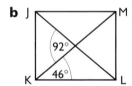 **c**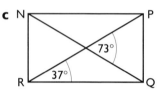

8 Copy each rectangle and give the size of as many lengths as you can. All sizes are in centimetres.

a 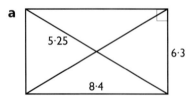 **b**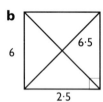

9 A garden patio has been arranged in congruent rectangles.
The distance AC = 2·6 metres.
AB = 1 metre. BC = 2·4 metres.
The grey section is a path. Calculate:

  a the perimeter of the patio

  b the length of edging needed for
    i BH   **ii** CG.

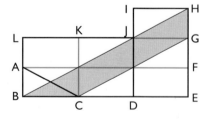

10 At a dangerous corner, chevrons are placed as a warning.
The design is based on four rectangles, each of which has a base of length 1·4 m and a diagonal of 1·9 m.

  a Calculate the perimeter of the shaded area.

  b The angle ABC = 43°.
    Calculate the size of all six angles in the shaded area.

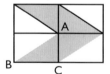

E

3 The rhombus and kite

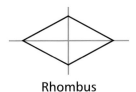

Rhombus

A **rhombus** is a quadrilateral with two axes of symmetry passing through the vertices.

A **kite** is a quadrilateral with one axis of symmetry passing through vertices.

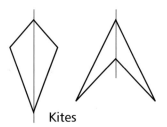

Kites

Example

Prove the sides of a rhombus are equal.
Reflecting in the axis PQ, we see that:

A → A	also	C → C
D → B		D → B
AD → AB		CD → CB

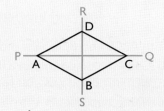

and so AD = AB   and so   CD = CB

Reflecting in the axis RS, we see that:

A → C
D → D
AD → CD

and so AD = CD so AD = AB = CD = CB

Exercise 3.1

1   For the rhombus ABCD above, prove:
   a   opposite angles are equal
   b   the diagonals bisect each other
   c   the diagonals intersect at right angles.

2   **a**   For the rhombus PQRS and the axis passing through Q and S:
      i   prove the four angles marked x are equal,
      ii   calculate the value of $x + y$
      iii calculate the sum of the four angles of a rhombus.

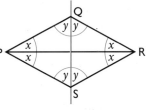

   b **i**   Show that the angles round the centre of this group of rhombuses is 360° and hence the rhombus tiles.
      ii   Prove that ABCD is a rectangle.

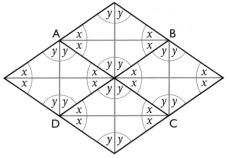

3 PRSU is a rectangle. QRTU is a rhombus.

   a How many right-angled triangles can you find in the diagram?

   b PQ = 5 cm, PU = 12 cm and UQ = 13 cm. Calculate the perimeter of
      i rectangle PRSU
      ii the rhombus QRTU.

   c Measuring to the nearest degree, it was found that ∠PQU = 67°. Calculate the size of
      i ∠UQT
      ii ∠QUR
      iii the angles of the rhombus.

4 Both ABCE and BCDE are rhombuses.

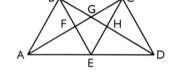

   a Copy the diagram and calculate the sizes of as many angles as you can.

   b Name two kites in the diagram.

   c **i** The line GE is drawn. Prove GE = GB.
      ii Name two other kites.

5 **a** Prove AC is bisected at right angles by the axis of symmetry BD.

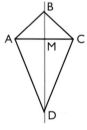

   b What is the sum of the four angles of the kite?

   c If ∠BAC = 50° and ∠ADC = 30°, calculate the size of each angle of the kite.

   d Congruent kites will tile in a regular fashion. Draw one such tiling.

Challenge

Within this picture of a toy teepee there are six kites.

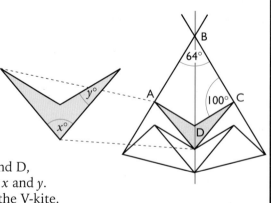

a Copy the diagram and identify each kite.

b The four V-kites are congruent. ∠ABC = 64°. ∠BCD = 100°.
   i By considering the angles round C, find a connection between x and y.
   ii By considering the angles round D, find another relation between x and y.
   iii Find the size of each angle of the V-kite.

Exercise 3.2

1 ABCD is a kite
A is the point (2, 0) and C is the point (8, 0).

  a State the coordinates of D if B is the point
      i (6, 2)   **ii** (4, 3)
      iii (3, 1)   **iv** (0, 3).

  b What is special about ABCD if B has
    an x-coordinate of 5?

  c What happens to the shape if B has
    an x-coordinate of 2?

  d What is special about the kite when B has an x-coordinate less than 2?

  e What is the connection between the x-coordinates of B and D?

2 The diagonals of a rhombus PQRS intersect at (3, 2).
P(5, 1) and Q(1, −2) are two of the vertices.

  a On a coordinate grid, draw the rhombus.

  b State the coordinates of   **i** R   **ii** S.

  c Find the mid-points of the sides PQ and RS.

  d State the coordinates of the mid-point of QR.

3 A(−2, −1), B(5, 5), C(8, 4) and D are the vertices of a kite.

  a Draw the kite.

  b State the coordinates of D.

  c State the point of intersection of the diagonals.

  d The point E lies on AC so that EBCD is a square.
    What are the coordinates of E?

4 A kite has vertices P(3, 2), Q(0, 4), R(−3, 2)
and S(0, −3).

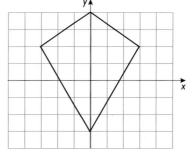

  a State the point of intersection of its
    diagonals.

  b The kite forms part of a tiling of
    congruent kites. Four such tiles have a
    side in common with PQRS. State the
    points of intersection of the diagonals
    of each of the four tiles.

  c **i**   What shape is formed when these four points are joined?
     ii Where is the point of intersection of its diagonals?

Rhombus summary	**Kite summary**
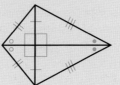	

4 The parallelogram and trapezium

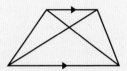 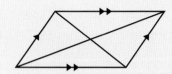

A **trapezium** is a quadrilateral with one pair of parallel sides.

The trapezium tiles.

A **parallelogram** is a quadrilateral with two pairs of parallel sides.

The parallelogram has a centre of symmetry and it tiles.

Example

Prove opposite angles are equal.

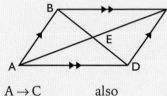

After a half-turn about E it becomes ...

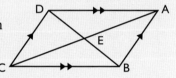

A → C	also	B → D
B → D		C → A
C → A		D → B

∠ABC → ∠CDA   ∠BCD → ∠DAB

So ∠ABC = ∠CDA   So ∠BCD = ∠DAB

Thus opposite angles are equal.

Exercise 4.1

1 Prove that:

  a the diagonals of the parallelogram bisect each other

  b opposite sides are equal.

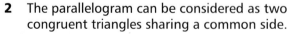

2 The parallelogram can be considered as two congruent triangles sharing a common side.

  a What do the four angles of a parallelogram add up to make?

  b What is the value of $x + y$?

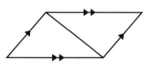 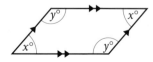

E

3 Calculate the value of the lettered angles in each diagram.

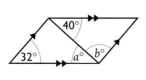 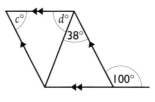 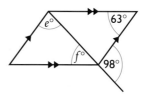

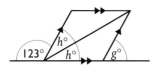 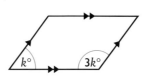 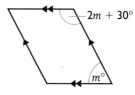

4 PQRS is a parallelogram whose diagonals intersect at T. Name:

  a four pairs of alternate angles
  b two pairs of corresponding angles
  c two pairs of vertically opposite angles.

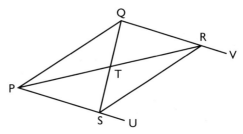

5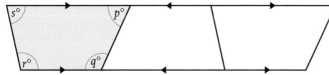

  a By considering the tiling of trapezia shown above, show that:
    i $p + q = 180$
    ii $s + r = 180$.
  b Calculate the missing angles.

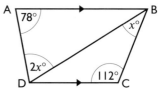

6 a Name two equal angles in the diagram.
  b If $\angle ABD = k°$, express k in terms of x.
  c Use triangle BCD to find another expression for k in terms of x.
  d Calculate the value of
    i x
    ii k.

7 MNKL is a trapezium with MN = NK.
  a Prove that the line KM cuts $\angle$NML in half.
  b Calculate the size of each angle in the diagram.

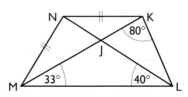

8   A modern picture frame is made as shown.
    It appears to be one square inside another.
    The sides of the squares are parallel.
    The green line is an axis of symmetry.
    Calculate the size of each angle in the picture.

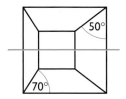

Challenge

Four congruent copies of this trapezium can be
combined to form an enlargement of itself.

The shape is symmetrical.

a   What are the sizes of the angles of the shape?
b   How much bigger is the larger version?

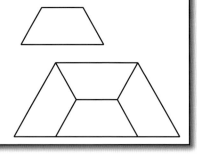

E

5 Classifying quadrilaterals

We can sort out the different types of triangles by asking yes/no questions about
the lengths of sides:

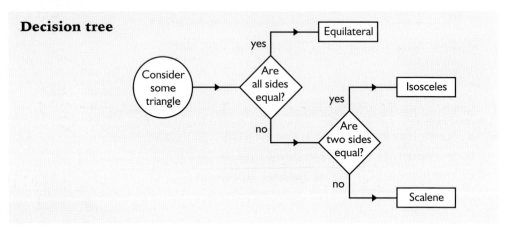

What sort of yes/no questions could we ask to sort the quadrilaterals into
different classes?

Exercise 5.1

1 Follow this decision tree with each of the named quadrilateral types.
State into which box each shape is put.

a rectangle
b square
c rhombus
d kite
e parallelogram
f trapezium

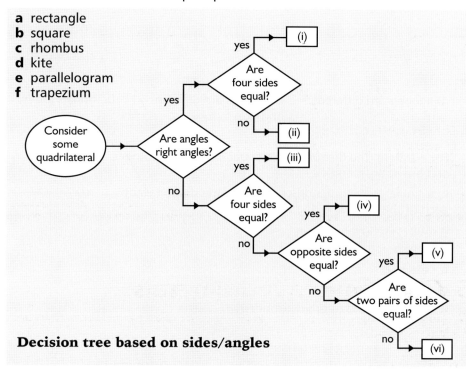

Decision tree based on sides/angles

E

2 Sort the same quadrilaterals using this decision tree.

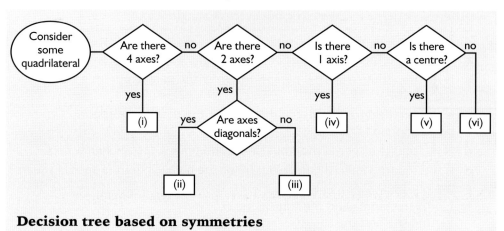

Decision tree based on symmetries

3 We might define the quadrilateral ABCD by two diagonals, line segments AC and BD.
The way these diagonals lie in relation to each other will dictate the type of quadrilateral we get.

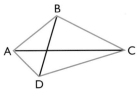

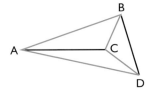

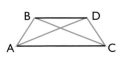

Diagonals are different and cross.

Diagonals are different and don't cross.

Diagonals are parallel!

For a square, the diagonals are equal, bisect each other and are at right angles.

In a similar way, find a description for the diagonals of each of the following quadrilaterals:

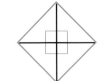

a the rectangle

b the rhombus

c the kite

d the parallelogram

e the trapezium (a brainstormer!)

4 A square is a special rectangle.
It has all the properties of the rectangle plus the extra property that adjacent sides are equal.

> Every square is a rectangle but not every rectangle is a square.

a Is the kite a special rhombus or the rhombus a special kite?

b Is the trapezium a special parallelogram or the parallelogram a special trapezium?

c Is the parallelogram a special rhombus or the rhombus a special parallelogram?

d Is the square a special rhombus or the rhombus a special square?

e Is the square a special parallelogram or the parallelogram a special square?

f What is the relation between
  i the rectangle and the trapezium
  ii the kite and the square
  iii the rectangle and the parallelogram?

6 Drawing polygons

When drawing a polygon we usually need a ruler, a protractor and a set of compasses.

Drawing a sketch first helps us plan the steps.

Example 1

Draw a quadrilateral with sides AB = 3 cm, BC = 4 cm, CD = 5 cm, DA = 6 cm and ∠ABC = 55°.

By examining the sketch, we can plan the steps:
• draw AB
• measure 55°
• draw BC
• draw arc, centre C radius 5
• draw arc, centre A radius 6
• identify the point D and draw shape.

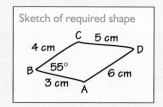

Once an accurate drawing is made other sizes can be measured. For example, the diagonal AC = 3·5 cm to 1 d.p.

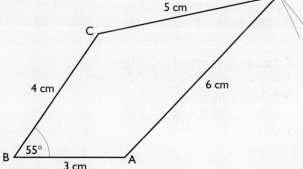

Example 2

Draw a *regular* pentagon of side 3 cm.
Regular means all sides are equal and all angles are equal.
Plan the steps:
• draw base
• draw 108°
• draw side
• continue clockwise.

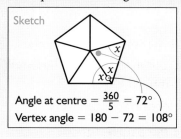

Angle at centre = $\frac{360}{5}$ = 72°
Vertex angle = 180 − 72 = 108°

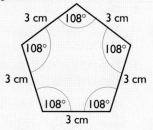

Exercise 6.1

1 **i** Make accurate drawings of the following sketches.
  ii Find the value of each letter by measurement.

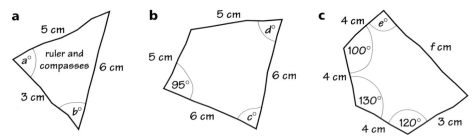

a 5 cm, ruler and compasses, 6 cm, $a°$, 3 cm, $b°$

b 5 cm, 5 cm, $d°$, 6 cm, 95°, 6 cm, $c°$

c 4 cm, $e°$, 100°, f cm, 4 cm, 130°, 120°, 4 cm, 3 cm

2 **a** Calculate the vertex angle of the regular hexagon.
  b Draw a regular hexagon with side 4 cm.
  c Measure the length of the longest diagonal.

3 **a** In this regular heptagon, calculate
    i $a°$ **ii** $b°$.
  b Draw a regular heptagon of
    side 4 cm.
  c The 50p piece is based on the
    heptagon.
    Arcs are drawn on each side using
    the opposite vertex as the centre.
    Convert your heptagon to a 50p piece shape.

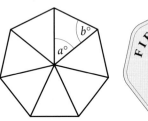

FIFTY PENCE

50

CHECK-UP

1 Here is a rectangle marked up to indicate its properties.

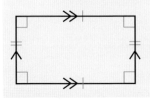

Arrows indicate parallel lines.
Squares represent right angles.
Marks represent equal lengths.

In a similar way, mark up the square, the rhombus, the kite, the
parallelogram and the trapezium.

2 PQ is an axis of symmetry of the rectangle ABCD.
  a Prove that ∠ABD = ∠BAC
  b Show that AE = EC.

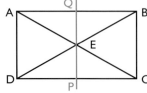

3 Find the size of each angle in:

   a the rhombus

   b the kite.

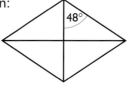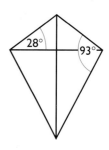

4 AC, HD and GE are parallel.
   CE, BF and AG are also parallel.
   BD is parallel to HF.
   CG is an axis of symmetry of the design.

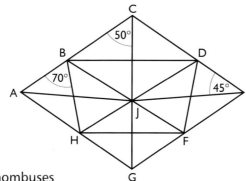

   a Name:
   i three rhombuses
   ii six parallelograms
   iii a trapezium without symmetry
   iv a trapezium with symmetry.
   b Find the size of as many angles as possible.

5 Name the quadrilaterals which have:
   a at least four axes of symmetry
   b exactly two axes of symmetry
   c a centre of symmetry
   d a centre of symmetry but no axes of symmetry
   e only one pair of parallel lines.

6 Draw a regular octagon of side 4 cm.

7 a Make an accurate drawing of this sketch.
   b Measure:
   i the diagonals AC and BD
   ii ∠ABC.

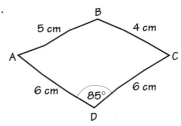

⑰ Three dimensions

A 3-D puzzle picture!

Hold this picture up very close to your face.

Let your eyes relax, then slowly move the picture away. Keep looking through the page.

Do not try to focus on the picture.

A 3-D image should appear.

---

1 Looking back ◀◀

Exercise 1.1

1   Name each solid.

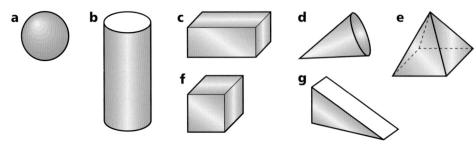

2 Which of these are nets of cubes?

a   b   c   d   e   f

3 Here is a picture of a cuboid and its net.

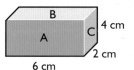

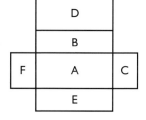

a   State the dimensions of rectangle A.

b   What other rectangle has the same dimensions?

c   Two rectangles are 2 cm by 4 cm. Which ones?

4 PQRSTU is a triangular prism.

a   How many faces does it have?

b   PQR is one triangular face. Name the other one.

c   Which edge is parallel to PQ?

d   How many rectangular faces does the prism have?

e   Which edges meet at the vertex R?

f   How many vertices does the prism have?

5 a   How many litres of liquid are in the jug?

b   Express this in millilitres.

6 Convert:

a   1250 ml into litres   b   3·4 kg into grams

c   900 g into kilograms   d   1·84 m into centimetres.

7 Calculate the total length of wire needed to make each of these skeleton models.

a

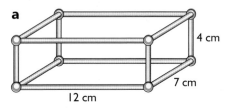

4 cm

7 cm

12 cm

b

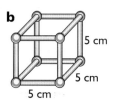

5 cm

5 cm

5 cm

2 Pyramids and prisms

To form a pyramid:

Take any 2-dimensional shape and a point A, not on the same surface.

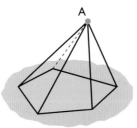

Join A to each vertex of the shape and a solid is outlined.

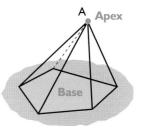

A pentagonal pyramid

The family of pyramids

Triangular pyramid
A tetrahedron

Square-based pyramid

Pentagonal pyramid

Hexagonal pyramid

Heptagonal pyramid

Circular pyramid
A cone

To form a prism:

Take any two congruent faces, e.g. triangular faces, ...

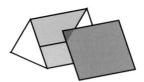

... and connect them by rectangles ...

to produce a prism, in this case a triangular prism.

The family of prisms

Pentagonal prism

Hexagonal prism

Heptagonal prism

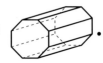

Octagonal prism

Circular prism
A cylinder

E

Exercise 2.1

1 Animal ornaments are sold in pyramid-shaped boxes.
The horse is in a square-based pyramid.

  a How many:
     i   faces   **ii**   edges   **iii**   vertices does this box have?

  b Name the shape of the box containing
     i   the mouse   **ii**   the penguin.

  c What shapes would be needed to make the penguin's box?

  d How many edges does the mouse's box have?

2 Individual chocolate boxes are in the
shape of triangular prisms.
Six of these boxes are packed
into a larger carton.

  a How many:
     i   faces   **ii**   edges   **iii**   vertices does the box have?

  b What shape is the larger box?

  c How many
     i   faces   **ii**   edges   **iii**   vertices does the larger box have?

3 **a** Write down the name of solid ABCDEF.

  b AFE is one triangular face.
  Write down the names of the others.

4 The German postage stamp commemorates
Euler finding a connection between faces,
vertices and edges for solids.

  a Copy and complete the table.

  b Can you explain the connection that Euler found?

  c Does it work for all solids?
  If not, explain for which solids the rule does not hold.

Solid	Faces (f)	Vertices (v)	Edges (e)	$f + v - e$
cuboid	6	8	12	2
tetrahedron				
pentagonal pyramid				
hexagonal pyramid				
triangular prism				
pentagonal prism				
cone				
sphere				

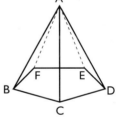

E

5 This solid is called an octahedron.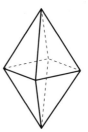

   a Explain why it is called an octahedron.

   b Write down the number of
     i faces
     ii edges
     iii vertices of the octahedron.

   c Does Euler's rule work for the octahedron?

Challenge

Lynne and Jason are making models.
They have a construction kit containing the following pieces:

8 equilateral triangles with sides 6 cm
8 isosceles triangles with sides 6 cm, 6 cm and 4 cm
8 rectangles 6 cm by 4 cm
6 squares 6 cm by 6 cm
4 squares 4 cm by 4 cm

What sort of solids can they make?
Name the solid and write down which pieces are needed to make it.

E

3 Drawing solids

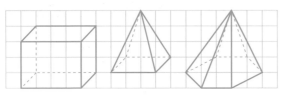 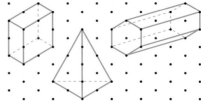

Pictures which represent solids can be drawn on squared paper ... or isometric paper.

Exercise 3.1

1 Make a copy of each of the above solids.
Label each drawing with the name of the solid represented.

2 Cuboids can be drawn easily on both types of paper.

   a Draw a picture to represent a cuboid which is 2 cm by 3 cm by 4 cm:
     i on squared paper
     ii on isometric dot paper.

   b Which method did you find easier?

3 Cuboid A has dimensions 3 by 1 by 2.

a Write down the dimensions of cuboids B and C.

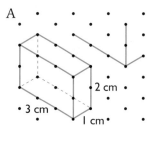

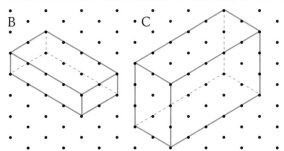

b On isometric dot paper, draw cuboids of dimensions:
  i $3 \times 2 \times 5$ **ii** $4 \times 4 \times 3$.

4 On squared or isometric dot paper, draw:
  a a pentagonal pyramid
  b a right-angled triangular prism
  c an octahedron.

4 Skeleton models

Sometimes we wish we could see through a shape to study its edges, vertices and hidden faces.

One way to study these is to make a model using straws, wire or cane to form the edges. Pipe cleaners, plastic connectors or plasticine are needed to join these edges at the vertices.

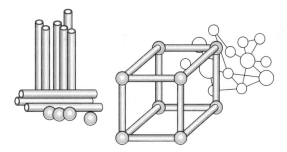

E

Scientists use models like these to study the shape of molecules.
This model of a salt crystal uses 12 rods and 8 connectors.

Exercise 4.1

1 Calculate the total length of the straws needed to make each model.

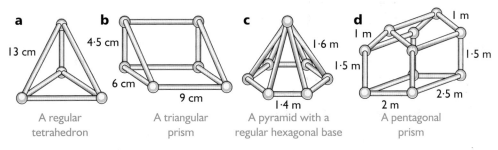

a	b	c	d
13 cm	4·5 cm, 6 cm, 9 cm	1·6 m, 1·5 m, 1·4 m	1 m, 1 m, 1·5 m, 2·5 m, 2 m
A regular tetrahedron	A triangular prism	A pyramid with a regular hexagonal base	A pentagonal prism

2 Calculate the total length of cane needed to make a skeleton model of:
  a a cube with sides 14 cm
  b a cuboid measuring 7 cm by 5·5 cm by 4 cm
  c a pentagonal pyramid with sloping edges 11 cm whose base is a regular pentagon of side 9 cm
  d an octagonal prism, with all edges 28 cm.

3 Mairi has 2·5 metres of cane.
  She wants to make a hexagonal pyramid with all edges the same length.
  a What is the largest length she can have if each is a whole number of centimetres?
  b How much cane is left over?

4 Aaron uses all of a 1·5 m length of wire to make the triangular prism shown. How long is the prism?

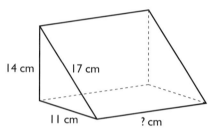

14 cm   17 cm
11 cm   ? cm

5 Eva uses all of a 3 m roll of wire to make a skeleton model of a cuboid.
  Its length is 31 cm and its breadth 23 cm.
  What is its height?

6 The total length of wire used for each model below is 180 cm. For each:
  a form an equation in x
  b solve it to find the lengths of the sides of the solid.

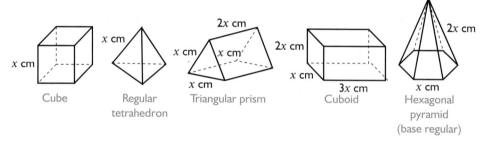

| Cube | Regular tetrahedron | Triangular prism | Cuboid | Hexagonal pyramid (base regular) |

x cm x cm x cm x cm x cm $2x$ cm x cm $2x$ cm $2x$ cm x cm $3x$ cm $2x$ cm x cm

5 Nets of pyramids and prisms

Some manufacturers are interested in finding the nets of pyramids and prisms in order to make boxes for their products.

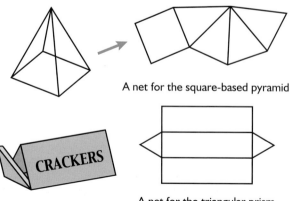

A net for the square-based pyramid

CRACKERS

A net for the triangular prism

E

Exercise 5.1

1 This is another net of a square-based pyramid. The grey areas are not part of the net, but are flaps for gluing it together.

  a Copy the net onto paper.

  b Cut it out and fold it to make the pyramid.

  c Two such pyramids are glued base to base. Name the solid formed.

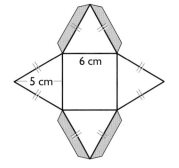

6 cm

5 cm

2 A name plate for a desk top has a net as shown on the right.

  a Copy the net and add gluing flaps.

  b Cut out the net and make the solid.

  c Name the solid.

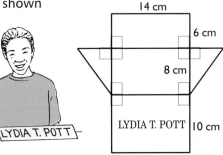

14 cm

6 cm

8 cm

LYDIA T. POTT

LYDIA T. POTT 10 cm

3 On isometric paper, draw the net of:

  a a regular tetrahedron   **b** a regular octohedron.

E

4 Which of these are nets of a triangular prism?

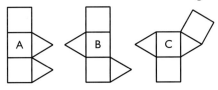

A   B   C

5 Archaeologists have found several examples of a variety of dice used by the Egyptians and Romans.

  a Make a copy of the net and form the solid.

  b What name would you give the solid?

  c Why is it important for the hexagons to be regular?

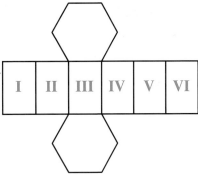

I II III IV V VI

6 Draw the net of a pyramid whose base is a regular pentagon with sides 5 cm. Its triangular sides are all isosceles and its slant height is 6 cm.

7 Identify the solids of which these are the nets.

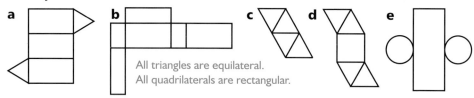

All triangles are equilateral.
All quadrilaterals are rectangular.

Challenge

This design has eight equilateral triangles and a square.

a Copy it on paper and cut it out.
b Make creases along BF, CG, GI and JC.
c Join CD to CB, GH to GF.
d Join JI to AE, JD to AB and IH to EF.
e Make a second identical solid.

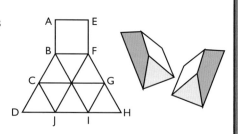

Can you sit these two solids together to form a regular tetrahedron?

6 Surface area

Example Find the total surface area of this cuboid.

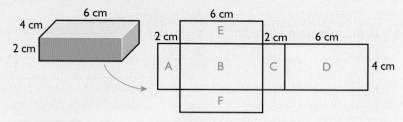

Rectangle		Area (cm²)
A	2 × 4	8
B	6 × 4	24
C	2 × 4	8
D	6 × 4	24
E	2 × 6	12
F	2 × 6	12
	Total	88

By adding the areas of all six faces we get the total surface area of the cuboid = 88 cm².

Exercise 6.1

1 This is a net of a cube.
It is made from six squares of side 5 cm.

    a Calculate the area of one square.

    b What is the total surface area of
the cube?

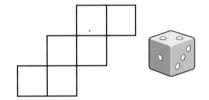

2 **a** Sketch the net of the cuboid.

    b Calculate the area of each face.

    c Work out the total surface area of the cuboid.

    d Each dimension of this cuboid is half the size
of those in the worked example.
Comment on the difference in their surface areas.

3 Here is the net of a cuboid.

    a Calculate the area of each face.

    b Work out the total surface area of
the cuboid.

    c What are the dimensions of the
cuboid?

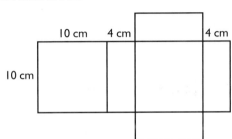

E

4 Bethany is going to paint the sides and top of
this box.

    a Calculate the area to be painted.

    b James has an open box of the same dimensions.
He is going to paint the sides and inside of the box.
What area will he paint?

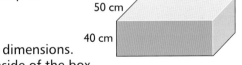

5 A formula for the surface area of a cuboid (S cm^2) is:

$$S = 2(ab + bc + ac)$$

    a Verify the formula works for a cuboid which is
3 cm × 4 cm × 5 cm by:

      i calculating the area of each face separately
and adding together

      ii using the formula.

    b Use the formula to calculate the surface area of the
following cuboids:

      i 10 cm × 6 cm × 4 cm

      ii 8 cm × 5 cm × 8 cm

    c Adapt the formula to give the surface area of a cube
of edge a cm.

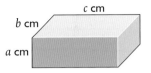

6 a Calculate the surface area of:
   i a cube of side 4 cm
   ii a cuboid of dimensions 6 cm × 5 cm × 3 cm
b Which has the greater surface area and by how much?

> **Reminder**
>
> Area of a triangle $(A \text{ cm}^2) = \frac{1}{2}ab$

Exercise 6.2

1 This is the net of a square-based pyramid. All triangular faces are congruent and isosceles.

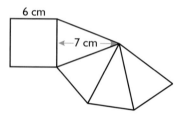

  a Calculate the area of:
    i the square base
    ii a triangular face.
  b Calculate the surface area of the pyramid.

2 a Sketch the net of this triangular prism.
  b Calculate:
    i the area of each face
    ii the total surface area.

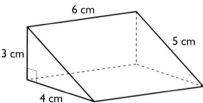

3 Calculate the surface area of each of the following solids.

a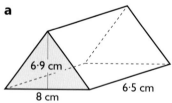

b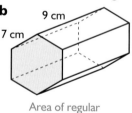
Area of regular hexagon = 127 cm²

c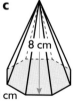
Area of regular octagon = 121 cm²

d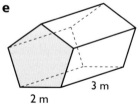

e
Area of regular pentagon = 6·9 cm²

f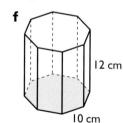
Area of regular octagon = 485 cm²

276

7 Volumes of cubes and cuboids

Reminders
1 cubic centimetre = 1 millilitre
1000 millilitres = 1 litre
1000 litres = 1 cubic metre
The **capacity** of a vessel is the
volume it can hold.

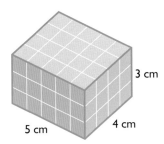

The volume of this
cuboid can be calculated
by counting cubes.
$5 \times 4 \times 3$
$= 20 \times 3$
$= 60 \text{ cm}^3$

3 cm

4 cm

5 cm

In general:
Volume = length × breadth × height
        = area of base × height

$\boxed{V = lbh}$ or $\boxed{V = Ah}$

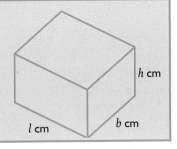

h cm

l cm b cm

E

Example 1   Find the volume of the washing machine in:
               a cubic metres   **b** cubic centimetres.

0·5 m

0·9 m

0·6 m

50 cm

90 cm

60 cm

For the formulae to work
all units must be consistent

$$1 \text{ m}^3 = 1\,000\,000 \text{ cm}^3$$

a $V = lbh$
       $= 0·5 \times 0·6 \times 0·9$
       $= 0·27 \text{ m}^3$

b $V = lbh$
       $= 50 \times 60 \times 90$
       $= 270\,000 \text{ cm}^3$

Example 2

Calculate the volume of the room.

$V = Ah$
    $= 25 \times 3$
    $= 75 \text{ m}^3$

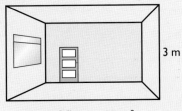

3 m

Area of floor = 25 m²

Example 3

Calculate the volume of the slab.
Choose metres or centimetres.
Here we have chosen centimetres.

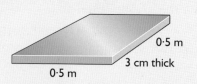

0·5 m
3 cm thick
0·5 m

$$V = 50 \times 50 \times 3$$
$$= 7500 \text{ cm}^3$$

Exercise 7.1

1 Calculate the volume of each cuboid.
Remember to use the correct units for volume.

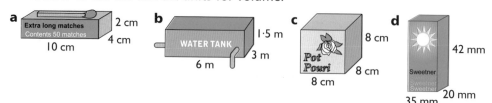

a Extra long matches / Contents 50 matches — 2 cm, 4 cm, 10 cm

b WATER TANK — 1·5 m, 3 m, 6 m

c Pot Pouri — 8 cm, 8 cm, 8 cm

d Sweetner — 42 mm, 20 mm, 35 mm

2 Calculate the volume of each box.

a Snowdrops Tissues — 5 cm, Area of base = 180 cm²

b PADDLING POOL — 0·7 m, Area of base = 6·4 m²

c Pewter Quaich — 8 cm, Area of base = 44 cm²

3 Calculate each volume correct to the nearest unit.

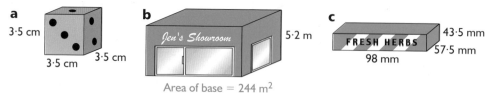

a 3·5 cm, 3·5 cm, 3·5 cm

b Jen's Showroom — 5·2 m, Area of base = 244 m²

c FRESH HERBS — 43·5 mm, 57·5 mm, 98 mm

4 Use the data in the table to calculate the volume of each cuboid.
Remember that units must be consistent.

Box	Length	Breadth	Height	Area of base
A	11 cm	9 cm	3·5 cm	
B	1·2 m	92 cm	1·3 m	
C			55 cm	5·25 m²
D	4·5 cm	12 mm	35 mm	
E			86 mm	10·5 cm²

Careful!

5 The base of a box has an area of 54 cm². The volume of the box is 378 cm³. Calculate the height of the box.

6 A tank must hold 6 cubic metres of water. Its base is a square of side 1·5 metres. What is the minimum height of the tank? Round your answer to 2 significant figures.

7 What size of cube would hold the same volume as a cuboid with dimensions 20 cm × 7·5 cm × 8 cm? (Round your answer to 2 significant figures.)

8 Calculate the missing dimension of each cuboid.

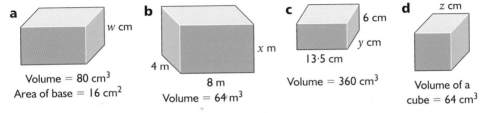

a Volume = 80 cm³
Area of base = 16 cm²

b 4 m, 8 m
Volume = 64 m³

c 6 cm, y cm, 13·5 cm
Volume = 360 cm³

d z cm
Volume of a cube = 64 cm³

Investigations

1 a Show that both these cuboids have the same volume.

b Work out the surface area of each cuboid. Which has the greater surface area?

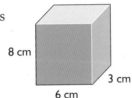
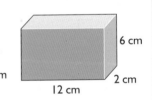

8 cm, 3 cm, 6 cm

6 cm, 2 cm, 12 cm

c Find different cuboids with volume 64 cubic centimetres. Use whole numbers only for the length, breadth and height. Work out the surface area of each cuboid. What are the dimensions of the cuboid with the smallest surface area?

2 In 1793 when the French scientists devised the metric system, they decided to call the weight of 1 cubic centimetre of water by the name 1 gram. Since 1000 cm³ = 1 litre, then 1 litre of water weighs 1 kilogram. They also decided to call the weight of 1 m³ of water 1 tonne.

a How many grams of water make a tonne weight?

One cubic centimetre of lead weighs approximately 11 g.
One cubic centimetre of gold weighs approximately 19 g.

On page 219 you read about how Archimedes was asked to find out whether a crown was made of pure gold or a mixture of gold and lead.

b Investigate how Archimedes was able to tell if the crown was pure gold or not; how he was able to find the volume of the crown without melting it down.

E

8 Volumes of prisms

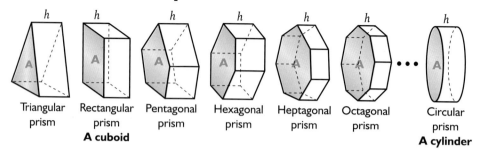

| Triangular prism | Rectangular prism **A cuboid** | Pentagonal prism | Hexagonal prism | Heptagonal prism | Octagonal prism | Circular prism **A cylinder** |

As with the cuboid, for the rest of the prisms,

volume = area of base × height. $\boxed{V = Ah}$

In the diagrams, the **base** has been highlighted in each case.
The **height** (h) is the distance between the congruent ends.

Example 1

Calculate the volume of this L-shaped prism.

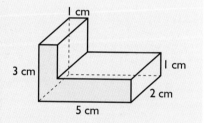

Answer:

The area of the base = 1 × 3 + 1 × 4
$$= 7 \text{ cm}^2$$
Volume = Ah = 7 × 2
$$= 14 \text{ cm}^3$$

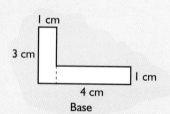

Example 2

Calculate the volume of this cylinder.
The base is a circle.

Area = $\pi r^2 = \pi \times 3 \times 3$
$$= 28 \cdot 3 \text{ cm}^2 \text{ (to 1 d.p.)}$$
Volume = 28·3 × 2
$$= 56 \cdot 6 \text{ cm}^3$$

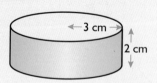

Exercise 8.1

1 Calculate the volume of each prism to the nearest cubic unit.

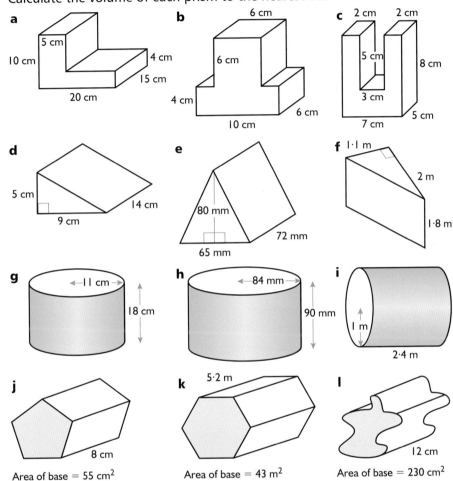

CHECK-UP

1 For each solid below   **i** give it a name   **ii** draw a net.

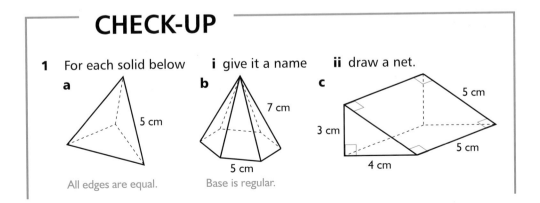

a 5 cm
All edges are equal.

b 7 cm, 5 cm
Base is regular.

c 5 cm, 3 cm, 5 cm, 4 cm

2 Calculate the total length of cane needed to make each model.

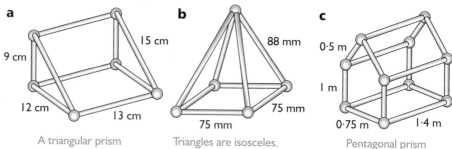

a

15 cm
9 cm
12 cm
13 cm

A triangular prism

b

88 mm
75 mm
75 mm

Triangles are isosceles.

c

0·5 m
1 m
0·75 m
1·4 m

Pentagonal prism

3 Calculate the volume of each cuboid

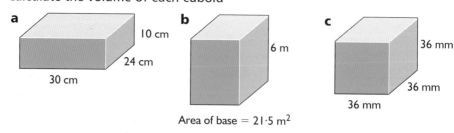

a

10 cm
24 cm
30 cm

b

6 m

Area of base = 21·5 m²

c

36 mm
36 mm
36 mm

4 A manufacturer makes 45 tonnes of powdered milk for orphan lambs.
   a How many kilograms is this?
   b The milk is put into 25 kg bags.
      How many bags of milk will there be?

5 **a** Calculate the capacity of each solid in litres.
   b Calculate the surface area of solids A and C.

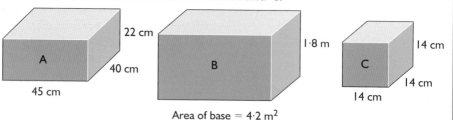

22 cm
A
40 cm
45 cm

1·8 m
B

Area of base = 4·2 m²

14 cm
C
14 cm
14 cm

6 Calculate the volume of each prism.

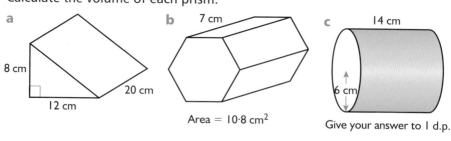

a

8 cm
20 cm
12 cm

b

7 cm

Area = 10·8 cm²

c

14 cm
6 cm

Give your answer to 1 d.p.

(18) Information handling 2

Technology has made this the Information Age.

Computers allow us to store vast amounts of data in **databases**.

We can use **spreadsheets** to organise and display data.

On the Internet we can find data on just about anything!

---

1 Looking back ◀◀

Exercise 1.1

1 James uses this spreadsheet to record the parts ordered for his workshop.

E5		× √					
	A	B	C	D	E	F	G
I	code	description	cost (£)	number			
2	9/115	switch	3.65	4			
3	1/960	bracket	8.99	7			
4	2/347	cable	10.25	I			
5							

  a What is in cell   **i** B1   **ii** C3   **iii** A4?

  b Name the cell containing   **i** cable   **ii** 1/960   **iii** 7.

  c Which cell is highlighted?

  d Which cell appears in the edit bar?

  e How many of item 2/347 are ordered?

  f What is the cost of the cable?

  g What is the code of the cheapest item?

2 The average demand for electricity from a certain power station over a
24-hour period is given in the table:

time	00 00	02 00	04 00	06 00	08 00	10 00	12 00	14 00	16 00	18 00	20 00	22 00	24 00
demand	18	9	8	10	26	37	35	28	34	36	28	25	18

a Copy and complete the
line graph to show the
demand over the 24 hours.

b Between which times
(approximately) is demand
  i below 10 000 units
  ii above 30 000 units?

c Describe the pattern in
electricity demand.

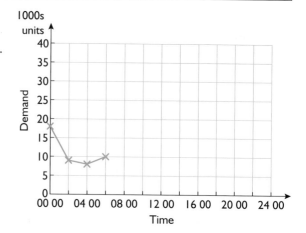

3 **a** What fraction of cinema goers went to the
  i matinée
  ii early evening
  iii evening programmes?

b If there were 220 tickets sold on the day of
this survey, how many were sold for the
  i matinée
  ii early evening
  iii evening programmes?

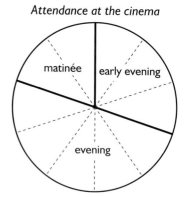

Attendance at the cinema

4 A travel agent recorded the number of holidays sold in one week for his most
popular destinations:

Holiday destination	America	France	Greece	Italy	Spain	Scandinavia	Turkey
Number of holidays	18	8	14	15	30	6	22

If you have access to a computer, enter the data in a spreadsheet.
Make a bar chart using the chart menu.
Try different options if possible.
Print out your results.
Otherwise, draw a bar chart by hand to illustrate this data.

2 Using spreadsheets: formulae

A spreadsheet will calculate if a **formula** is entered in a cell.
A formula always starts with '=' and can include mathematical operations like +, −, *(multiply), /(divide).

Example

The results of a maths competition are shown on the screen.

formula

| E2 | × √ | =B2+C2+D2 |

	A	B	C	D	E	
I	team	mental	speed	problems	total	
2	Greens	19	25	9		
3	Reds	15	20	13		
4	Blues	20	21	15		
5						

53 will be displayed here when this formula is entered.

The spreadsheet will calculate the total for the Greens when the formula '=B2+C2+D2' is entered by typing it in and pressing <Return>.

If we put a *similar* formula into cell E3, namely '=B3+C3+D3', we get the total for the Reds. Here we use the word *similar* to indicate that the formula will do a similar job.

A formula '=B2+B3+B4' will add the scores in the mental section.

A similar formula '=C2+C3+C4' will add the scores in the speed section.

Exercise 2.1

1

| DI | × √ | |

	A	B	C	D	E
I	2	6	18		
2					
3					

In the above spreadsheet, work out what number will appear in cell D1 when the formula entered in D1 is:

a =2+A1   **b** =A1+B1   **c** =A1*B1   **d** =C1−A1−B1
e =C1/3   **f** =C1/B1   **g** =(B1+C1)/2   **h** =(A1+B1)/A1
i =(A1+B1+C1)/13   **j** =5*A1+3*B1+C1

2 In the example about the maths competition, what formula should be entered in

    a E3 to calculate the total for the Reds

    b E4 to calculate the total for the Blues?

3 The Greens convince their teacher, Mrs Young, that their solution to a problem marked wrong is in fact correct. Mrs Young gives them an extra two marks.
  a Which cell does the teacher change?
  b What is now entered in this cell?
  c What effect does this have on cell E2?

4 Mrs Young would like to know the mean marks for each section of the maths competition.
  a What formula, entered in row 5, would give the mean score in
    i the mental   **ii** the speed   **iii** the problems section?
  b Using the corrected marks, what values would these formulae produce in cells
    i B5   **ii** C5   **iii** D5?
  c In which section were the highest marks scored on average?

5 **a** If a *similar* formula to that in cell B5 were entered in cell E5, what information would it give you?
  b Using the corrected marks, what value would cell E5 contain?

6 If you have access to a computer enter the corrected data from the example and also the given formula in cell C2.
  a To copy cell E2 into E3, E4 and E5:
    ● click on E2 and *drag* down to E5 to highlight the cells
    ● click on '**Fill down**' from the '**Edit**' menu.
    Note that this puts similar formulae into cells E3, E4 and E5 and not the same formula.
  b Enter formulae in the cells B4, C4, D4 and E4 to show Mrs Young all the mean values.

7 A packaging company is interested in knowing the volume and surface areas of various boxes as shown in the spreadsheet.

E6	× √								
	A	B	C	D	E	F	G	H	I
I	box	length	breadth	height	volume	area of top	area of side	total surface area	
2	P	20	20	20					
3	Q	20	20	30					
4	R	30	30	10					
5	S	30	30	20					
6	T	40	40	10					

If you have access to a computer, try to make the spreadsheet and print your result.

  a What formula should be entered in   **i** E2   **ii** F2   **iii** G2?
  b If *similar* formulae are entered in rows 3 to 6, copy and complete the spreadsheet table, showing all the entries so far.
  c Which box has the biggest volume?
  d The formula =2*F2+4*G2 is entered in cell H2. H2 is now copied down to H6. What values will appear in cells H2 to H6?
  e Does the box with the biggest surface area have the biggest volume?

3 Displaying data: line graphs

Reminder:
Line graphs with straight line segments are good for showing how something changes with time and make **trends** easier to spot.

Curved line graphs can be used when some underlying law is likely to connect the quantities or when you expect that all changes are gradual and predictable.

Exercise 3.1

1 On a winter's morning the outside temperature was recorded every hour as shown in the table.

   a Plot these temperatures with 'time of day' on the horizontal axis.

   b Join the points with straight lines.

   c Describe the change in temperature on this morning.

5 a.m.	−1 °C
6 a.m.	−1 °C
7 a.m.	0 °C
8 a.m.	2 °C
9 a.m.	6 °C
10 a.m.	7 °C
11 a.m.	7 °C
12 noon	10 °C

2 Stephen works in a factory making electrical components.
He starts work at 8 a.m. and by 10 a.m. has made 12 components.
By 1 p.m. he has made 30 components.

   a Show this information on a graph, joining the points with a straight line.
   (The larger the graph, the more accurate your answers.)

   b Explain why your graph should go through the point (8 a.m., 0).

   c How many components had Stephen probably made after one hour?

   d How many would you expect him to have made by 12 noon?

   e How long would you expect it to take him to make 20 components?

3 The profits of a small company at the end of the year for the seven years up to 2002 are shown in the table.

Year	1996	1997	1998	1999	2000	2001	2002
Profits (£1000s)	85	90	82	94	95	105	108

   a Show these results in a line graph.
   (Make your vertical scale start at £80 000.)

   b Describe the trend in these results.

   c In which year did profits
   i fall
   ii first go over £100 000?

E

4 a What would be a suitable title for this graph?

b In the first two years of life are boys or girls more likely to grow faster?

c i At what ages are boys and girls likely to be the same height?

ii How tall are they likely to be then?

d How much taller are boys than girls at the age of 18 years on average?

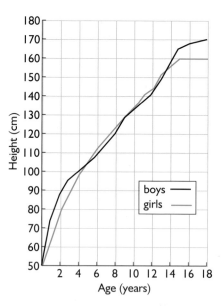

5 If you have access to a computer, try to enter the data for questions **1** through to **4** into a spreadsheet. Choose the correct sort of graph required from the chart menu. Experiment with different styles if possible.

E

4 Displaying data: pie charts

Reminder:

Pie charts are good for comparing categories of data.

The angle at the centre of each sector indicates the frequency in each category.

To make measuring angles easier, make your pie charts at least 6 cm across.

Exercise 4.1

1 I spend 30% of my time sleeping, 25% of my time at school and the rest of my time at leisure.

a Copy and complete the table.

b Draw a pie chart to illustrate this data. Use a protractor to measure the angles. Label the sectors or make a key.

Sleeping	30% of 360° = ...
School time	25% of 360° = ...
The rest (leisure)	360° − ... = ...

2 A pie chart in a safety leaflet shows the ages of those injured by fireworks.

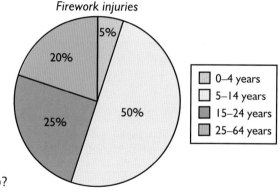

Firework injuries

5%
20%
50%
25%

☐ 0–4 years
☐ 5–14 years
■ 15–24 years
☐ 25–64 years

a What is the total percentage shown in the pie chart?

b Which age group had the largest number of injuries?

c Which age group had no injuries?

d What percentage of injuries are in the under 15 age group?

e If the total number of injuries shown in the pie chart is 240, how many were in the under fives age group?

3 Sixty pupils were asked what they ate when they went to the cinema. 30% said they ate popcorn, 60% said ice cream, 5% said sweets and the rest said they ate nothing.

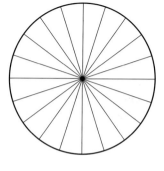

a A pie chart is divided into 20 equal sectors as shown. How many sectors would represent:
  i popcorn
  ii ice cream
  iii sweets?

b How many of the 60 pupils said they ate
  i popcorn
  ii nothing?

c Suggest a title for the pie chart.

4 This pie chart shows how a family spends its income:
25% on housing and travel   15% on clothing
20% on food   12% on leisure
20% on taxes
Anything left is saved.

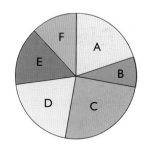

a Say which sector represents each category.

b If this family's income is £30 000 each year, how much does it:
  i spend on food
  ii spend on leisure
  iii save?

c Suggest a title for the pie chart.

5 If you have access to a computer, try to enter the data for questions 1 through to 4 into a spreadsheet. Choose the correct sort of graph required from the chart menu. Experiment with different styles if possible.

E

When raw data are given, the size of the sector representing each category can be calculated as follows:

- Find what fraction of the time the category occurred.
- Find that fraction of 360°.

Example

In a class of 30 students, 12 were fair-haired, 10 were dark-haired and the rest were red-heads. Draw a pie chart to illustrate the data.

12 out of 30 means $\frac{12}{30}$ were fair-haired.
$\frac{12}{30}$ of $360° = 144°$

10 out of 30 means $\frac{10}{30}$ were dark-haired.
$\frac{10}{30}$ of $360° = 120°$

8 out of 30 means $\frac{8}{30}$ were red-headed.
$\frac{8}{30}$ of $360° = 96°$

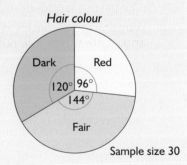

Hair colour

Sample size 30

Exercise 4.2

E

1   Sixty pupils were asked what sort of crisps they preferred. 12 preferred plain, 21 preferred cheese and onion and the rest chose salt and vinegar.

a   Copy and complete the table.

Flavour	Frequency	Fraction	Angle
plain	12		
cheese and onion	21	$\frac{21}{60} = \frac{7}{20}$	$\frac{7}{20} \times 360° = 126°$
salt and vinegar			
Total:	60	check total:	

b   Draw a pie chart. Add a key or labels and a title.
Use a protractor to measure the angles.

2   Each pupil from class 1P said which school day they preferred.
The results are shown in the table.

a   Make a table like the one in the previous question.

b   Show this information in a pie chart.

Day	Frequency
Monday	3
Tuesday	3
Wednesday	4
Thursday	6
Friday	8

3 A sample of 50 people were asked which Sunday newspaper they read most often.
The table shows the results.

  a Draw a pie chart, adding a key or labels and a title.
(Show your calculations.)

  b Why doesn't it matter that some angles are not whole numbers?

Newspaper	Frequency
Scotland on Sunday	15
Sunday Post	10
Sunday Times	4
Observer	5
Sunday Mirror	9
Herald on Sunday	7

4 a Calculate the fraction of cars which were manufactured in each country.

  b If there were 60 cars in the car park, work out how many cars came from each country.

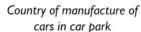

Country of manufacture of cars in car park

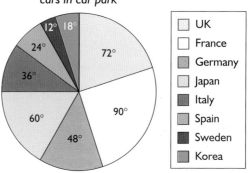

- UK
- France
- Germany
- Japan
- Italy
- Spain
- Sweden
- Korea

E

5 Tony and Sue wanted to know the age mix of the guests at their wedding.
The pie chart shows the results.

  a Use a protractor to measure each angle.

  b There were 100 guests.
How many were in each age group?

  c Your answers must be whole numbers. Why?

Wedding guests

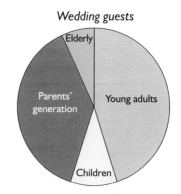

6 If you have access to a computer, try to enter the data for questions 1 through to 4 into a spreadsheet.
Choose the correct sort of graph required from the chart menu.
Experiment with different styles if possible.

5 Other data displays: stem and leaf

A **stem and leaf** diagram is a useful way to:

● order the data
● create a diagram in which all the data is recorded
● create a diagram whose overall shape is similar to a bar graph.

(Unfortunately most spreadsheets do not produce stem and leaf diagrams from their chart menu.)

The diagram is formed in two stages:

● doing a rough sort using 'stems' by reading through the data line by line
● sorting the 'leaves' in each stem.

Example

In a survey, 20 cinema goers were asked their ages as they bought tickets for a film. Their ages were:

24, 16, 23, 17, 17, 20, 19, 25, 24, 26, 27, 19, 18, 21, 29, 33, 16, 16, 34, 32.

Make a stem and leaf diagram with the data.

1st stage: Decide on the stems – 'teens', 'twenties', 'thirties' – and sort the list into these three categories.
(Note that 24 has a stem of 2 and a leaf of 4.)

```
1│6 7 7 9 9 8 6 6
```
stems ⟶ 2│4 3 0 5 4 6 7 1 9 ◀── leaves
```
3│3 4 2
```

2nd stage: Sort the leaves, putting the smallest nearest the stem. Add a key, title and state the sample size. This is known as an **ordered** stem and leaf diagram.

title ⟶ **Age of cinema goers (years)**

```
1│6 6 6 7 7 8 9 9
2│0 1 3 4 4 5 6 7 9
3│2 3 4
```

sample ⟶ $n = 20$ 1│6 means 16 years of age ◀── key
size

Exercise 5.1

1 Make a list of all the raw data used to create these stem and leaf diagrams.

a Heights of seedlings

```
 8 | 1  5  8
 9 | 2  2  3  5  7  9
10 | 1  1  1  4  8
11 | 2
```

$n = 15$ 8|1 means 8·1 cm

b Salesmen's weekly kitchen sales

```
0 | 3  4  5  8  8  9
1 | 0  2  2  2  5
2 | 1
```

$n = 12$ 0|3 means 3 kitchens

c Holiday prices

```
3 | 2  3  3  6  7  7
4 | 1  4  5  5  5  5  9
5 | 2  5  8
6 | 1
```

$n = 17$ 3|2 means £320

2 For each data set in question **1**, state
 i the size of the sample
 ii the least value in the data set
 iii the greatest value in the data set
 iv the mode (the value which occurs most frequently).

3 Here are the prices of bicycles in a shop given to the nearest £10:

  £240, £90, £120, £520, £140, £250, £360,
  £170, £290, £300, £400, £280, £250, £220.

```
0 |
1 |
2 | 4
3 |
4 |
5 |
```

a Copy and complete the first stage of the stem and leaf diagram.

b Complete the second stage by sorting the leaves, adding a key and a title, and stating the sample size.

4 The scores for 24 competitors in a trampolining competition were recorded as follows:

| 8·6 | 7·9 | 8·2 | 8·5 | 9·4 | 7·4 | 8·6 | 9·2 | 8·4 | 8·5 | 9·6 | 8·6 |
| 8·0 | 8·1 | 7·8 | 9·0 | 8·6 | 8·7 | 9·0 | 9·3 | 7·9 | 7·6 | 9·1 | 8·9 |

a Make a rough sort of the data using three stems.

b Complete an ordered stem and leaf diagram.

5 Class 1X collected information on how long it took them to get to school in the mornings on average. Here are the results (in minutes):

25	12	15	25	10	8	15	20	25	35	10	3
5	24	15	12	18	1	5	15	8	7	16	30
24	30	25	14	10	20	5	15	12	23	9	8

a Make a stem and leaf diagram.

b What is the sample size?

c What are   **i** the shortest   **ii** the longest times?

d Which times are more frequent: less than 10 minutes, 10 or more but less than 20, 20 or more but less than 30, 30 or more?

e How many pupils take

    i less than 15 minutes   **ii** more than 25 minutes on average?

f What is the modal time?

g What is the median time?

6 Other data displays: scatter graphs

Many statistical diagrams illustrate just one quantity (or variable), for example a bar chart might show 'the height of pupils in a class' or 'test marks in maths'. Often it's the relationship between two quantities which is important, for example:

- 'How are height and weight connected?'
- 'Is there a relationship between marks in a non-calculator test and a test where calculators are allowed?'

A **scatter graph** can be used to illustrate such relationships.
Each pair of data is plotted as a point on the graph. *Do not join up the points!*

Example

The marks of 10 pupils in both a non-calculator test, out of 20, and a test where calculators are allowed, out of 50, are given.

	Amy	Brian	Chris	Dave	Euan	Fiona	Greg	Helen	Iain	John
Non-calculator	17	13	18	12	16	20	14	13	14	18
Calculator	40	35	50	28	34	47	39	32	33	47

If there is a relationship between these marks, it will be easier to spot on the graph. Plot the non-calculator marks horizontally (on the x-axis), and the calculator marks vertically (on the y-axis), e.g. Amy's results are plotted as (17, 40).

Notice the axes do not have to cross at the origin, (0, 0).

The scatter graph shows there is a fairly strong association between the marks in the two tests.

The higher the mark in one, the higher the mark in the other tends to be. Here the two quantities tend to increase together. We can say there is a **positive correlation** between the two quantities. If one quantity tends to decrease as the other increases we can say there is a **negative correlation** between the two quantities.

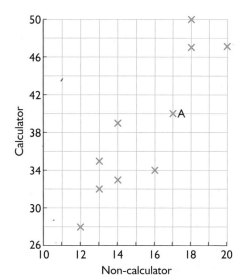

Exercise 6.1

1

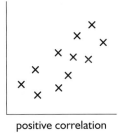

positive correlation

A

no correlation

B

negative correlation

C

Which diagram, A, B or C, is likely to represent the relationship between:

a height *and* shoe size

b number of people employed in the job *and* number of articles completed

c age of an adult *and* height of an adult

d time spent watching TV *and* time spent doing homework

e number of empty seats in a cinema *and* profits on a film

f time spent travelling *and* distance travelled on a motorway

g age of a child *and* size of birthday cake

h distance travelled on a train *and* cost of journey

i length of hair *and* age of teenager

2 **Discrete** data is data which can be counted; **continuous** data is data which is measured. For example, the number of pupils in a class is discrete, but the height of these pupils is continuous. For the variables in question **1a–i**, say whether data is discrete or continuous.

3 The scatter graph shows data collected at a youth club.

  a Does pocket money tend to be higher or lower for younger youth club members?

  b Does pocket money tend to be higher or lower for older youth club members?

  c Say whether the relationship is positive or negative.

Youth club pocket money

4

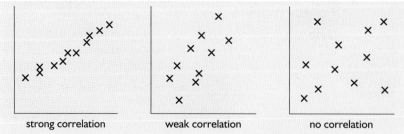

strong correlation   weak correlation   no correlation

Say whether these variables have a weak or strong, positive or zero or negative correlation.

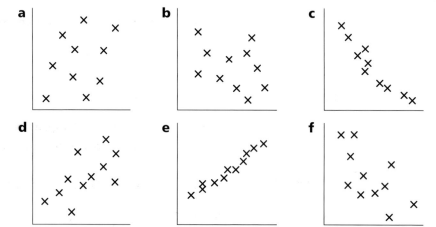

5 For this group of friends, draw a scatter graph showing how many brothers or sisters they have versus their pocket money. Plot the number of siblings horizontally with a scale from 0 to 5, and pocket money vertically with a scale from 0 to 14.

	Amy	Brian	Chris	Dave	Euan	Fiona	Greg	Helen	Iain	John
Number of siblings	2	0	1	0	3	2	1	1	5	2
Pocket money (£)	5	14	10	10	8	12	9	12·50	5	9

  a From the scatter graph can you say what sort of relationship exists between pocket money and number of brothers and sisters for this group?

  b Copy and complete the sentence 'Pocket money for a single child tends ... ..., whereas pocket money when there are several children in the family tends ... ...'

F

6 For this group of pupils, draw a scatter graph showing how maths test marks vary with English test marks. Plot the maths marks on a scale from 60 to 100, and English marks on a scale from 50 to 90.

Pupil	1	2	3	4	5	6	7	8	9	10
Maths marks (%)	70	68	87	99	93	76	87	84	94	82
English marks (%)	62	72	79	84	54	68	69	73	88	70

a From the scatter graph can you say what sort of relationship exists between maths and English test marks for this group?

b Copy and complete the sentence 'Maths and English test marks have a .... correlation. So, in general, the higher the maths mark, the ...... the English mark tends to be.'

c What can you say about pupil 5?

Challenge

Try to create the scatter diagrams for questions **4** and **5** using a spreadsheet.

F

7 Probability

Data is often collected in order to find out how likely something is to happen.

The **probability** or chance that something happens is measured on a scale from 0 to 1.

It can also be described using words, such as *likely* or *unlikely*, but these words are often too vague.

If an event is *certain* to happen, it has a probability of 1.

If an event is *impossible*, it has a probability of 0.

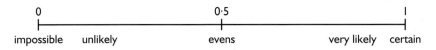

In situations when all possible outcomes are equally likely, it is possible to calculate the probability of that event using the formula:

$$\text{Probability of an event} = \frac{\text{number of ways that event can occur}}{\text{total number of different outcomes}}$$

Example

For a fair dice, each number is equally likely to be rolled. What is the probability of rolling a 3?

$$\text{Probability of rolling a 3} = \frac{\text{number of threes on the dice}}{\text{total number of faces}} = \frac{1}{6}$$

If you needed a three to win a game, would you say that rolling a three was unlikely?

Probably. Winning in this case is less likely than not winning.

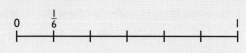

Exercise 7.1

1 You throw a dice. How would you describe the probability of these events? (Choose from the words *certain*, *evens* or *impossible*.)
Rolling   **a**   a 7   **b**   any number from 1 to 6
                 c   an odd number   **d**   a 4, 5 or 6.

2 You shuffle a pack of cards and deal. How would you describe the probability of these events? (Choose from *likely*, *unlikely*, *very likely* or *very unlikely*.)
Dealing   **a**   a red ace   **b**   the Queen of Spades
                 c   anything but a king   **d**   a picture card.

3 Choose words to describe the probability of these events.
   a A person wins the lottery.
   b You go to school next Monday.
   c You forget your calculator for a maths lesson.
   d Your friend is left-handed.

4 Draw a line, scaled from 0 to 1, showing roughly where the probabilities of the events in the previous question lie.

5 Find the probability of each of these events, giving your answer as a fraction. With a fair dice, rolling
   a a 6   **b** a 1 or 2   **c** an even number   **d** any number but a 6.

6 In a game of 'Fish', you hold seven cards in your hand. The next player chooses a card unseen from your hand. Your cards are:

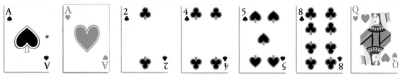

Assuming each card is equally likely to be chosen, find the probability that from your hand the next player chooses
   a a queen   **b** an ace   **c** a club   **d** any card but the aces.

7 You take two cards from a shuffled pack of 52 cards and keep them.
They are both hearts.
What is the probability that the next card you take is another heart?

8 You roll two dice. There are 36 possible outcomes such as (1, 2), (2, 1) or a double (2, 2).

  a List all the possible outcomes in the event 'doubles'.

  b Find the probability of rolling a 'double'.

  c List all the possible outcomes in the event 'total score of 11 or more'.

  d Find the probability of a 'total score of 10 or more'.

9 In a game of dominoes, seven dominoes are chosen at random by each player.
(Remember each domino has two numbers from: blank, 1, 2, 3, 4, 5 or 6.)

  a Copy and complete this list of possible dominoes: (blank, blank), (blank, 1), (blank, 2), (blank, 3), (blank, 4), (blank, 5), (blank, 6), (1, 1), (1, 2), (1, ...), ...

  b How many dominoes are there?

  c Find the probability that a player chooses:
    i 'double blank'
    ii any double
    iii any domino with a blank
    iv any domino with at least one 4
    v any domino without a blank.

10 A whole number is chosen at random from 1 to 50. By listing all the outcomes in these events, find the probability that the number is:

  a even   **b** less than 10   **c** more than 10

  d a square number   **e** a prime number.

11 In a game of noughts and crosses, all things being equal, what is the probability that the first player plays

  a in a corner   **b** in the centre   **c** any other square?

F
E

CHECK-UP

1 Sandy's science class is growing seedlings. Sandy records the height of his seedlings each week.

Week	1	2	3	4	5	6	7	8	9	10
Height (cm)	0	1	2·1	3·6	5·5	7·4	8·5	9·1	9·4	9·5

  a Choosing suitable scales, show the data on a graph.
As the change is expected to be gradual, join the points with a smooth curve.

  b Describe the growth over the 10-week period.

2 Mrs Taylor analysed the marks in the end-of-year exam.
240 pupils took the exam.
Use the pie chart to find how many pupils scored:
  a less than 30%
  b 30% to 49%
  c 50% to 79%
  d 80% and over.

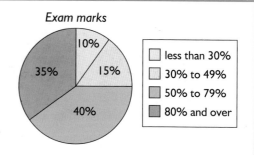

Exam marks

□ less than 30%
□ 30% to 49%
■ 50% to 79%
■ 80% and over

3 A botanist counted the number of different plant species found in a random selection of metre squares in a park. The results are given in the table.

5	26	13	31	8	14
12	20	7	6	5	12
10	19	13	9	15	23
8	14	17	11	22	13

  a Construct a stem and leaf diagram to illustrate these results.
  b What are the smallest and largest data values?
  c What is the modal value?

4 During the summer holidays, Jamil went on several bike rides. He noted the distances shown on his odometer and compared them with the distances he had estimated for his trip before he went.
(All distances are in kilometres.)

Trip	1	2	3	4	5	6	7	8	9
Odometer (km)	7	15	8	12	18	15	20	10	14
Estimate (km)	6	12	6	12	19	13	18	10	12

  a Draw a scatter diagram to illustrate the data.
  b Say whether the relationship is **i** weak or strong **ii** positive or negative.

5 Four books of raffle tickets were sold for a prize. Each book had 30 tickets and were coloured red, blue, green and yellow.
  a Sarah bought ticket 'red 3'. What is the probability she wins the prize?
  b Jane bought five tickets 'green 1–5'. What is the probability she wins the prize?
  c What is the probability that the winning colour is yellow?
  d What is the probability that the winning number is 30?